Garfield
tips the scales

BY JIM DAVIS

Ballantine Books • New York

A Ballantine Book
Published by The Random House Publishing Group
Copyright © 1984, 2004 by PAWS, Inc. All Rights Reserved.

All rights reserved under International and Pan-American Copyright Conventions. Published in the United States by The Random House Publishing Group, a division of Random House, Inc., New York, and simultaneously in Canada by Random House of Canada Limited, Toronto. Originally published in slightly different form by The Random House Publishing Group, a division of Random House, Inc., in 1984.

Ballantine and the Ballantine colophon are registered trademarks of Random House, Inc.

"GARFIELD" and the GARFIELD characters are registered and unregistered trademarks of PAWS, Inc.

www.ballantinebooks.com

Library of Congress Control Number: 2003097616

ISBN 0-345-46909-7

Manufactured in the United States of America

First Colorized Edition: July 2004

10 9 8 7 6 5 4 3 2 1

THE SHOCKING TRUTH...REVEALED!!

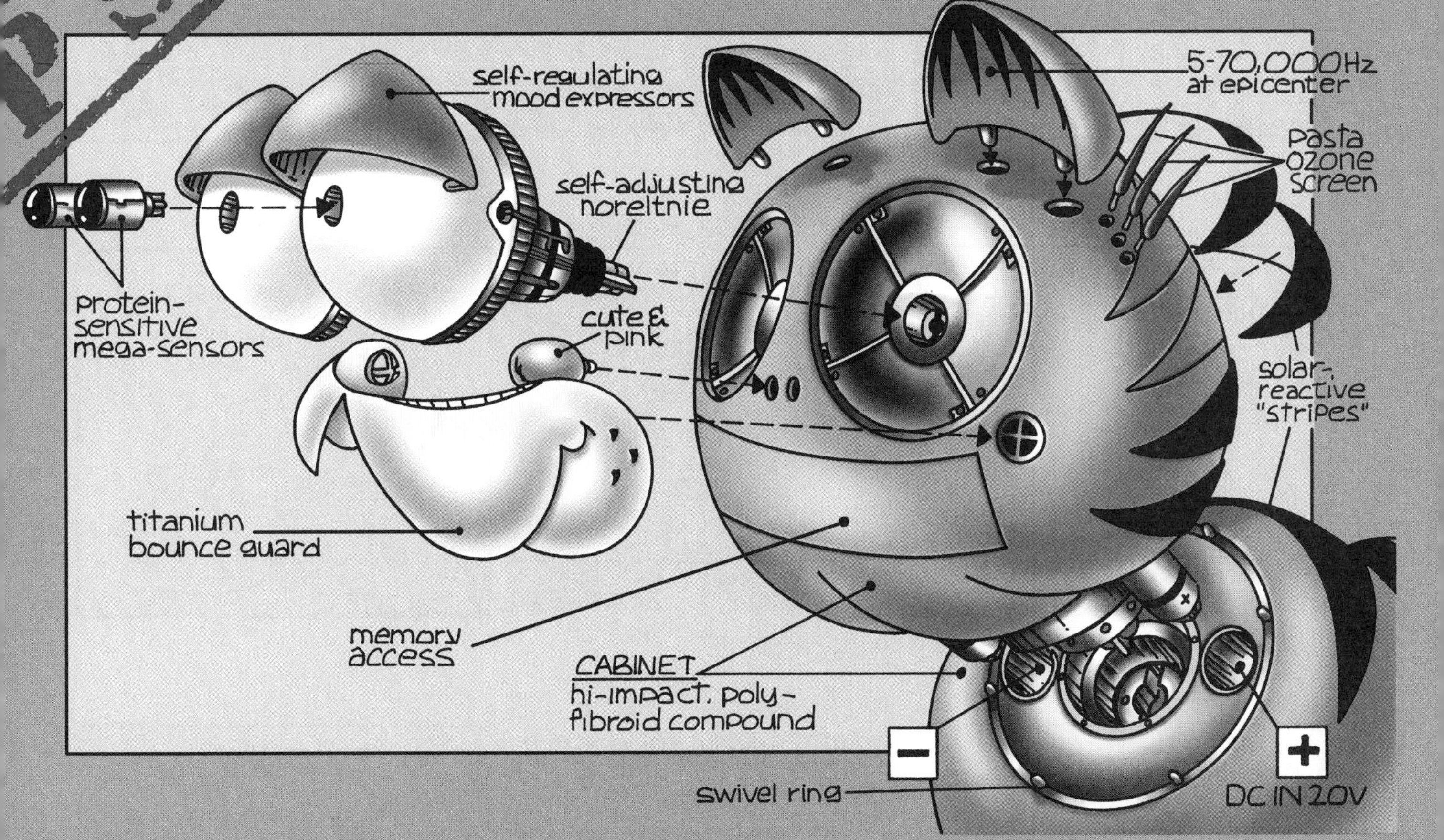

self-regulating mood expressors
5-70,000Hz at epicenter
pasta ozone screen
self-adjusting noreltnie
protein-sensitive mega-sensors
cute & pink
solar-reactive "stripes"
titanium bounce guard
memory access
CABINET
hi-impact. poly-fibroid compound
swivel ring
DC IN 20V

MAJOR COMIC STRIP CHARACTER REPLACED BY A MACHINE!

Rumors are running rampant that Garfield the cat has retired to a South Sea island and has been replaced by a bionic duplicate. This schematic mysteriously ended up in the hands of the publisher. Fact . . . or fiction? Read this book and determine for yourself.

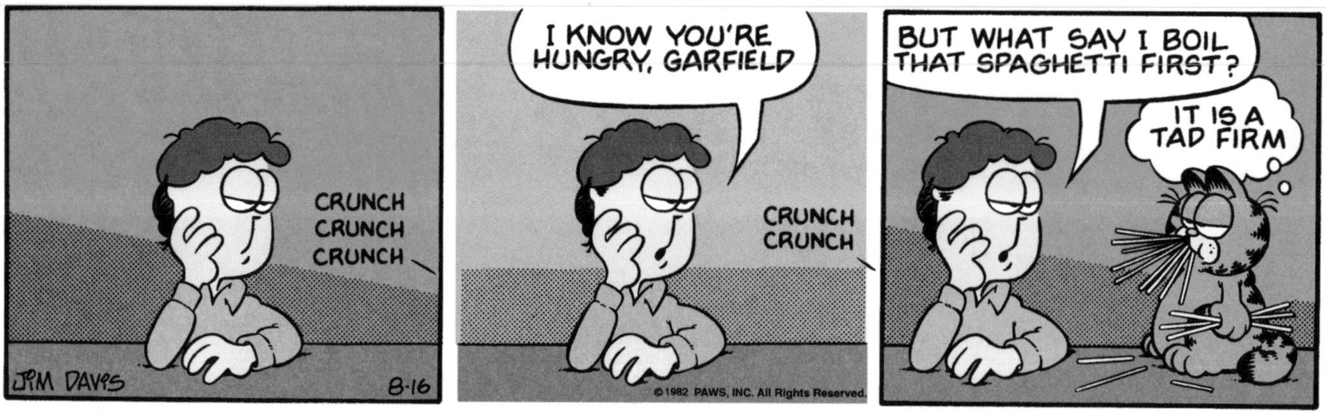
JIM DAVIS
8-16
CRUNCH
CRUNCH
CRUNCH
I KNOW YOU'RE HUNGRY, GARFIELD
CRUNCH
CRUNCH
© 1982 PAWS, INC. All Rights Reserved.
BUT WHAT SAY I BOIL THAT SPAGHETTI FIRST?
IT IS A TAD FIRM

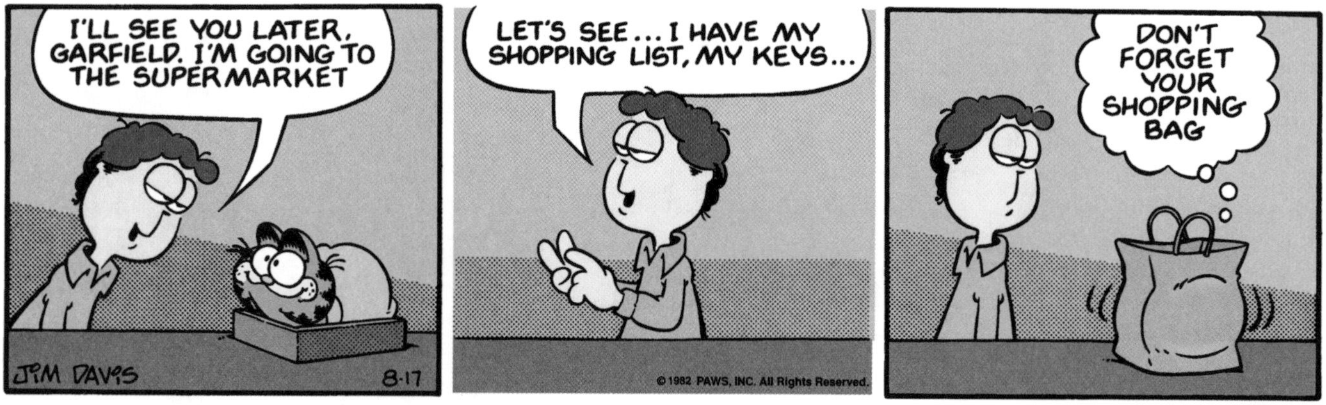
I'LL SEE YOU LATER, GARFIELD. I'M GOING TO THE SUPERMARKET
JIM DAVIS
8-17
LET'S SEE... I HAVE MY SHOPPING LIST, MY KEYS...
© 1982 PAWS, INC. All Rights Reserved.
DON'T FORGET YOUR SHOPPING BAG

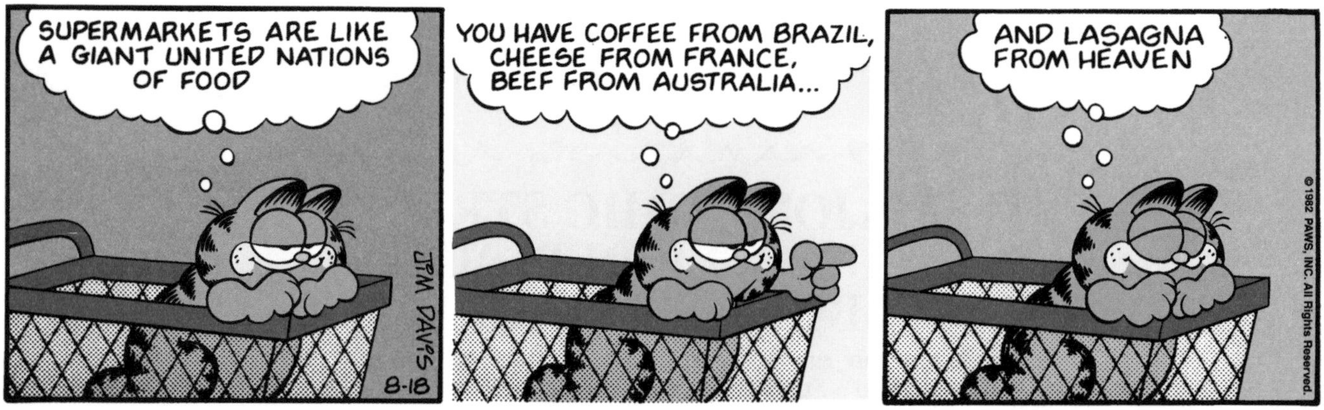
SUPERMARKETS ARE LIKE A GIANT UNITED NATIONS OF FOOD
JIM DAVIS
8-18
YOU HAVE COFFEE FROM BRAZIL, CHEESE FROM FRANCE, BEEF FROM AUSTRALIA...
AND LASAGNA FROM HEAVEN
© 1982 PAWS, INC. All Rights Reserved.

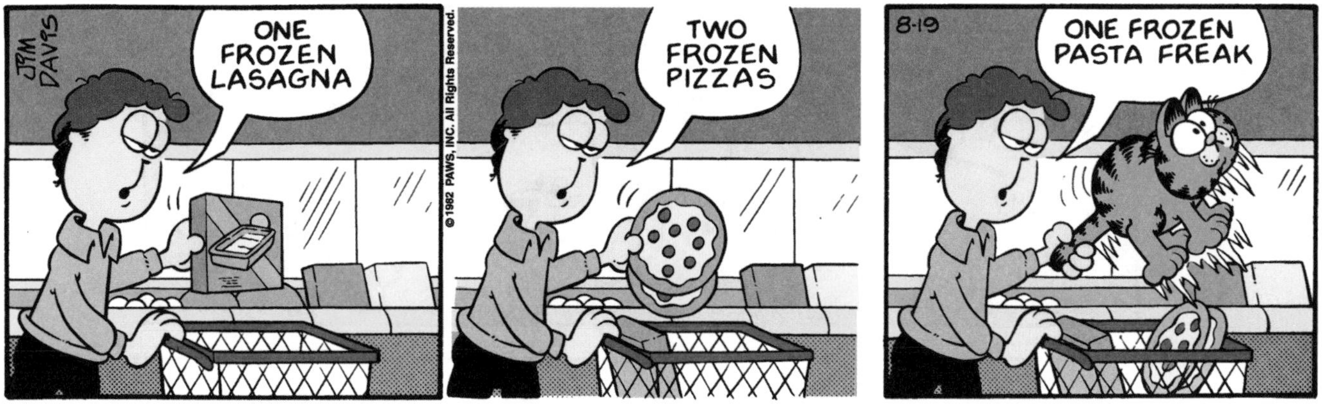
JIM DAVIS
ONE FROZEN LASAGNA
© 1982 PAWS, INC. All Rights Reserved.
TWO FROZEN PIZZAS
8-19
ONE FROZEN PASTA FREAK

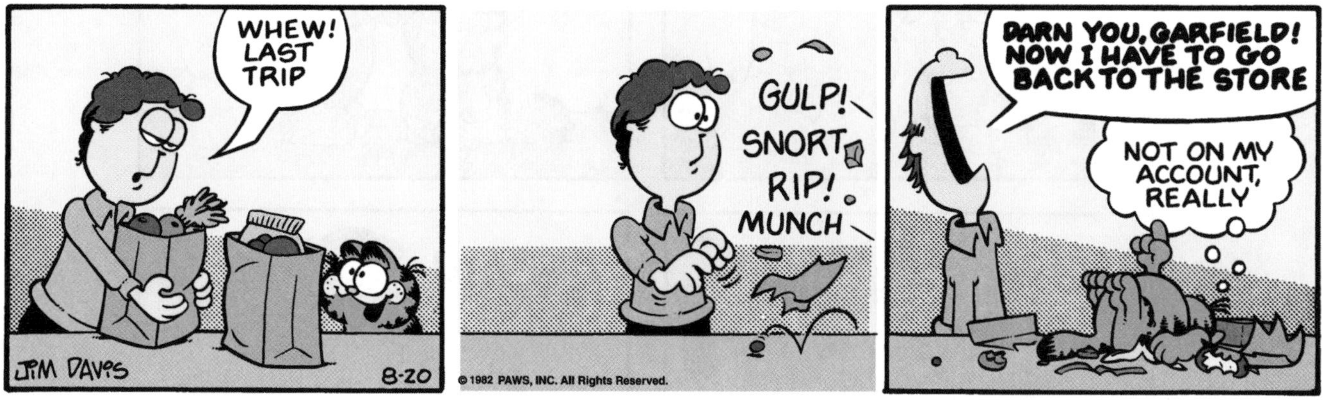
WHEW! LAST TRIP
JIM DAVIS
8-20
GULP!
SNORT
RIP!
MUNCH
© 1982 PAWS, INC. All Rights Reserved.
DARN YOU, GARFIELD! NOW I HAVE TO GO BACK TO THE STORE
NOT ON MY ACCOUNT, REALLY

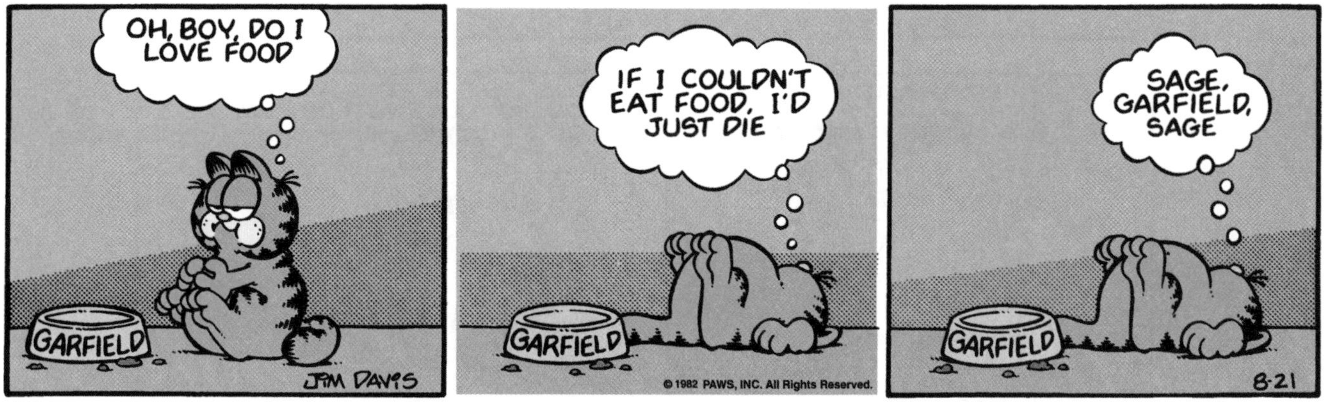
OH, BOY, DO I LOVE FOOD
GARFIELD
JIM DAVIS
IF I COULDN'T EAT FOOD, I'D JUST DIE
GARFIELD
© 1982 PAWS, INC. All Rights Reserved.
SAGE, GARFIELD, SAGE
GARFIELD
8-21

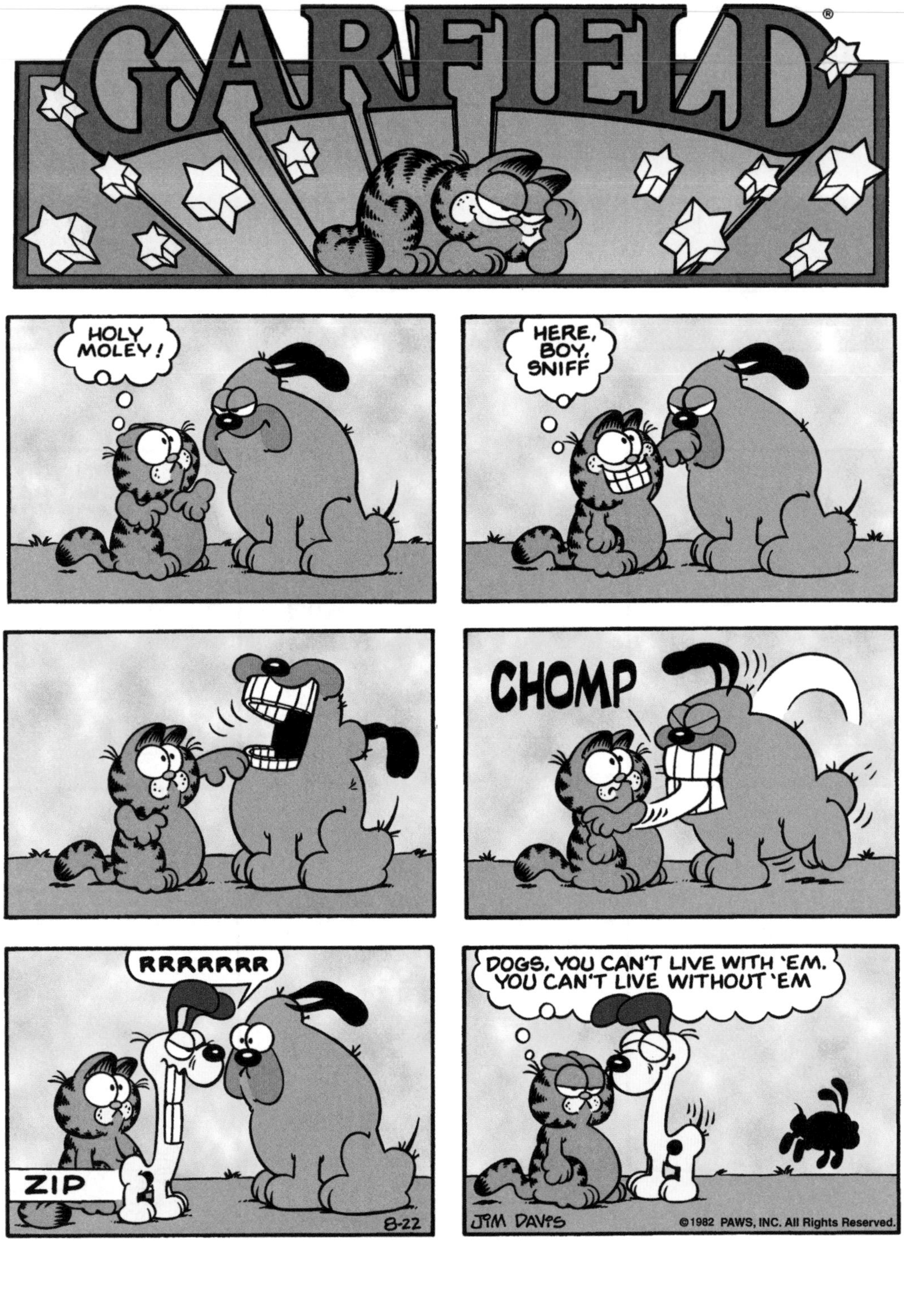
GARFIELD®
HOLY MOLEY!
HERE, BOY, SNIFF
CHOMP
RRRRRRRR
ZIP
DOGS, YOU CAN'T LIVE WITH 'EM. YOU CAN'T LIVE WITHOUT 'EM
8-22
JIM DAVIS
©1982 PAWS, INC. All Rights Reserved.

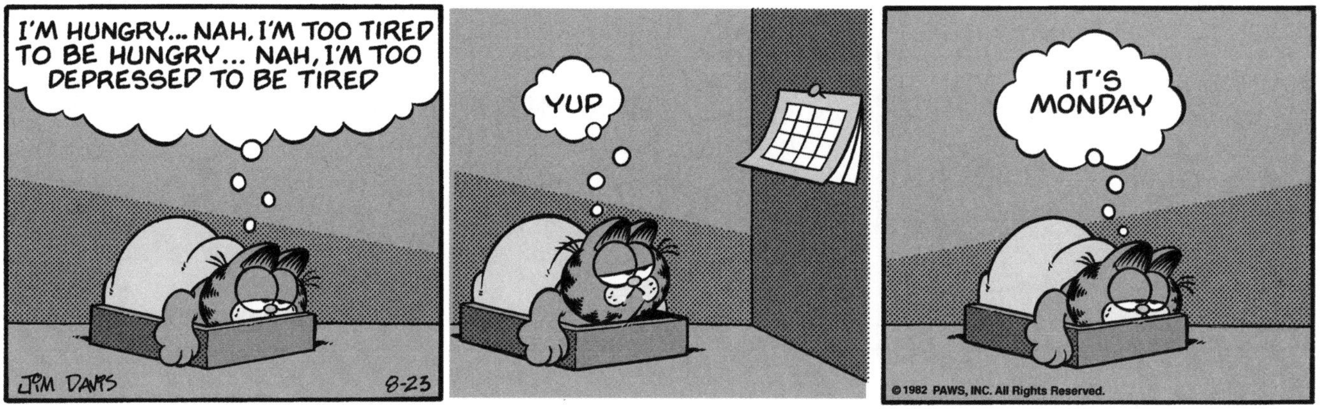
I'M HUNGRY... NAH, I'M TOO TIRED TO BE HUNGRY... NAH, I'M TOO DEPRESSED TO BE TIRED
JIM DAVIS
8-23
YUP
IT'S MONDAY
© 1982 PAWS, INC. All Rights Reserved.

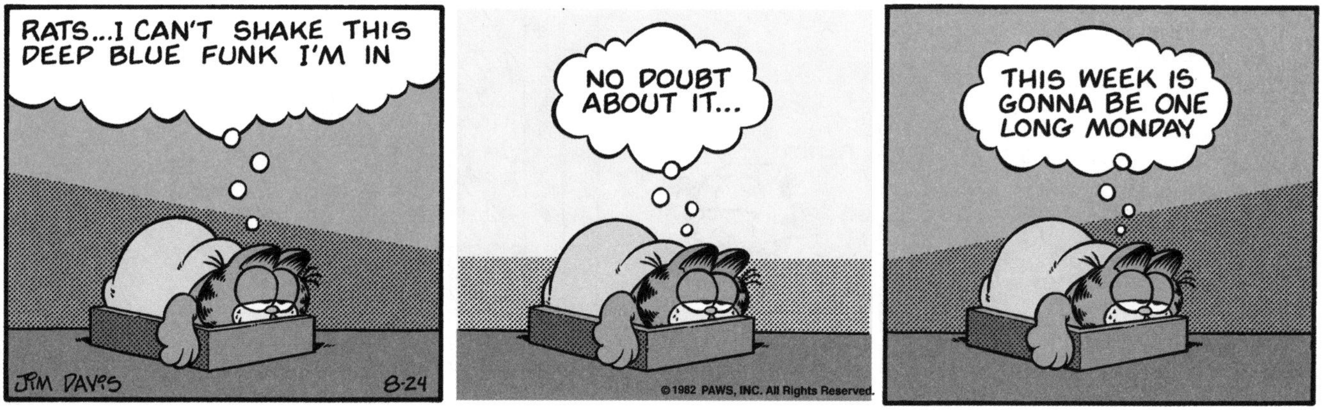
RATS...I CAN'T SHAKE THIS DEEP BLUE FUNK I'M IN
JIM DAVIS
8-24
NO DOUBT ABOUT IT...
© 1982 PAWS, INC. All Rights Reserved.
THIS WEEK IS GONNA BE ONE LONG MONDAY

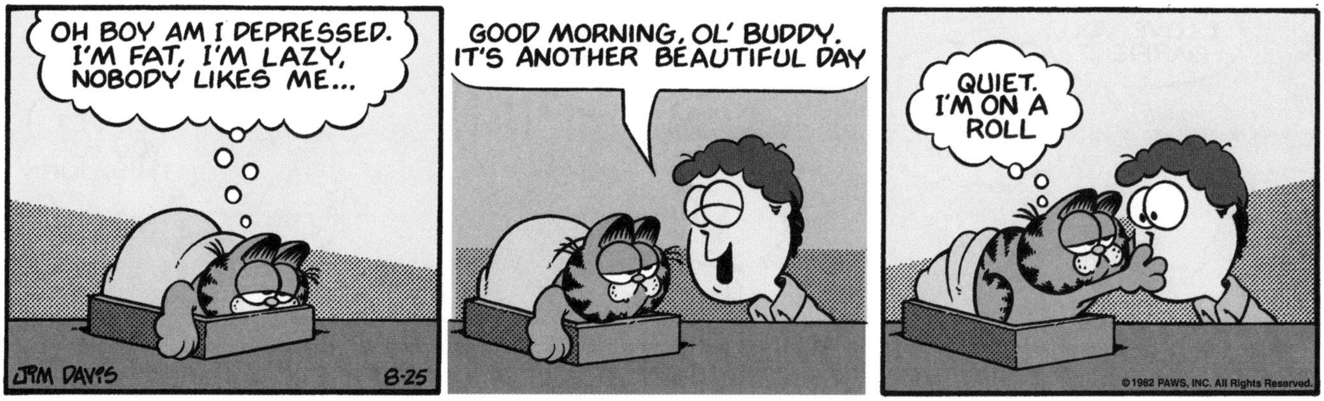
OH BOY AM I DEPRESSED. I'M FAT, I'M LAZY, NOBODY LIKES ME...
JIM DAVIS
8-25
GOOD MORNING, OL' BUDDY. IT'S ANOTHER BEAUTIFUL DAY
QUIET. I'M ON A ROLL
© 1982 PAWS, INC. All Rights Reserved.

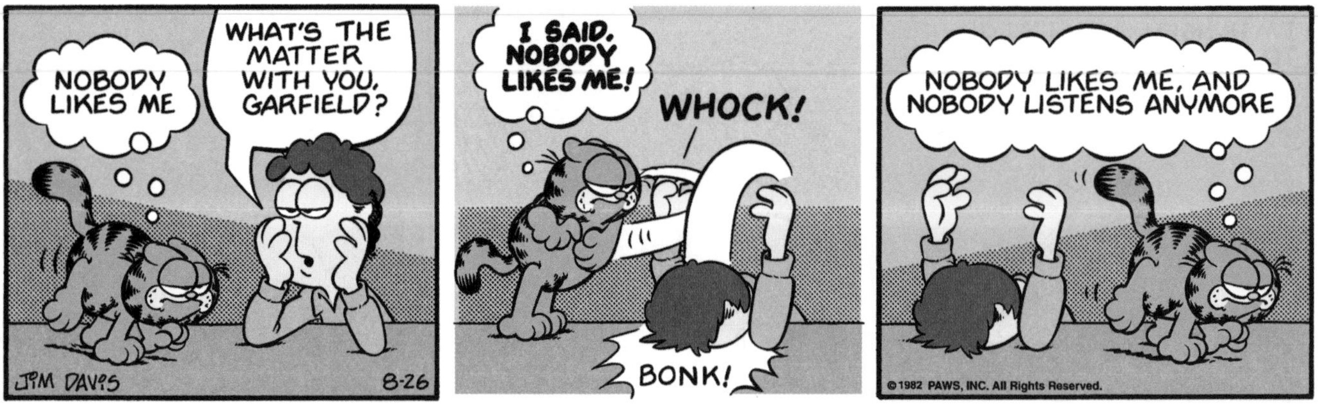
NOBODY LIKES ME
WHAT'S THE MATTER WITH YOU, GARFIELD?
JIM DAVIS
8-26
I SAID, NOBODY LIKES ME!
WHOCK!
BONK!
NOBODY LIKES ME, AND NOBODY LISTENS ANYMORE
© 1982 PAWS, INC. All Rights Reserved.

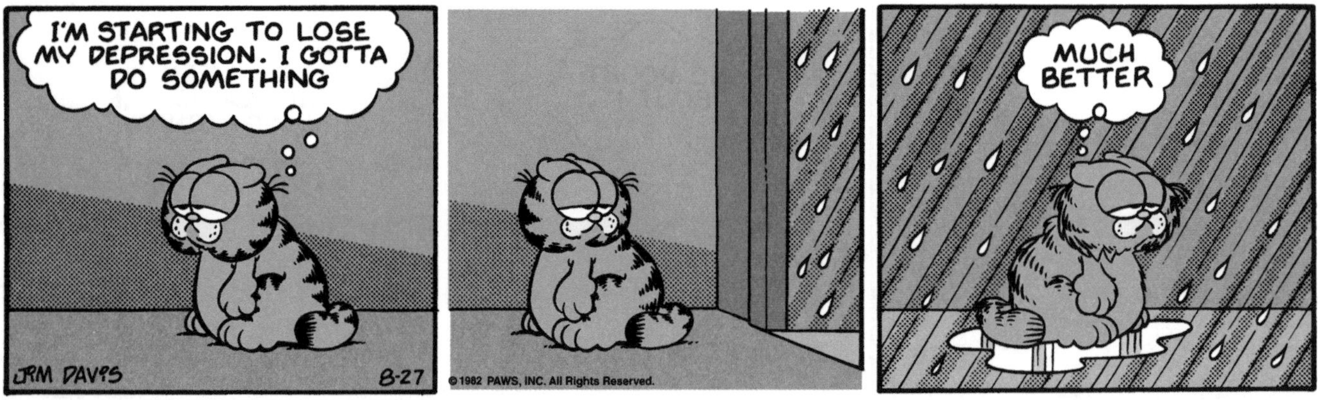
I'M STARTING TO LOSE MY DEPRESSION. I GOTTA DO SOMETHING
JIM DAVIS
8-27
© 1982 PAWS, INC. All Rights Reserved.
MUCH BETTER

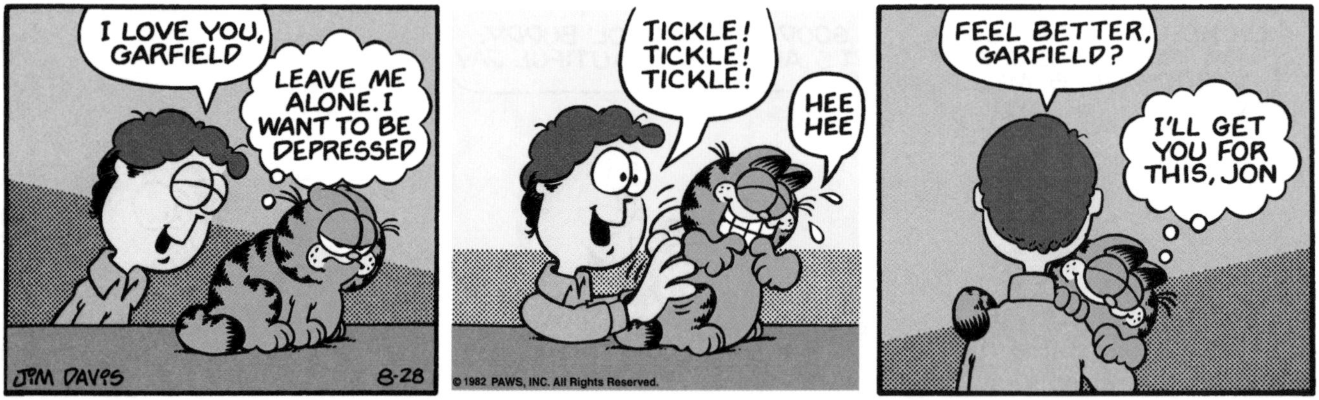
I LOVE YOU, GARFIELD
LEAVE ME ALONE. I WANT TO BE DEPRESSED
JIM DAVIS
8-28
TICKLE! TICKLE! TICKLE!
HEE HEE
© 1982 PAWS, INC. All Rights Reserved.
FEEL BETTER, GARFIELD?
I'LL GET YOU FOR THIS, JON

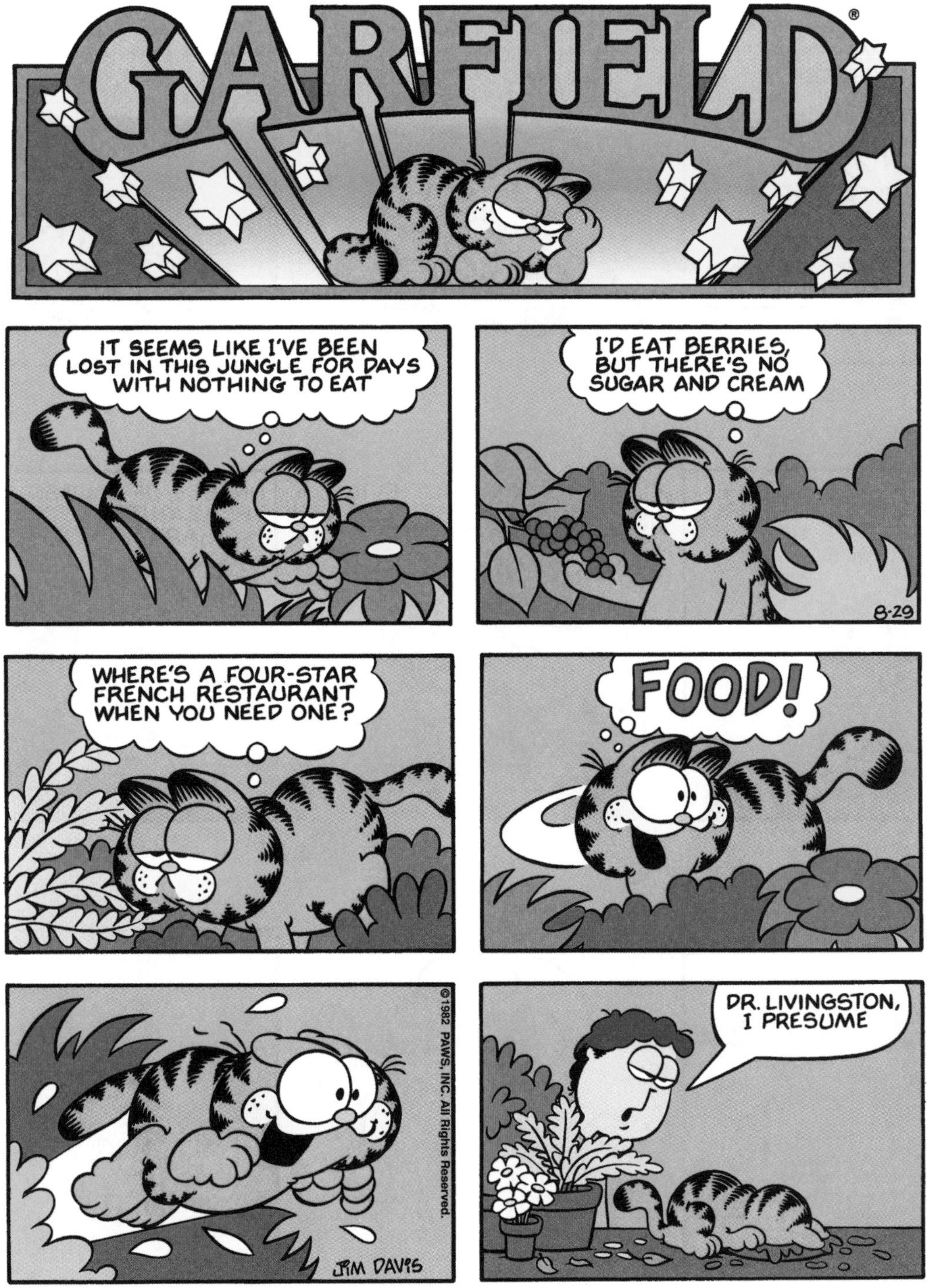
GARFIELD®
IT SEEMS LIKE I'VE BEEN LOST IN THIS JUNGLE FOR DAYS WITH NOTHING TO EAT
I'D EAT BERRIES, BUT THERE'S NO SUGAR AND CREAM
8-29
WHERE'S A FOUR-STAR FRENCH RESTAURANT WHEN YOU NEED ONE?
FOOD!
© 1982 PAWS, INC. All Rights Reserved.
JIM DAVIS
DR. LIVINGSTON, I PRESUME

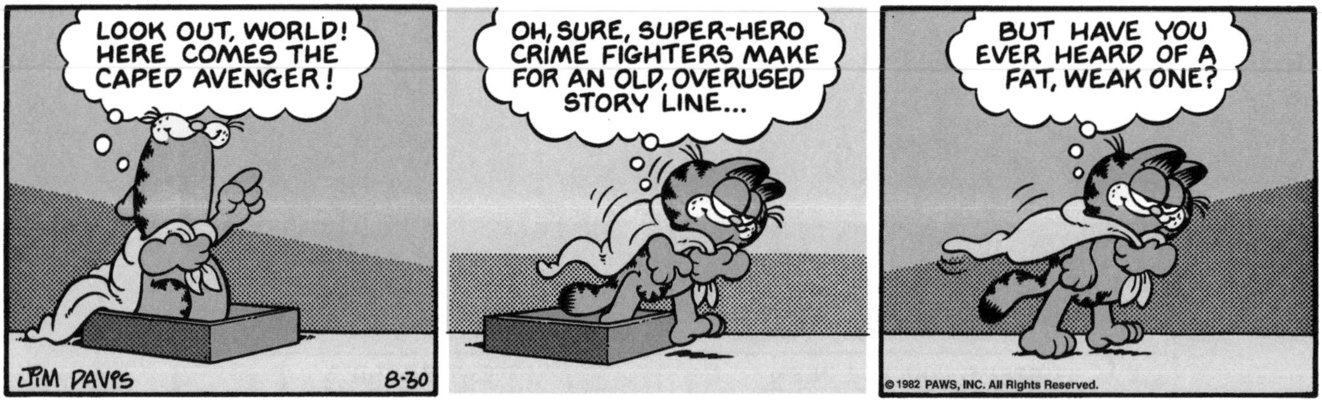
LOOK OUT, WORLD! HERE COMES THE CAPED AVENGER!
JIM DAVIS
8-30
OH, SURE, SUPER-HERO CRIME FIGHTERS MAKE FOR AN OLD, OVERUSED STORY LINE...
BUT HAVE YOU EVER HEARD OF A FAT, WEAK ONE?
© 1982 PAWS, INC. All Rights Reserved.

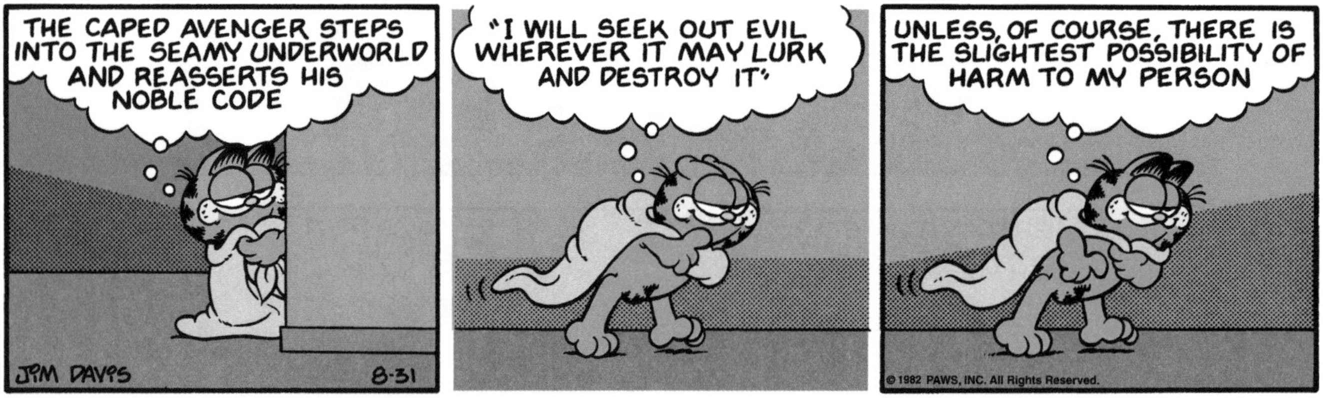
THE CAPED AVENGER STEPS INTO THE SEAMY UNDERWORLD AND REASSERTS HIS NOBLE CODE
JIM DAVIS
8-31
"I WILL SEEK OUT EVIL WHEREVER IT MAY LURK AND DESTROY IT"
UNLESS, OF COURSE, THERE IS THE SLIGHTEST POSSIBILITY OF HARM TO MY PERSON
© 1982 PAWS, INC. All Rights Reserved.

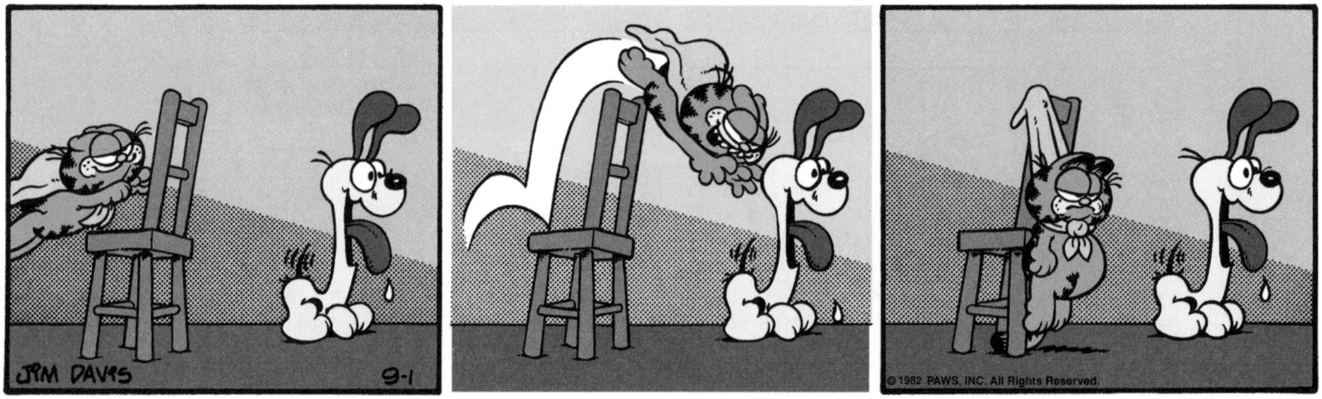
JIM DAVIS
9-1
© 1982 PAWS, INC. All Rights Reserved.

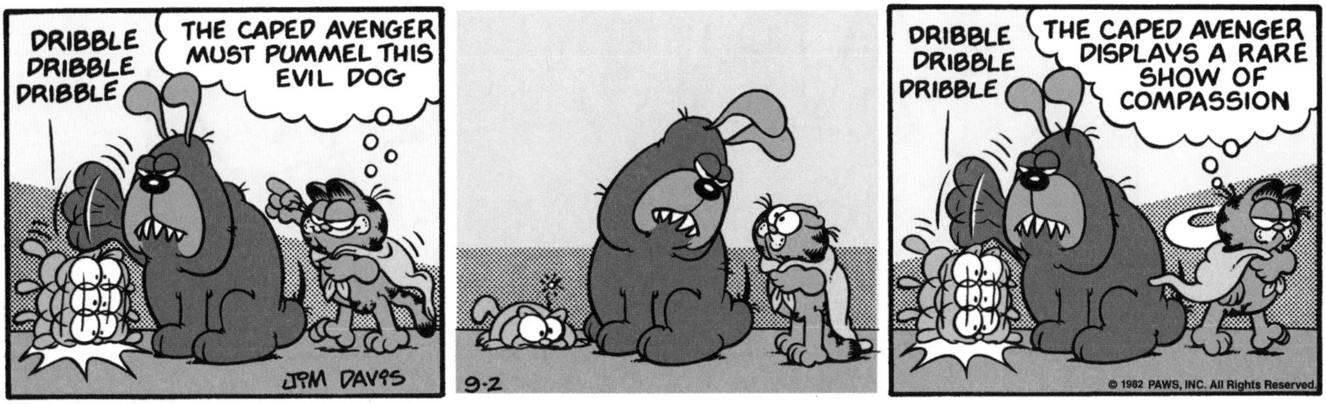
DRIBBLE DRIBBLE DRIBBLE
THE CAPED AVENGER MUST PUMMEL THIS EVIL DOG
JIM DAVIS
9-2
DRIBBLE DRIBBLE DRIBBLE
THE CAPED AVENGER DISPLAYS A RARE SHOW OF COMPASSION
© 1982 PAWS, INC. All Rights Reserved.

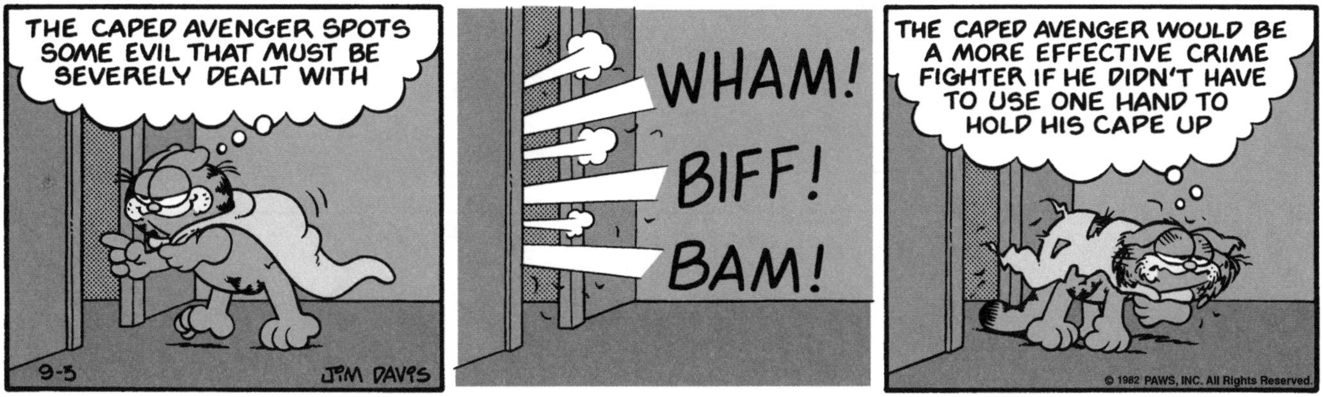
THE CAPED AVENGER SPOTS SOME EVIL THAT MUST BE SEVERELY DEALT WITH
9-3
JIM DAVIS
WHAM!
BIFF!
BAM!
THE CAPED AVENGER WOULD BE A MORE EFFECTIVE CRIME FIGHTER IF HE DIDN'T HAVE TO USE ONE HAND TO HOLD HIS CAPE UP
© 1982 PAWS, INC. All Rights Reserved.

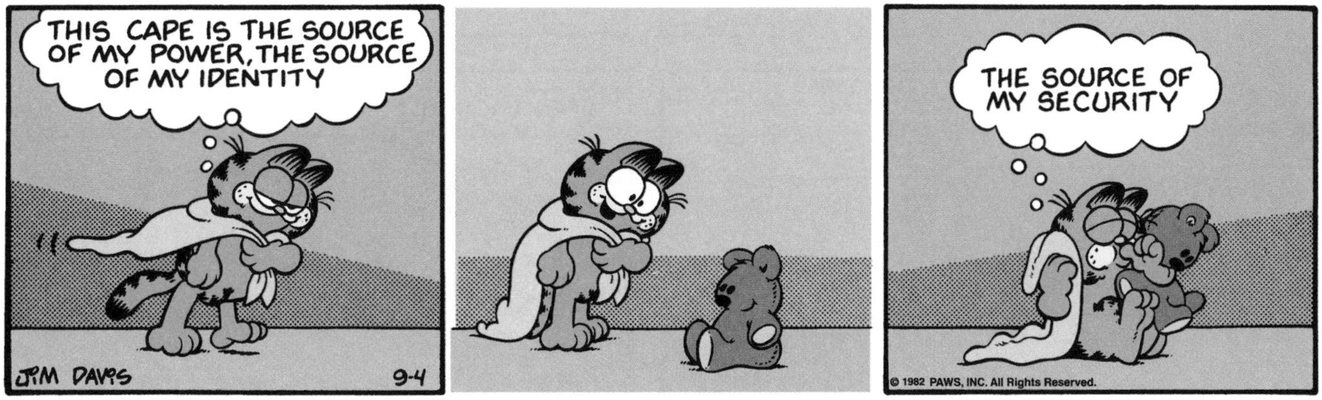
THIS CAPE IS THE SOURCE OF MY POWER, THE SOURCE OF MY IDENTITY
JIM DAVIS
9-4
THE SOURCE OF MY SECURITY
© 1982 PAWS, INC. All Rights Reserved.

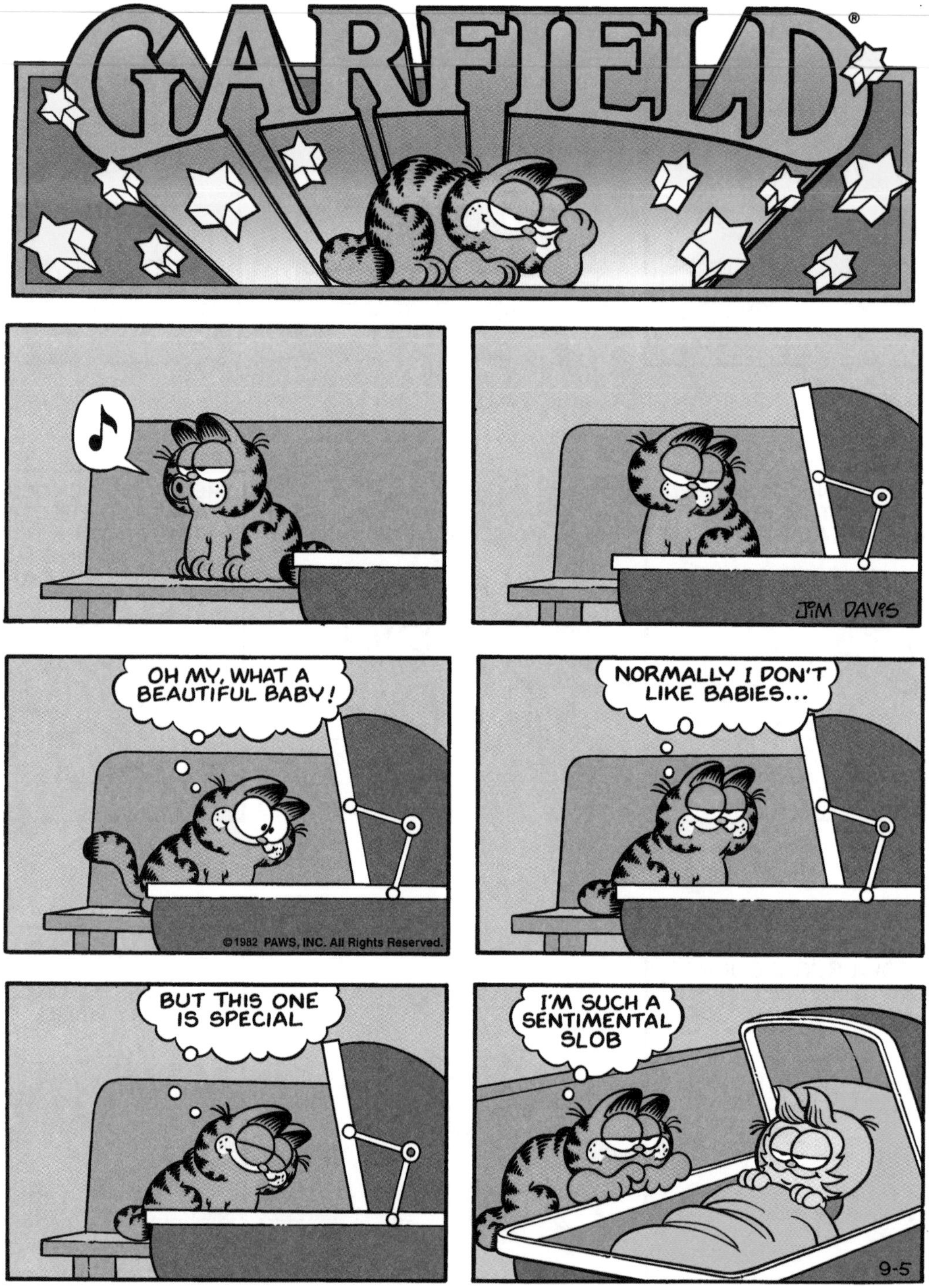
GARFIELD
JIM DAVIS
OH MY, WHAT A BEAUTIFUL BABY!
NORMALLY I DON'T LIKE BABIES...
BUT THIS ONE IS SPECIAL
I'M SUCH A SENTIMENTAL SLOB
©1982 PAWS, INC. All Rights Reserved.
9-5

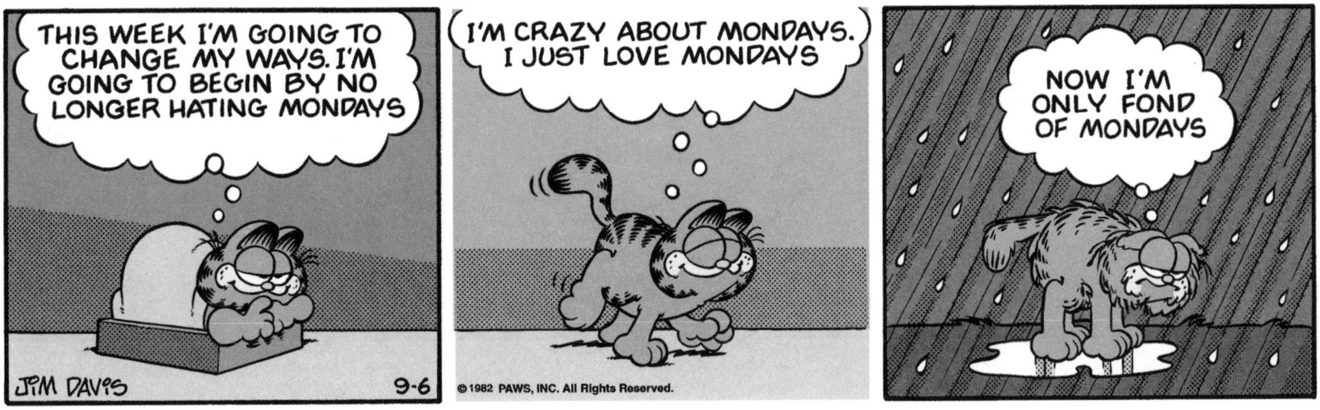
THIS WEEK I'M GOING TO CHANGE MY WAYS. I'M GOING TO BEGIN BY NO LONGER HATING MONDAYS
JIM DAVIS
9-6
I'M CRAZY ABOUT MONDAYS. I JUST LOVE MONDAYS
© 1982 PAWS, INC. All Rights Reserved.
NOW I'M ONLY FOND OF MONDAYS

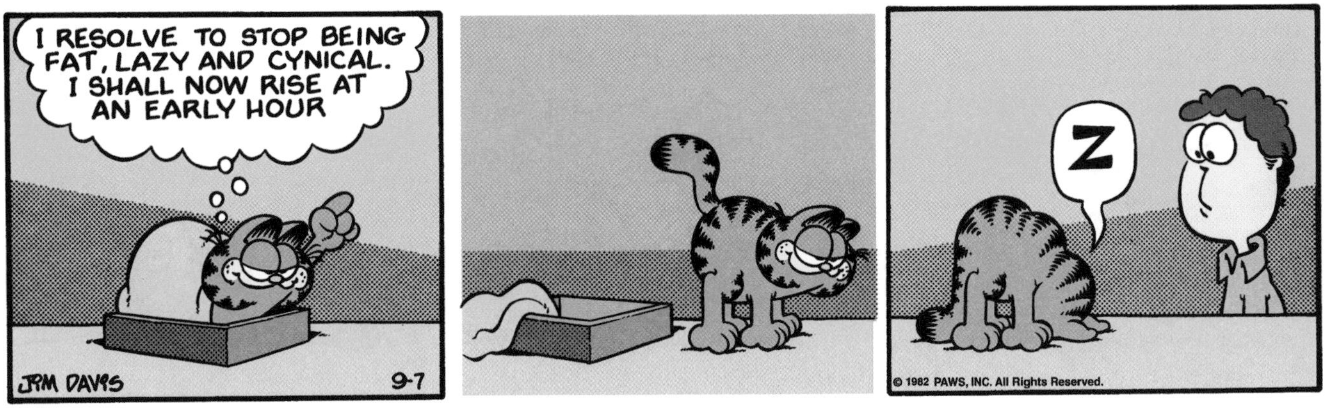
I RESOLVE TO STOP BEING FAT, LAZY AND CYNICAL. I SHALL NOW RISE AT AN EARLY HOUR
JIM DAVIS
9-7
Z
© 1982 PAWS, INC. All Rights Reserved.

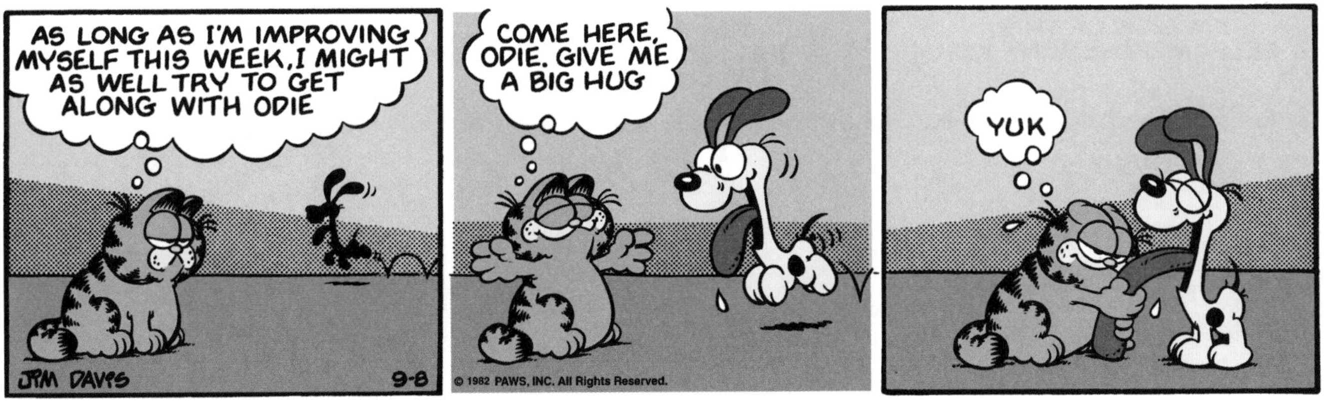
AS LONG AS I'M IMPROVING MYSELF THIS WEEK, I MIGHT AS WELL TRY TO GET ALONG WITH ODIE
JIM DAVIS
9-8
COME HERE, ODIE. GIVE ME A BIG HUG
© 1982 PAWS, INC. All Rights Reserved.
YUK

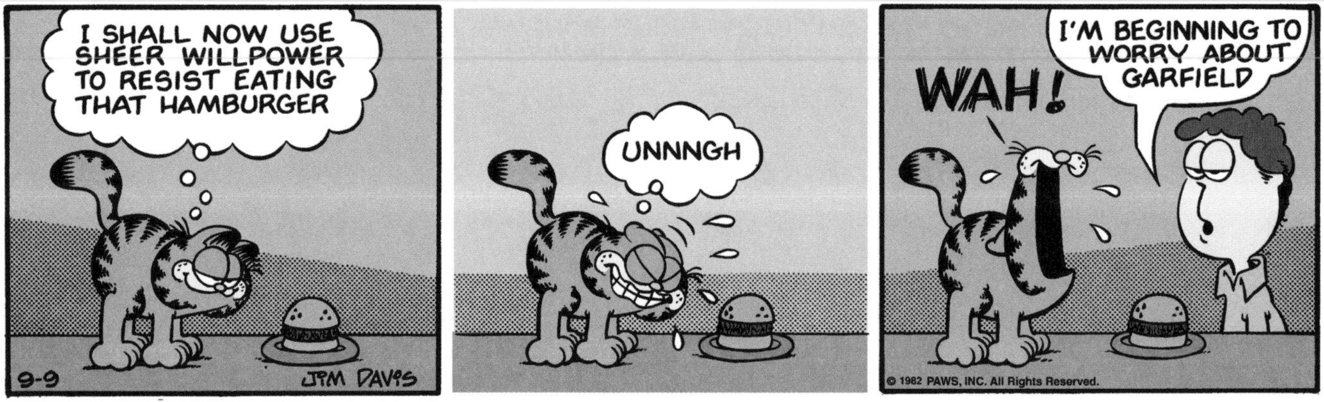
I SHALL NOW USE SHEER WILLPOWER TO RESIST EATING THAT HAMBURGER
9-9
JIM DAVIS
UNNNGH
WAH!
I'M BEGINNING TO WORRY ABOUT GARFIELD
© 1982 PAWS, INC. All Rights Reserved.

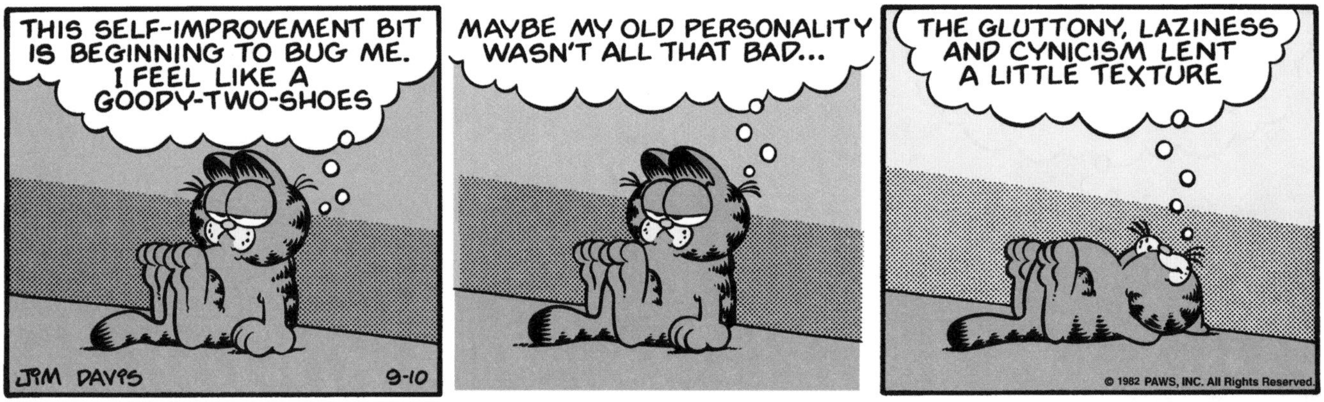
THIS SELF-IMPROVEMENT BIT IS BEGINNING TO BUG ME. I FEEL LIKE A GOODY-TWO-SHOES
JIM DAVIS
9-10
MAYBE MY OLD PERSONALITY WASN'T ALL THAT BAD...
THE GLUTTONY, LAZINESS AND CYNICISM LENT A LITTLE TEXTURE
© 1982 PAWS, INC. All Rights Reserved.

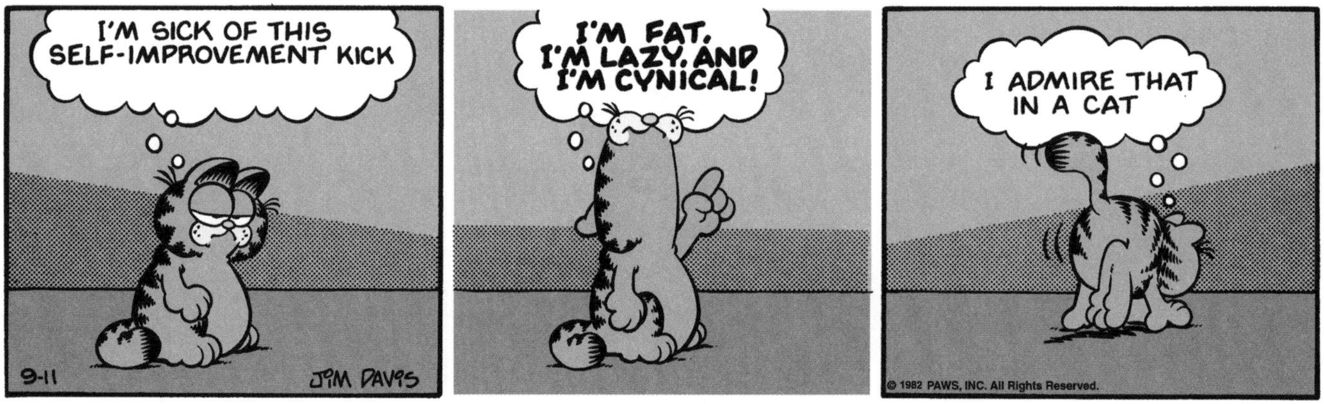
I'M SICK OF THIS SELF-IMPROVEMENT KICK
9-11
JIM DAVIS
I'M FAT. I'M LAZY. AND I'M CYNICAL!
I ADMIRE THAT IN A CAT
© 1982 PAWS, INC. All Rights Reserved.

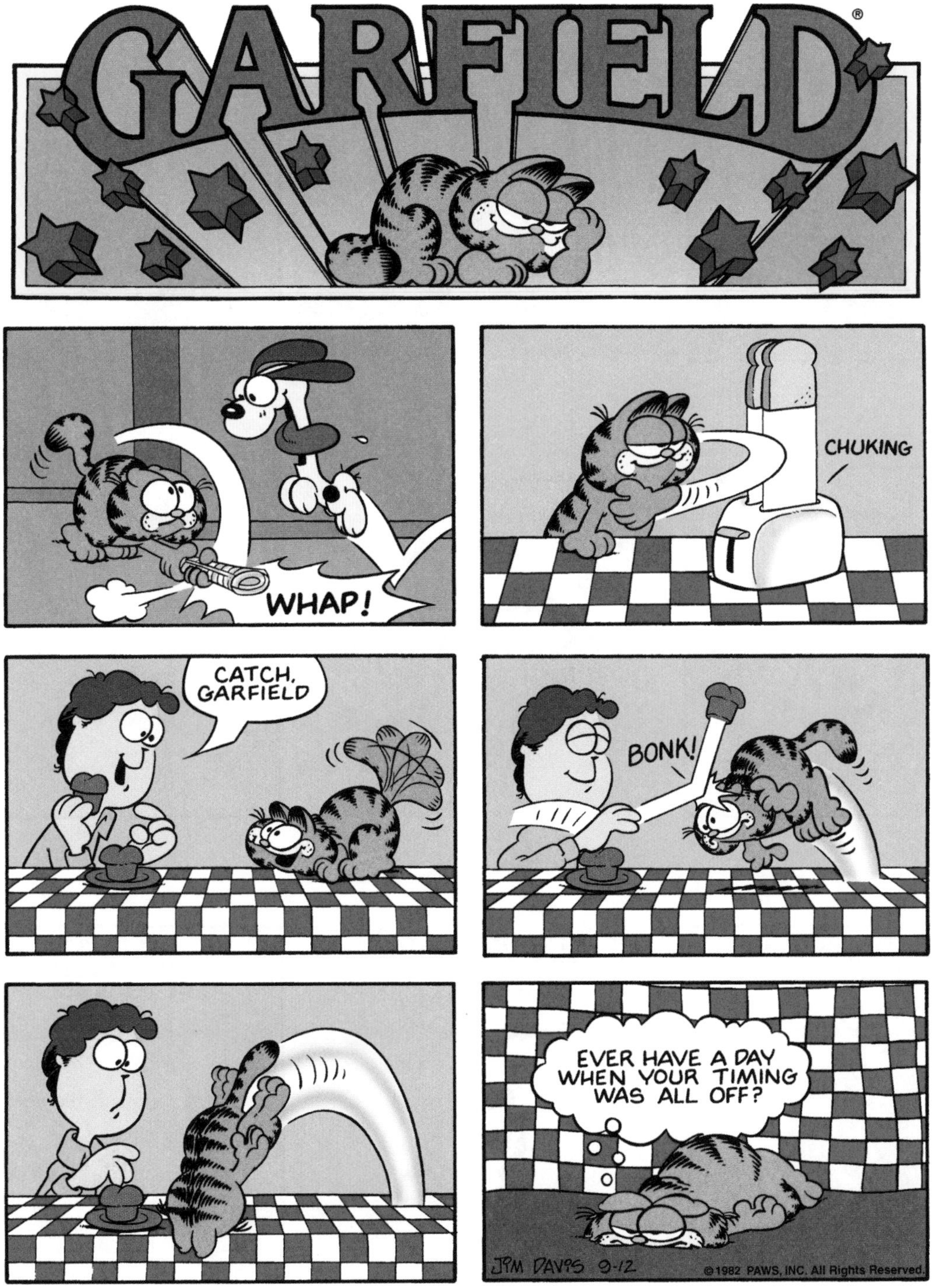
GARFIELD®
WHAP!
CHUKING
CATCH, GARFIELD
BONK!
EVER HAVE A DAY WHEN YOUR TIMING WAS ALL OFF?
JIM DAVIS 9-12
©1982 PAWS, INC. All Rights Reserved.

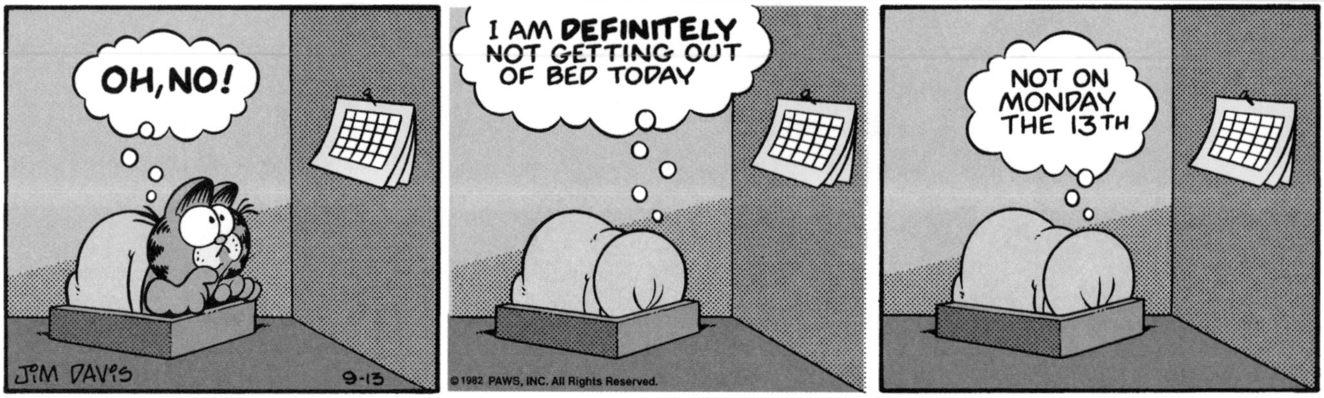
OH, NO!
JIM DAVIS
9-13
I AM DEFINITELY NOT GETTING OUT OF BED TODAY
© 1982 PAWS, INC. All Rights Reserved.
NOT ON MONDAY THE 13TH

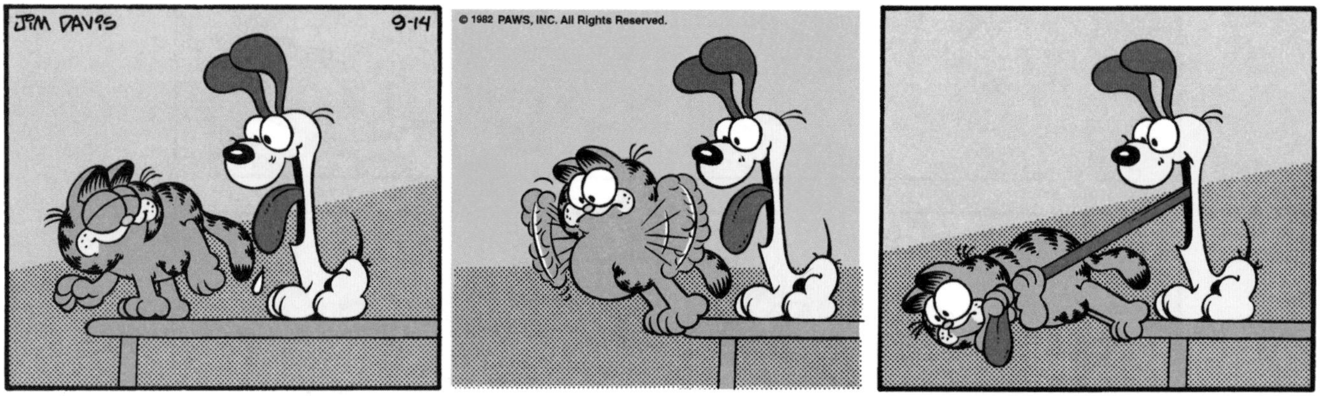
JIM DAVIS
9-14
© 1982 PAWS, INC. All Rights Reserved.

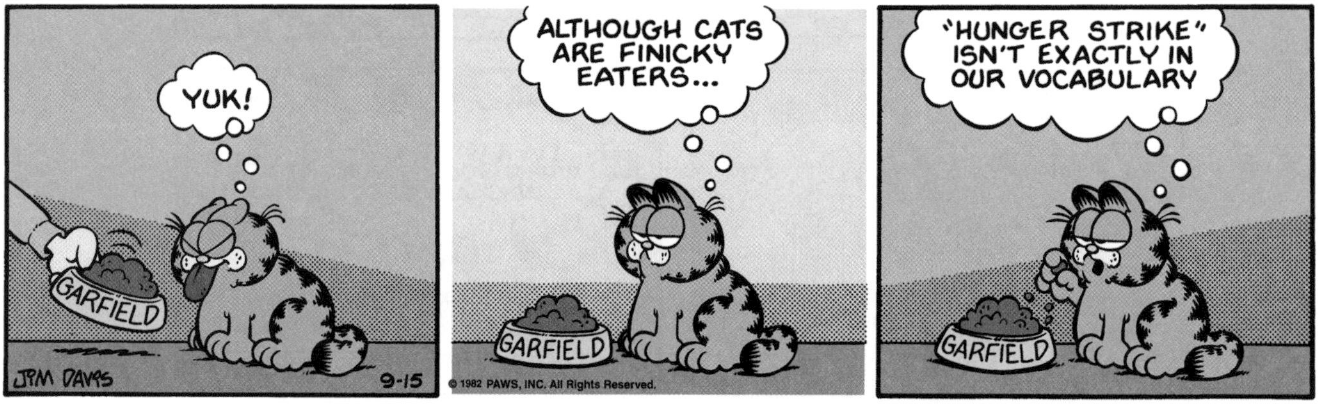
YUK!
GARFIELD
JIM DAVIS
9-15
ALTHOUGH CATS ARE FINICKY EATERS...
GARFIELD
© 1982 PAWS, INC. All Rights Reserved.
"HUNGER STRIKE" ISN'T EXACTLY IN OUR VOCABULARY
GARFIELD

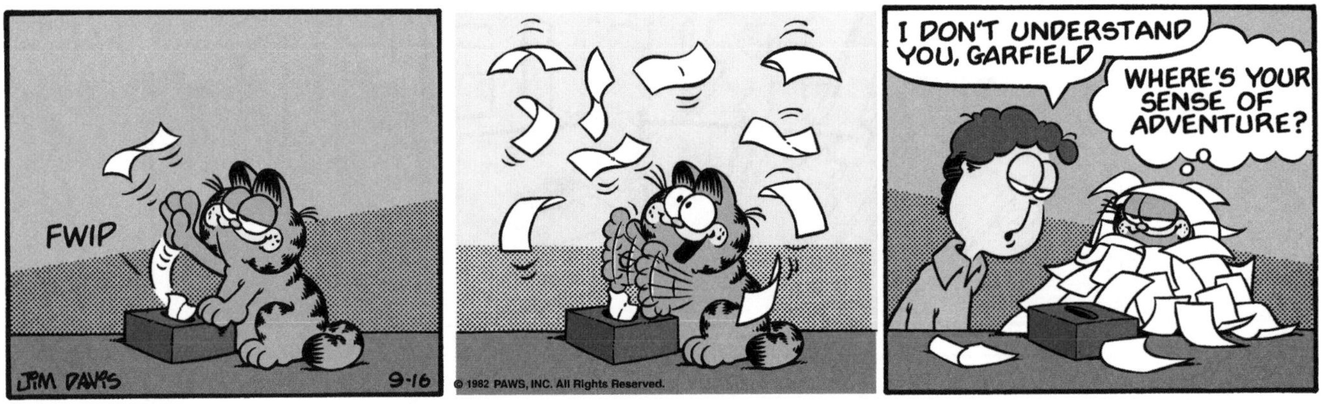
FWIP
JIM DAVIS
9-16
© 1982 PAWS, INC. All Rights Reserved.
I DON'T UNDERSTAND YOU, GARFIELD
WHERE'S YOUR SENSE OF ADVENTURE?

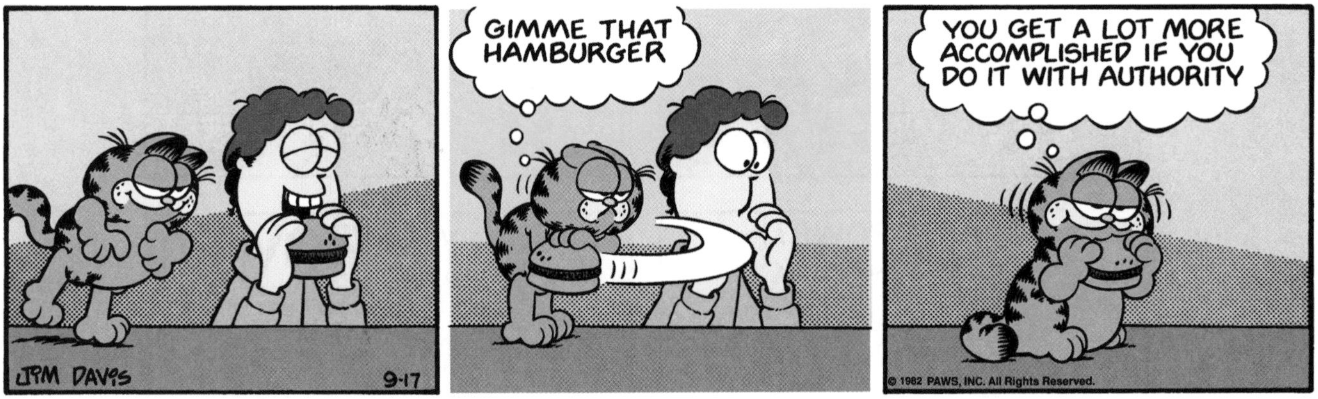
JIM DAVIS
9-17
GIMME THAT HAMBURGER
YOU GET A LOT MORE ACCOMPLISHED IF YOU DO IT WITH AUTHORITY
© 1982 PAWS, INC. All Rights Reserved.

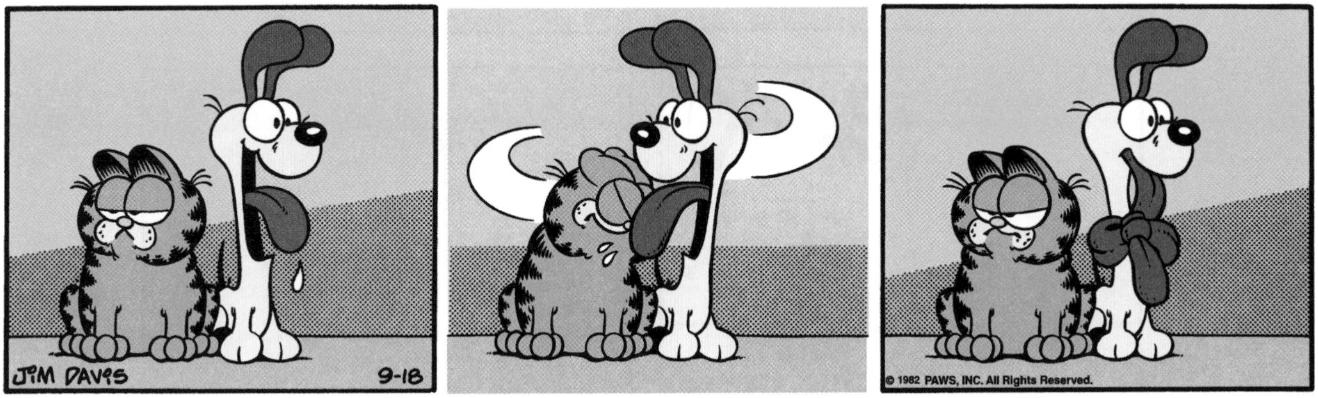
JIM DAVIS
9-18
© 1982 PAWS, INC. All Rights Reserved.

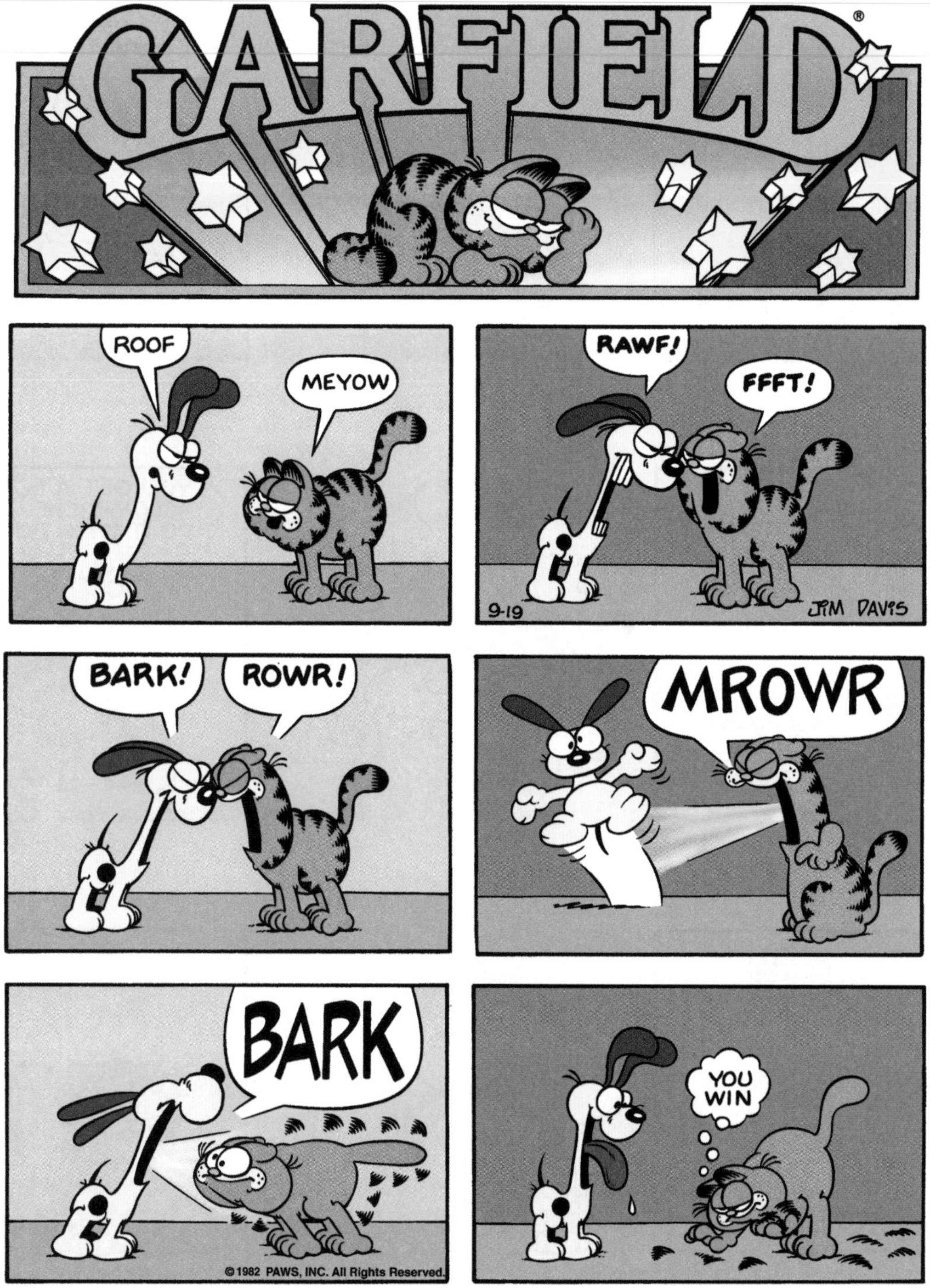
GARFIELD®
ROOF
MEYOW
RAWF!
FFFT!
9-19
JIM DAVIS
BARK!
ROWR!
MROWR
BARK
© 1982 PAWS, INC. All Rights Reserved.
YOU WIN

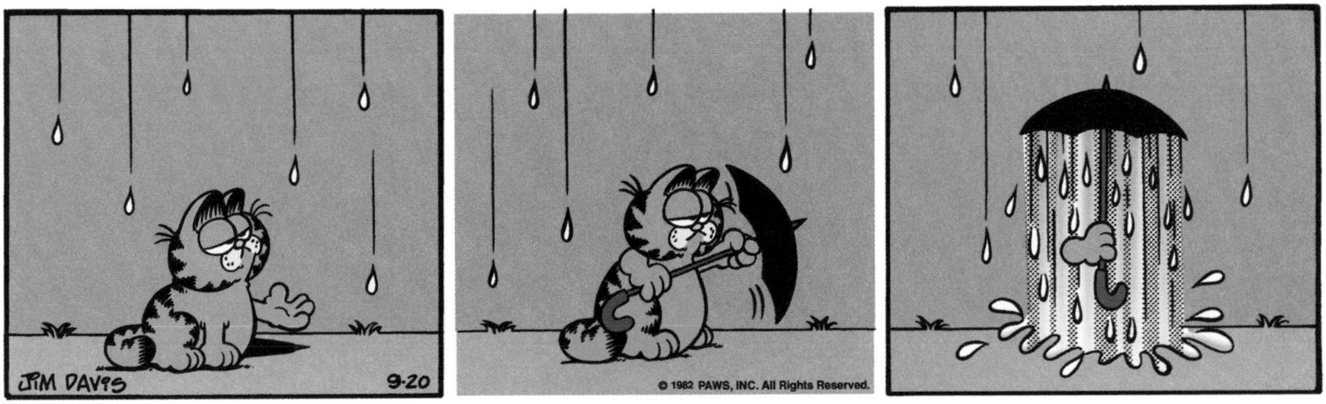
JIM DAVIS
9-20
© 1982 PAWS, INC. All Rights Reserved.

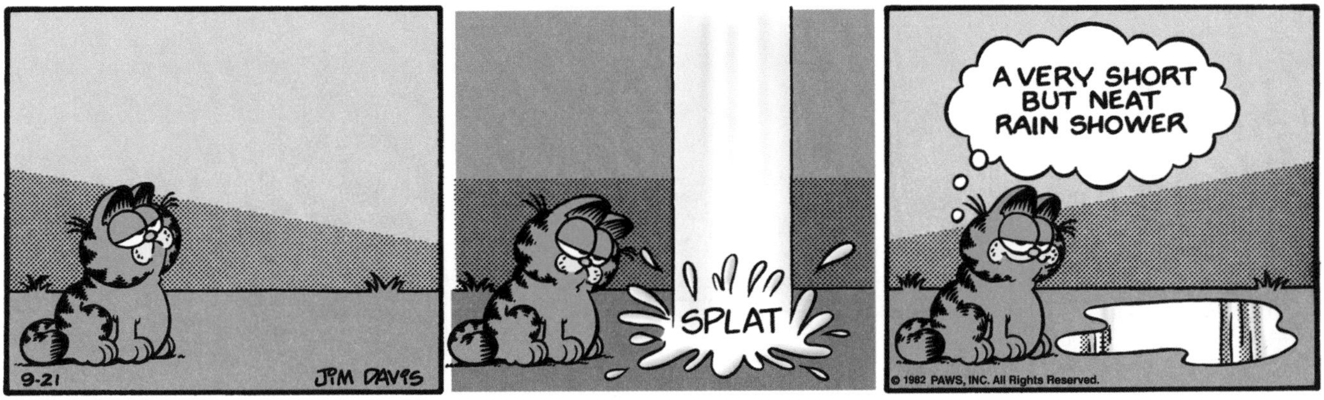
9-21
JIM DAVIS
SPLAT
A VERY SHORT BUT NEAT RAIN SHOWER
© 1982 PAWS, INC. All Rights Reserved.

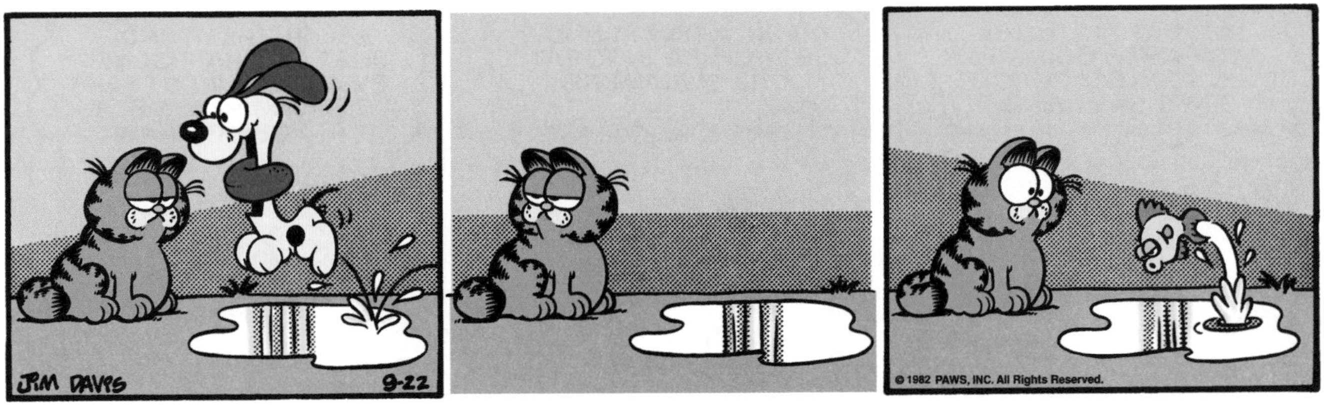
JIM DAVIS
9-22
© 1982 PAWS, INC. All Rights Reserved.

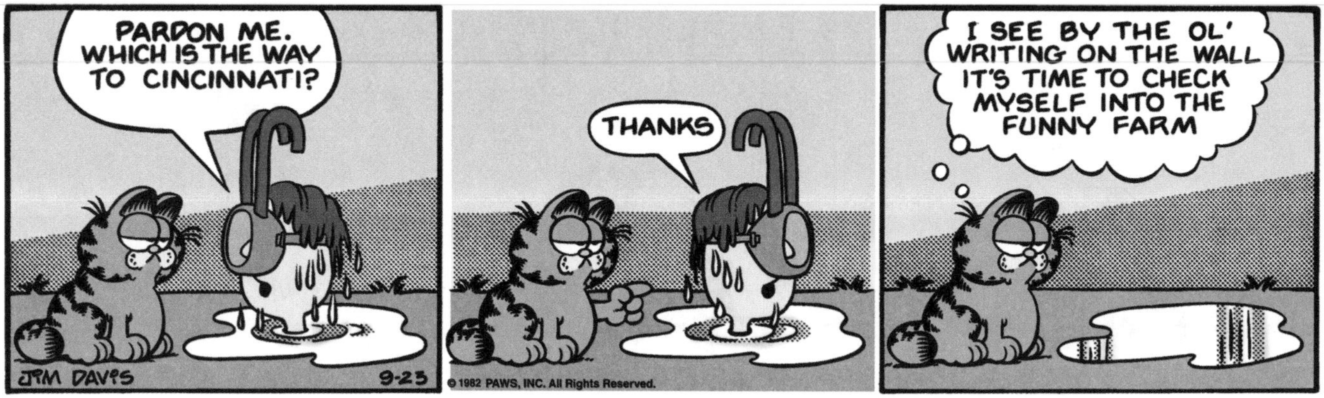
PARDON ME. WHICH IS THE WAY TO CINCINNATI?
JIM DAVIS
9-23
THANKS
© 1982 PAWS, INC. All Rights Reserved.
I SEE BY THE OL' WRITING ON THE WALL IT'S TIME TO CHECK MYSELF INTO THE FUNNY FARM

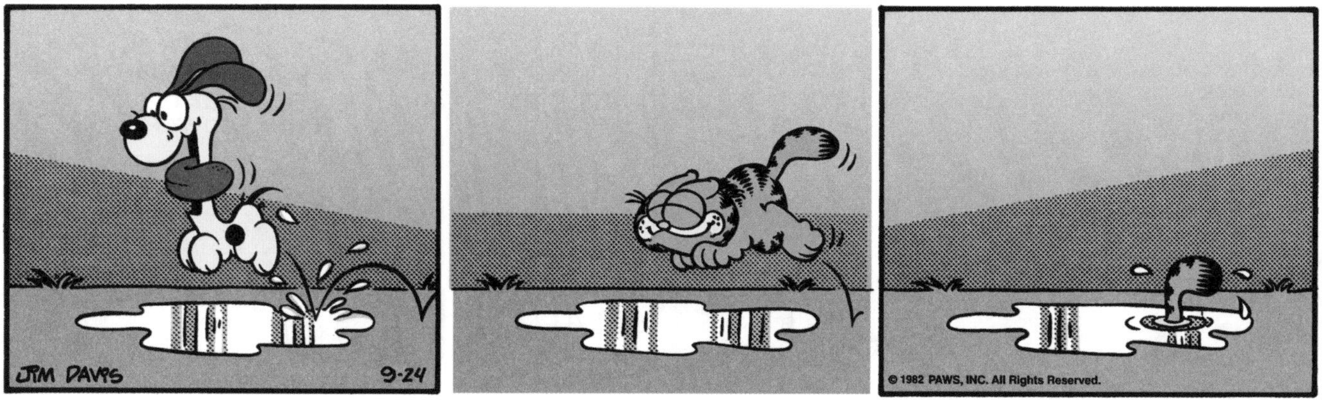
JIM DAVIS
9-24
© 1982 PAWS, INC. All Rights Reserved.

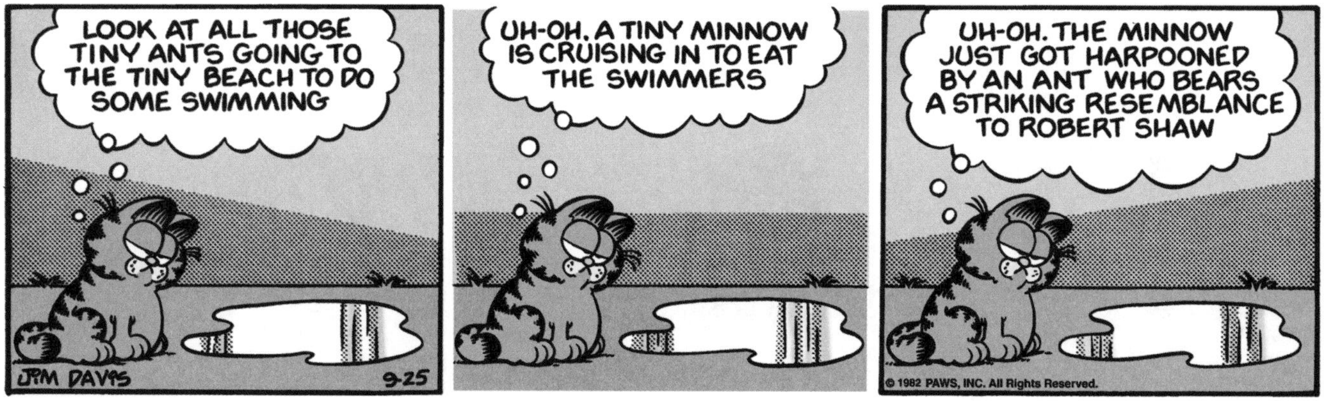
LOOK AT ALL THOSE TINY ANTS GOING TO THE TINY BEACH TO DO SOME SWIMMING
JIM DAVIS
9-25
UH-OH. A TINY MINNOW IS CRUISING IN TO EAT THE SWIMMERS
UH-OH. THE MINNOW JUST GOT HARPOONED BY AN ANT WHO BEARS A STRIKING RESEMBLANCE TO ROBERT SHAW
© 1982 PAWS, INC. All Rights Reserved.

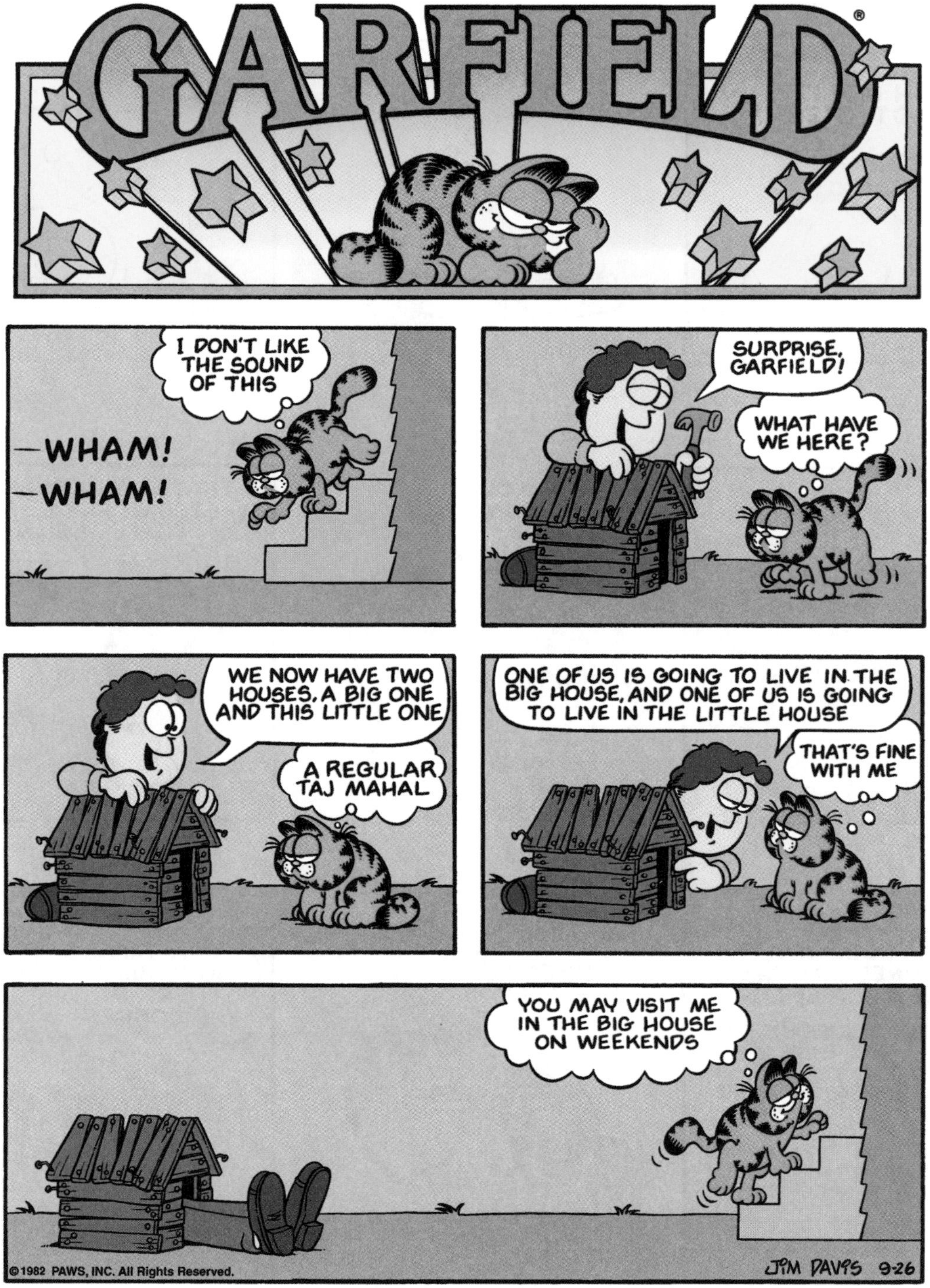
GARFIELD
WHAM!
WHAM!
I DON'T LIKE THE SOUND OF THIS
SURPRISE, GARFIELD!
WHAT HAVE WE HERE?
WE NOW HAVE TWO HOUSES, A BIG ONE AND THIS LITTLE ONE
A REGULAR TAJ MAHAL
ONE OF US IS GOING TO LIVE IN THE BIG HOUSE, AND ONE OF US IS GOING TO LIVE IN THE LITTLE HOUSE
THAT'S FINE WITH ME
YOU MAY VISIT ME IN THE BIG HOUSE ON WEEKENDS
JIM DAVIS 9-26

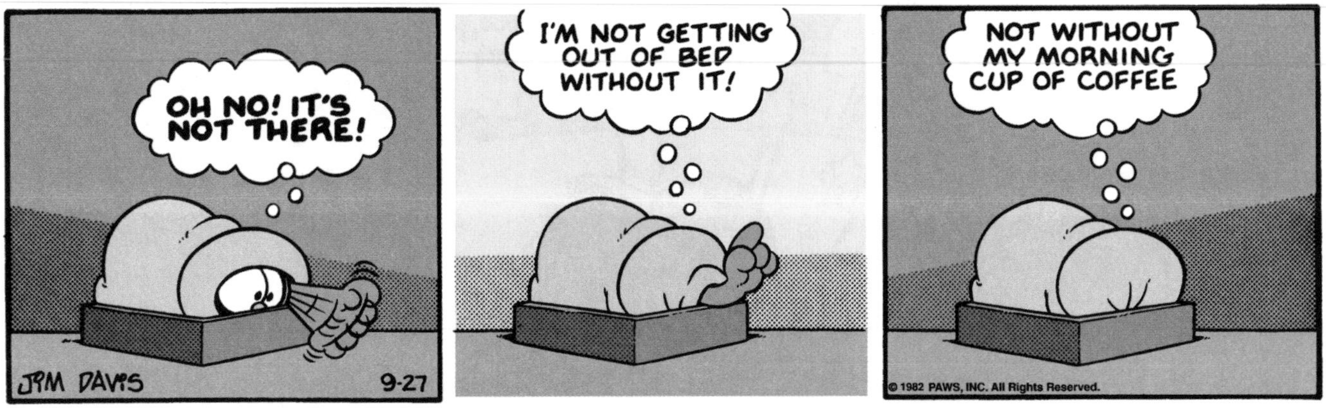
OH NO! IT'S NOT THERE!
I'M NOT GETTING OUT OF BED WITHOUT IT!
NOT WITHOUT MY MORNING CUP OF COFFEE
JIM DAVIS
9-27
© 1982 PAWS, INC. All Rights Reserved.

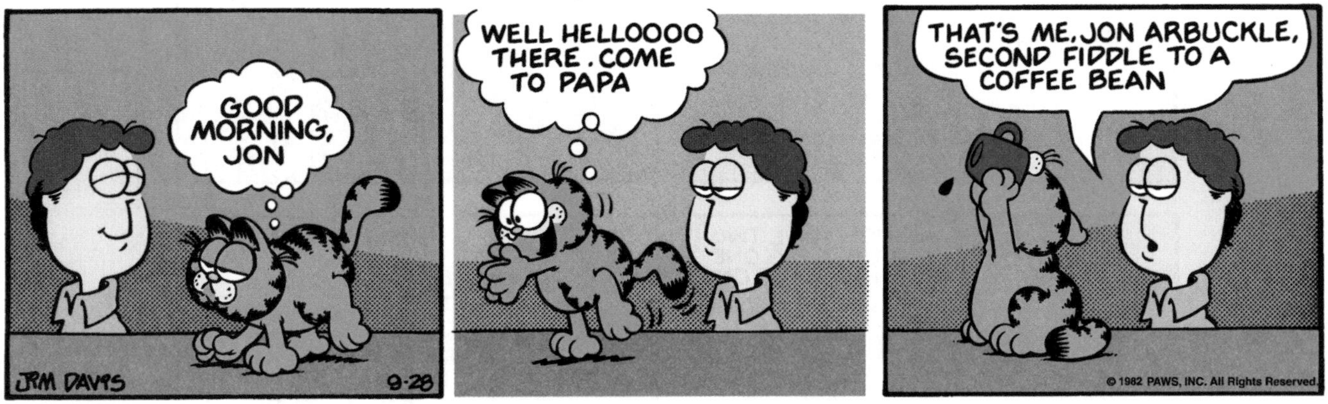
GOOD MORNING, JON
WELL HELLOOOO THERE. COME TO PAPA
THAT'S ME, JON ARBUCKLE, SECOND FIDDLE TO A COFFEE BEAN
JIM DAVIS
9-28
© 1982 PAWS, INC. All Rights Reserved.

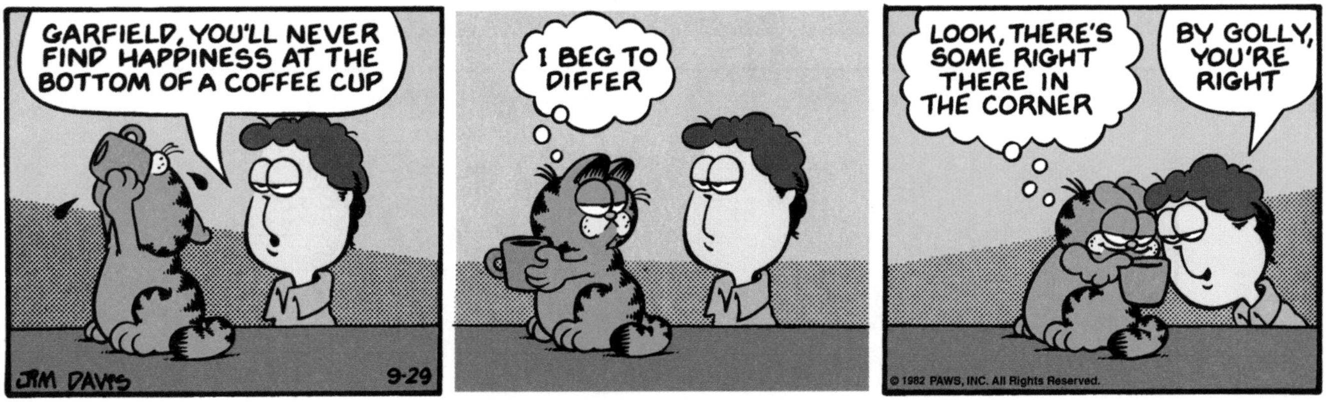
GARFIELD, YOU'LL NEVER FIND HAPPINESS AT THE BOTTOM OF A COFFEE CUP
I BEG TO DIFFER
LOOK, THERE'S SOME RIGHT THERE IN THE CORNER
BY GOLLY, YOU'RE RIGHT
JIM DAVIS
9-29
© 1982 PAWS, INC. All Rights Reserved.

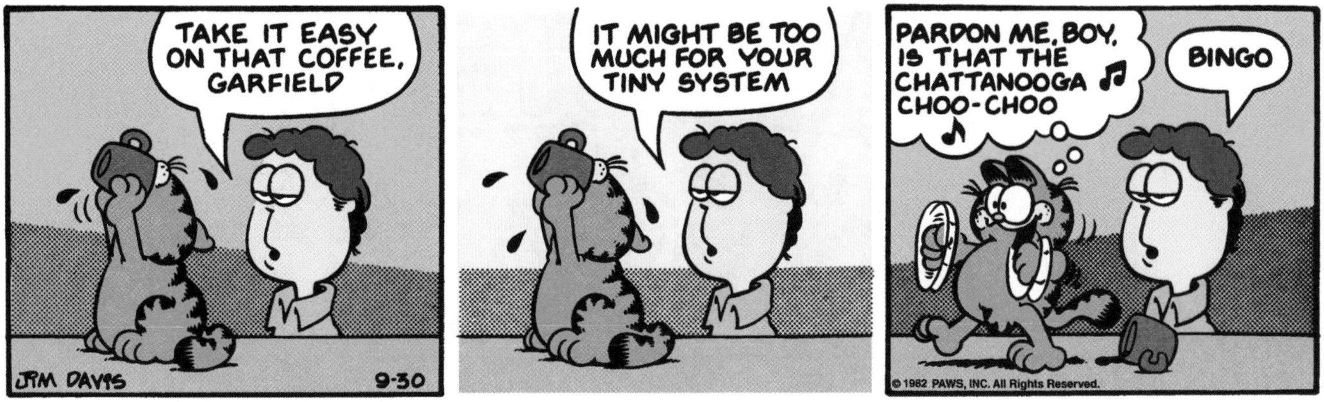
TAKE IT EASY ON THAT COFFEE, GARFIELD
JIM DAVIS
9-30
IT MIGHT BE TOO MUCH FOR YOUR TINY SYSTEM
PARDON ME, BOY, IS THAT THE CHATTANOOGA CHOO-CHOO
BINGO
© 1982 PAWS, INC. All Rights Reserved.

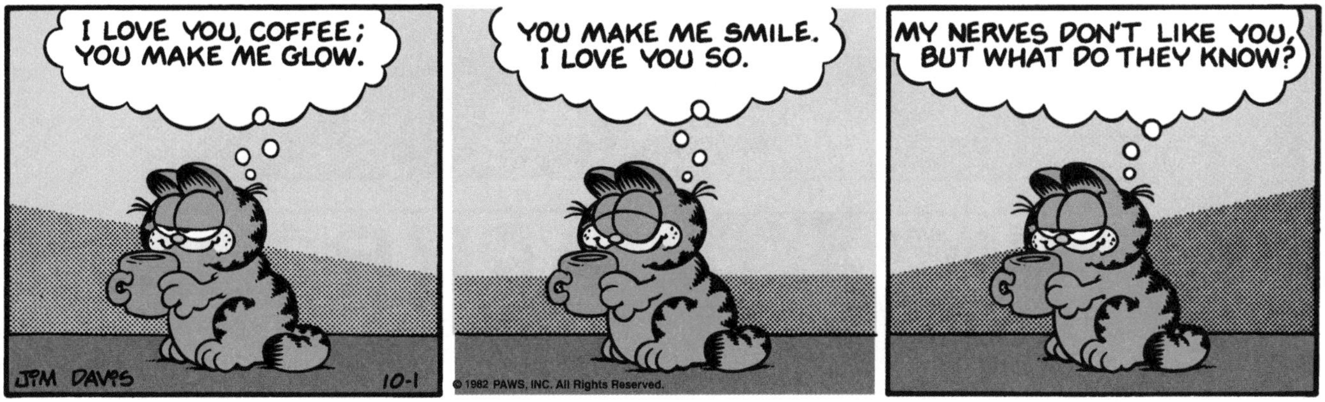
I LOVE YOU, COFFEE; YOU MAKE ME GLOW.
JIM DAVIS
10-1
YOU MAKE ME SMILE. I LOVE YOU SO.
© 1982 PAWS, INC. All Rights Reserved.
MY NERVES DON'T LIKE YOU, BUT WHAT DO THEY KNOW?

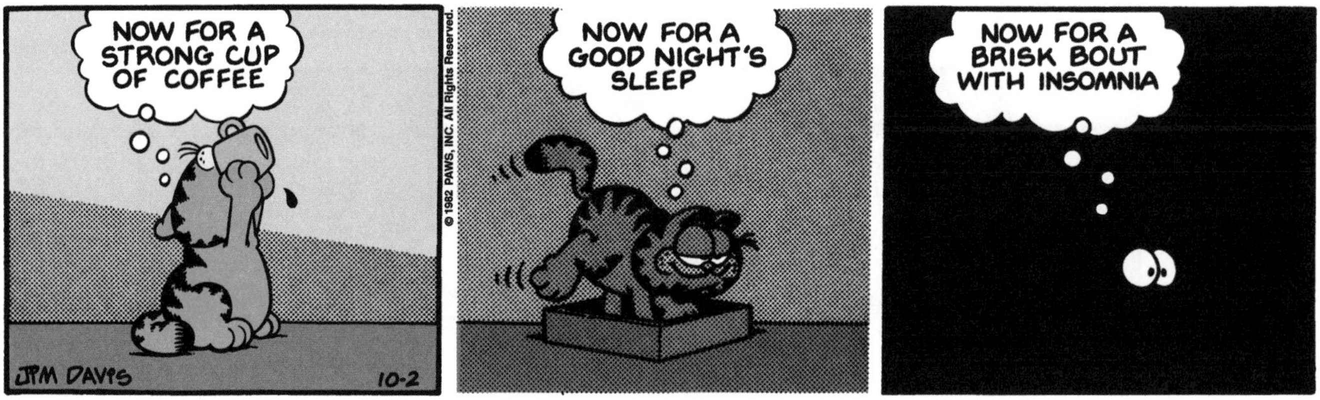
NOW FOR A STRONG CUP OF COFFEE
JIM DAVIS
10-2
© 1982 PAWS, INC. All Rights Reserved.
NOW FOR A GOOD NIGHT'S SLEEP
NOW FOR A BRISK BOUT WITH INSOMNIA

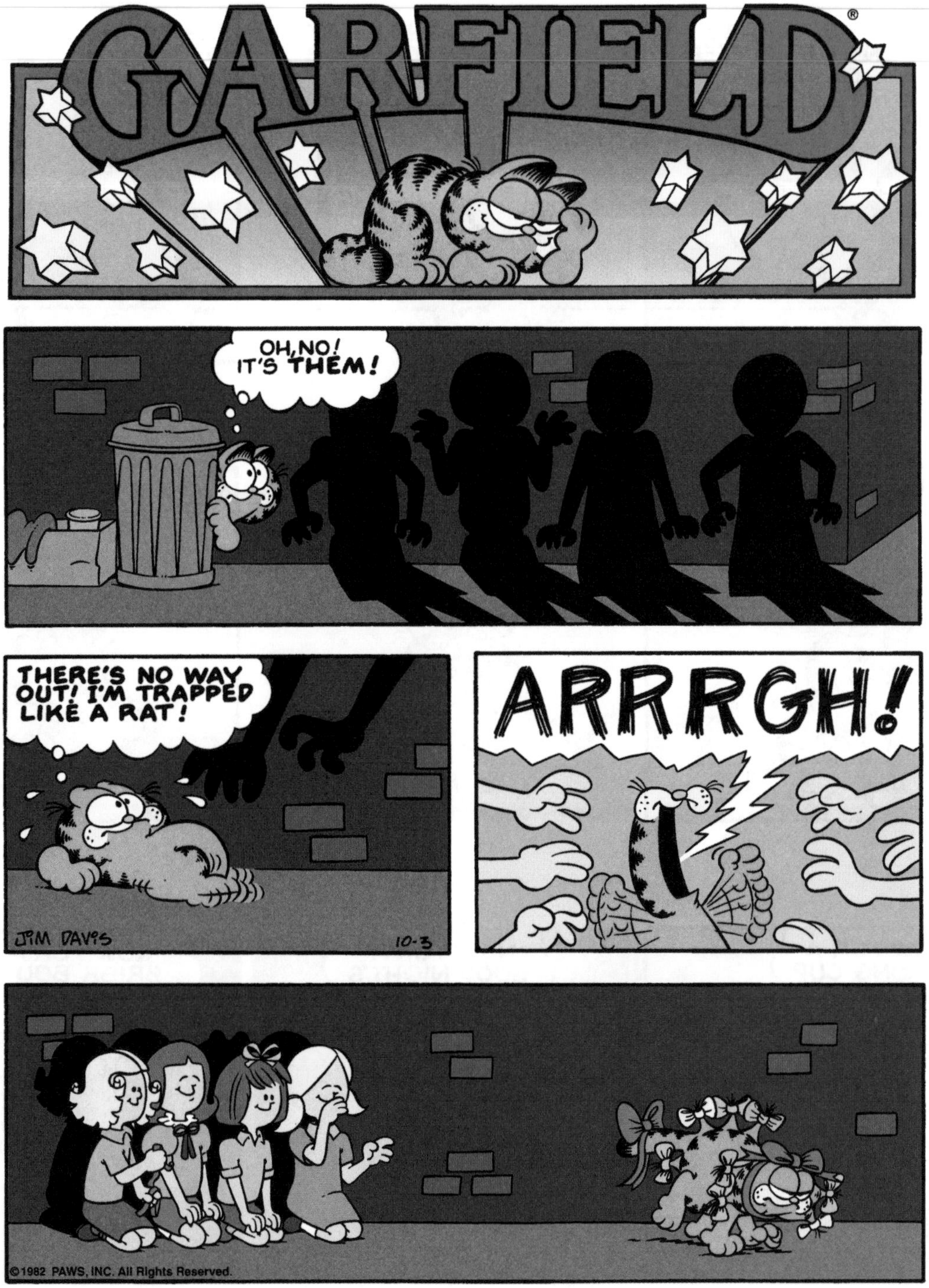
GARFIELD®
OH, NO! IT'S THEM!
THERE'S NO WAY OUT! I'M TRAPPED LIKE A RAT!
JIM DAVIS
10-3
ARRRGH!
©1982 PAWS, INC. All Rights Reserved.

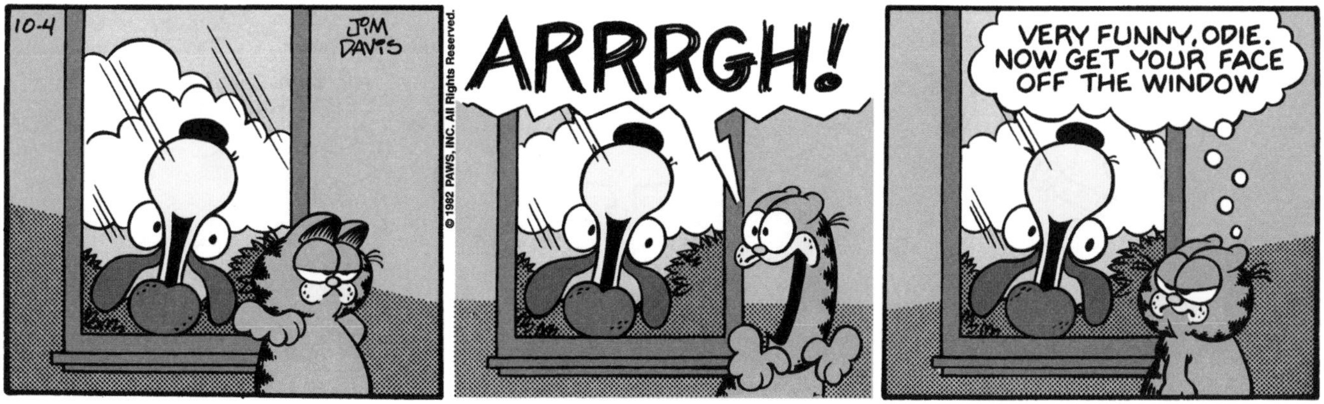
10-4
JIM DAVIS
© 1982 PAWS, INC. All Rights Reserved.
ARRRGH!
VERY FUNNY, ODIE. NOW GET YOUR FACE OFF THE WINDOW

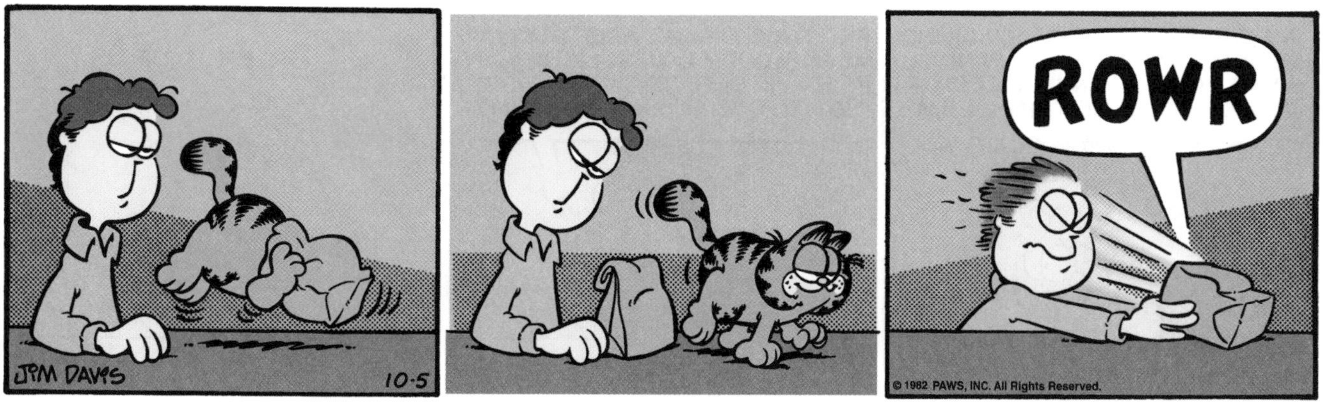
JIM DAVIS
10-5
ROWR
© 1982 PAWS, INC. All Rights Reserved.

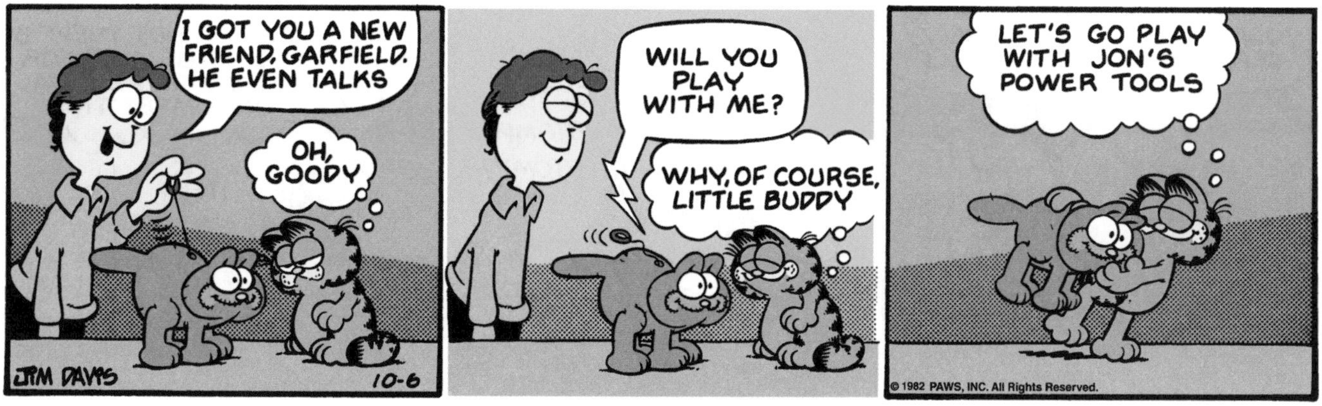
I GOT YOU A NEW FRIEND, GARFIELD. HE EVEN TALKS
OH, GOODY
JIM DAVIS
10-6
WILL YOU PLAY WITH ME?
WHY, OF COURSE, LITTLE BUDDY
LET'S GO PLAY WITH JON'S POWER TOOLS
© 1982 PAWS, INC. All Rights Reserved.

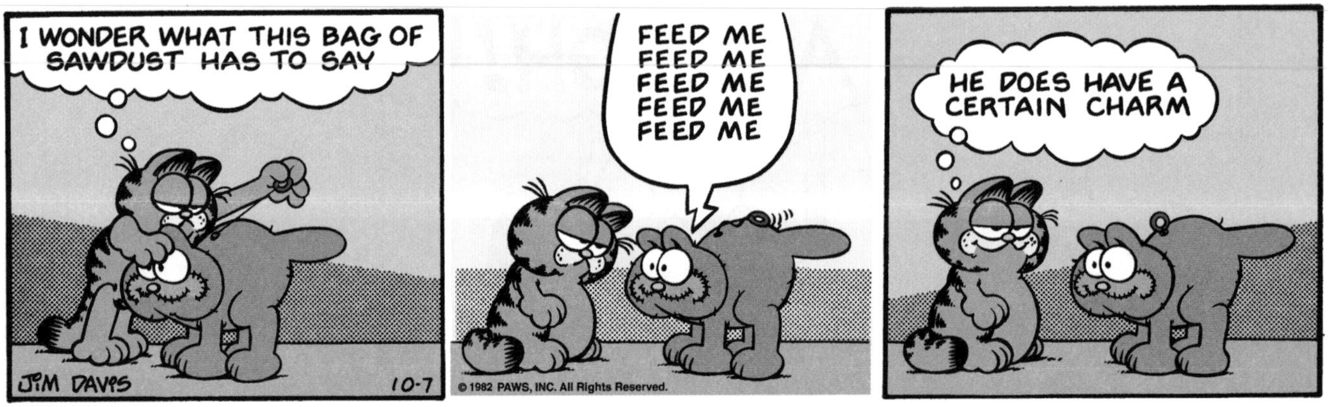
I WONDER WHAT THIS BAG OF SAWDUST HAS TO SAY
JIM DAVIS
10-7
FEED ME
FEED ME
FEED ME
FEED ME
FEED ME
© 1982 PAWS, INC. All Rights Reserved.
HE DOES HAVE A CERTAIN CHARM

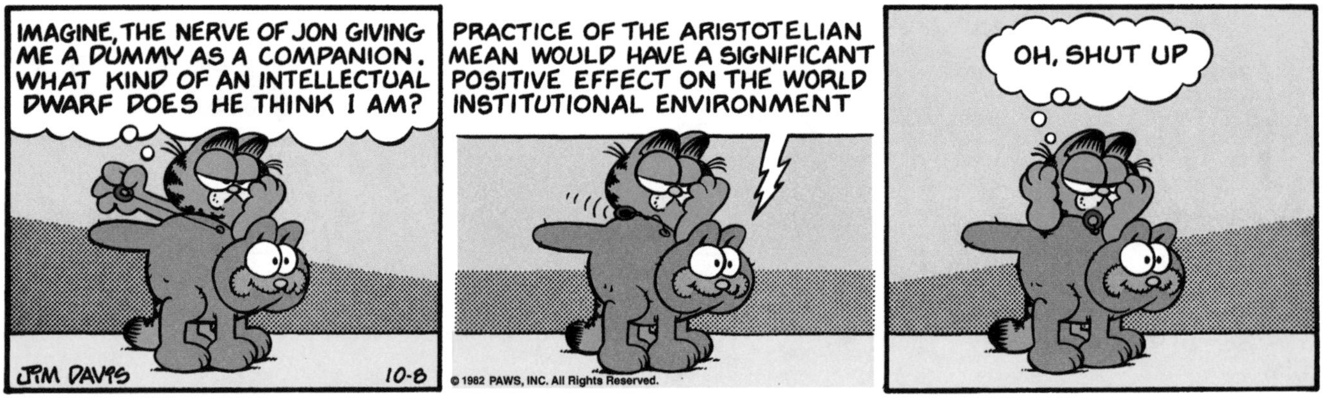
IMAGINE, THE NERVE OF JON GIVING ME A DUMMY AS A COMPANION. WHAT KIND OF AN INTELLECTUAL DWARF DOES HE THINK I AM?
JIM DAVIS
10-8
PRACTICE OF THE ARISTOTELIAN MEAN WOULD HAVE A SIGNIFICANT POSITIVE EFFECT ON THE WORLD INSTITUTIONAL ENVIRONMENT
© 1982 PAWS, INC. All Rights Reserved.
OH, SHUT UP

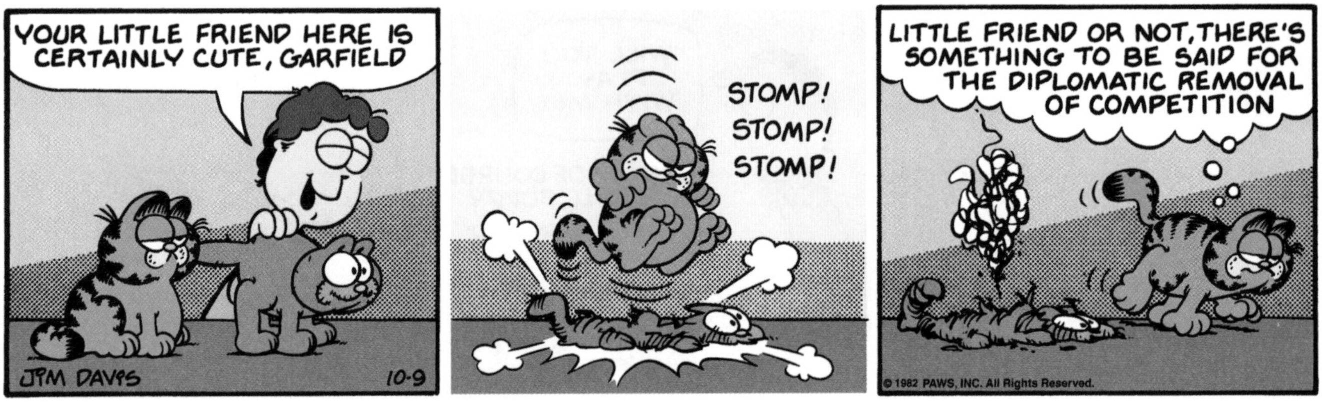
YOUR LITTLE FRIEND HERE IS CERTAINLY CUTE, GARFIELD
JIM DAVIS
10-9
STOMP!
STOMP!
STOMP!
LITTLE FRIEND OR NOT, THERE'S SOMETHING TO BE SAID FOR THE DIPLOMATIC REMOVAL OF COMPETITION
© 1982 PAWS, INC. All Rights Reserved.

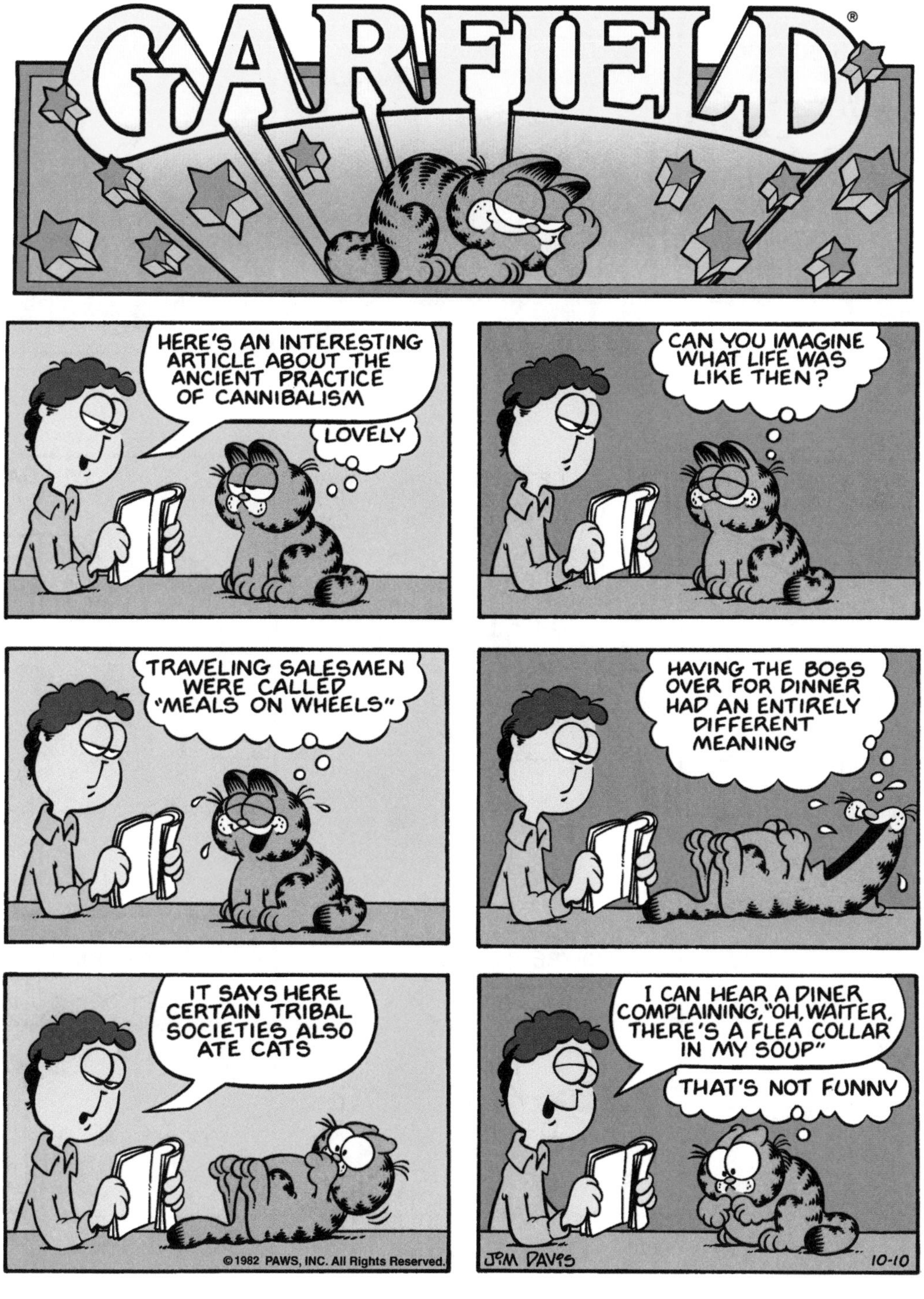
GARFIELD®
HERE'S AN INTERESTING ARTICLE ABOUT THE ANCIENT PRACTICE OF CANNIBALISM
LOVELY
CAN YOU IMAGINE WHAT LIFE WAS LIKE THEN?
TRAVELING SALESMEN WERE CALLED "MEALS ON WHEELS"
HAVING THE BOSS OVER FOR DINNER HAD AN ENTIRELY DIFFERENT MEANING
IT SAYS HERE CERTAIN TRIBAL SOCIETIES ALSO ATE CATS
I CAN HEAR A DINER COMPLAINING, "OH, WAITER, THERE'S A FLEA COLLAR IN MY SOUP"
THAT'S NOT FUNNY
© 1982 PAWS, INC. All Rights Reserved.
JIM DAVIS
10-10

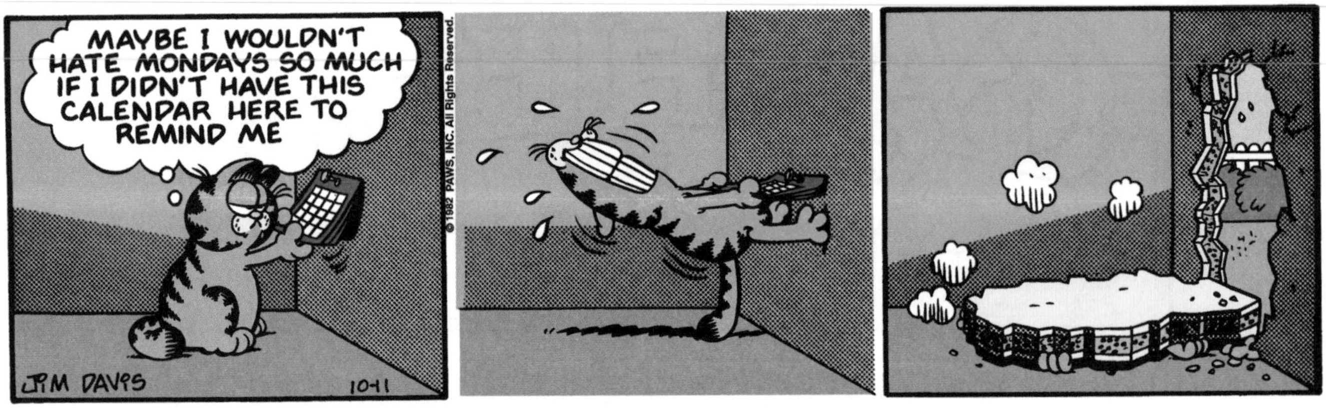
MAYBE I WOULDN'T HATE MONDAYS SO MUCH IF I DIDN'T HAVE THIS CALENDAR HERE TO REMIND ME
JIM DAVIS 10-11
© 1982 PAWS, INC. All Rights Reserved.

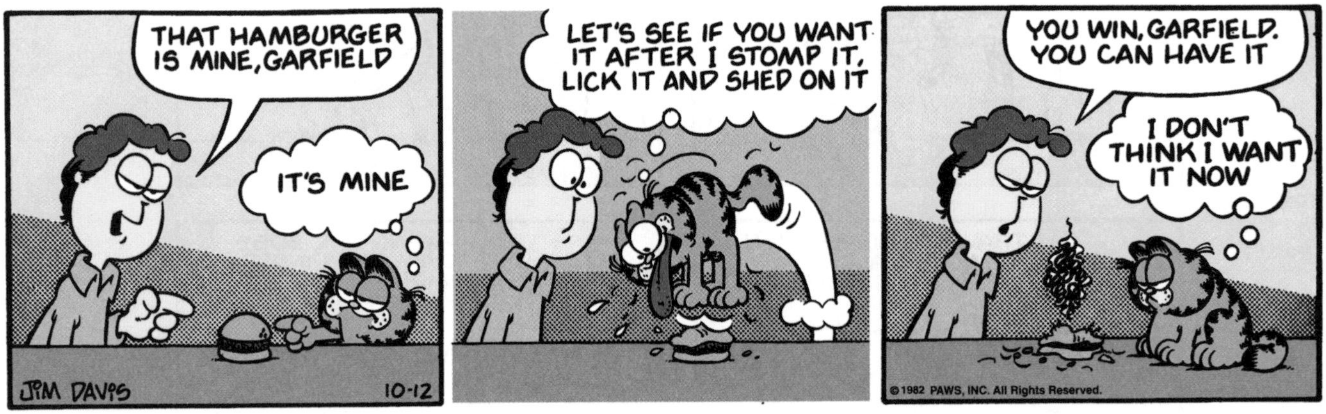
THAT HAMBURGER IS MINE, GARFIELD
IT'S MINE
JIM DAVIS 10-12
LET'S SEE IF YOU WANT IT AFTER I STOMP IT, LICK IT AND SHED ON IT
YOU WIN, GARFIELD. YOU CAN HAVE IT
I DON'T THINK I WANT IT NOW
© 1982 PAWS, INC. All Rights Reserved.

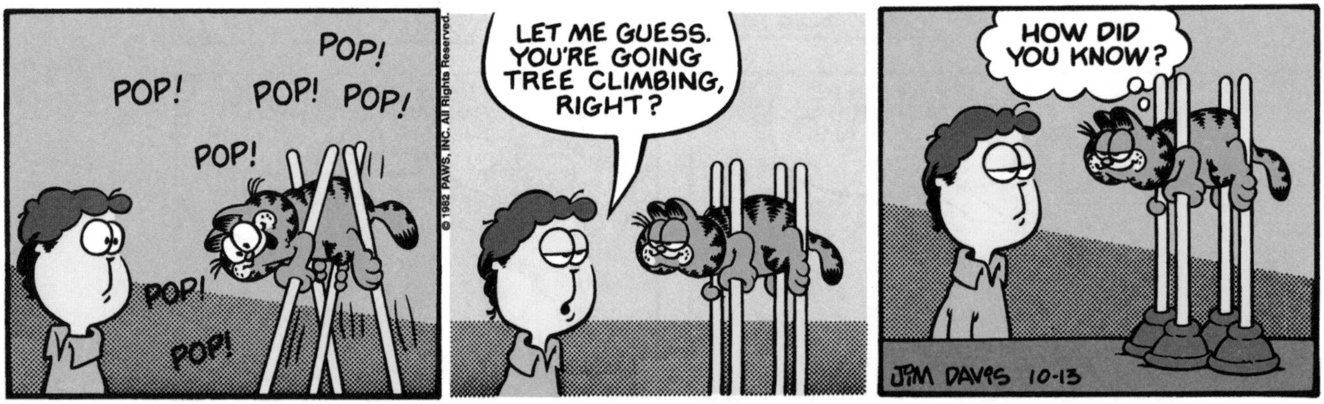
POP!
POP!
POP! POP!
POP!
POP!
POP!
© 1982 PAWS, INC. All Rights Reserved.
LET ME GUESS. YOU'RE GOING TREE CLIMBING, RIGHT?
HOW DID YOU KNOW?
JIM DAVIS 10-13

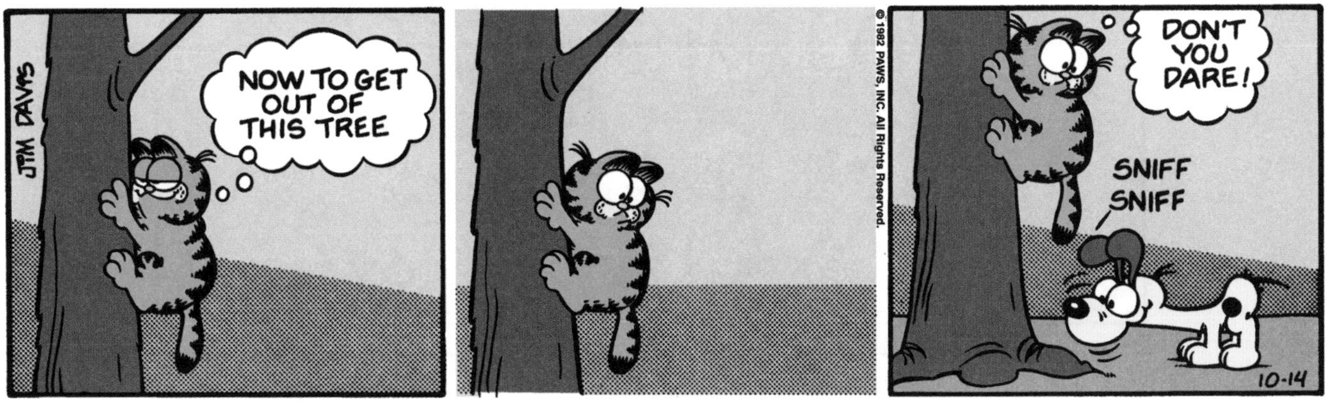
JIM DAVIS
NOW TO GET OUT OF THIS TREE
© 1982 PAWS, INC. All Rights Reserved.
DON'T YOU DARE!
SNIFF SNIFF
10-14

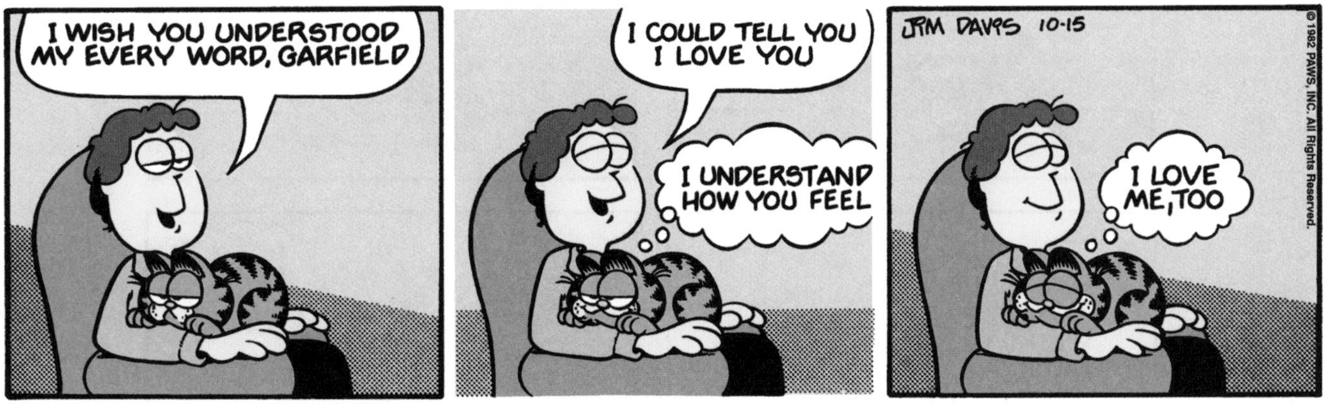
I WISH YOU UNDERSTOOD MY EVERY WORD, GARFIELD
I COULD TELL YOU I LOVE YOU
I UNDERSTAND HOW YOU FEEL
JIM DAVIS 10-15
I LOVE ME, TOO
© 1982 PAWS, INC. All Rights Reserved.

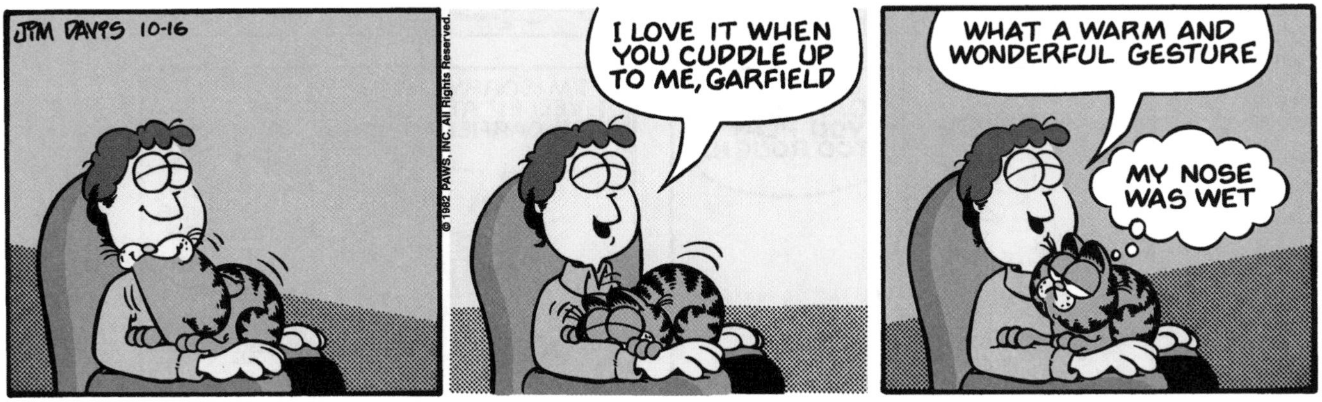
JIM DAVIS 10-16
© 1982 PAWS, INC. All Rights Reserved.
I LOVE IT WHEN YOU CUDDLE UP TO ME, GARFIELD
WHAT A WARM AND WONDERFUL GESTURE
MY NOSE WAS WET

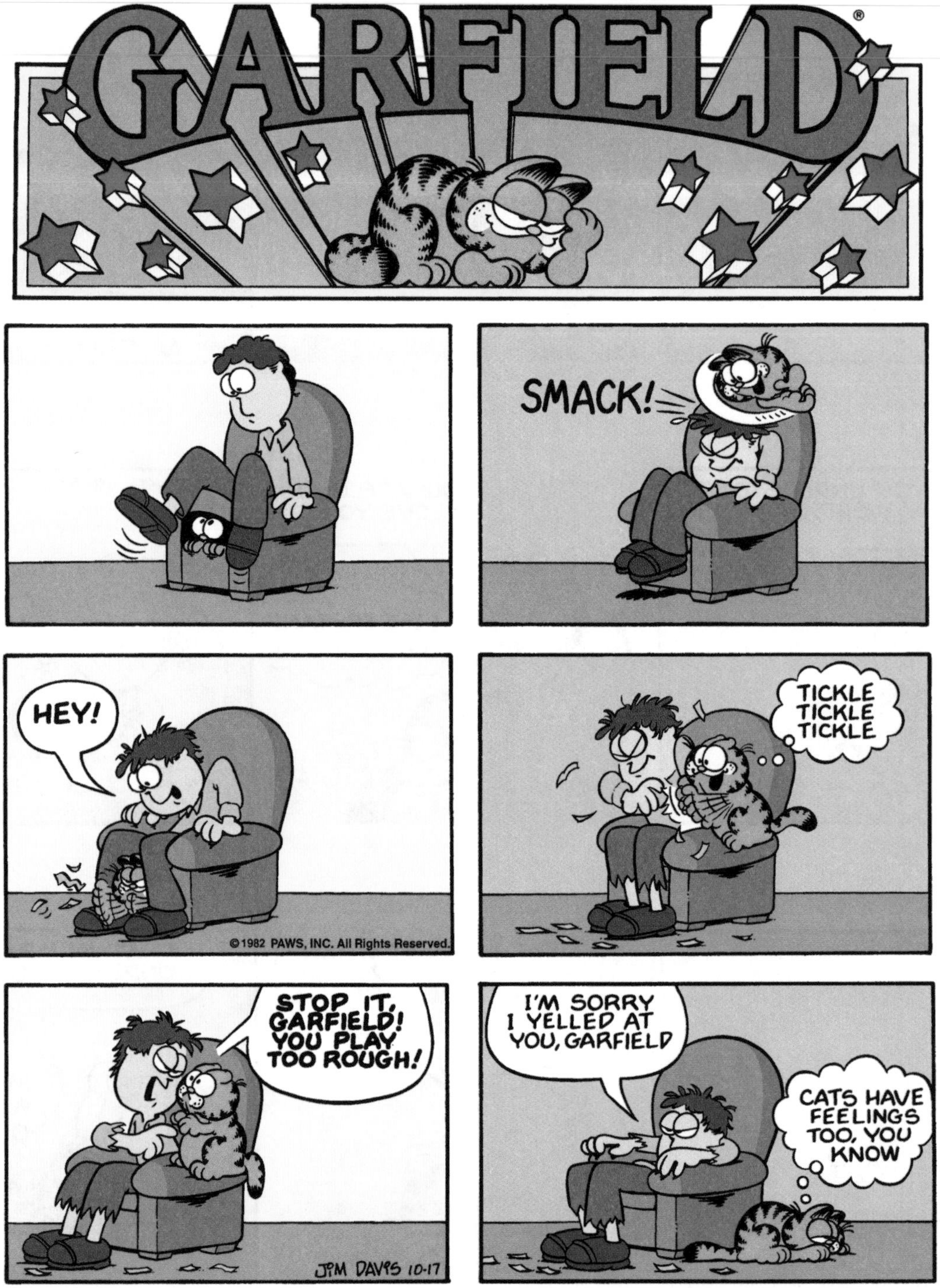
GARFIELD®
SMACK!
HEY!
© 1982 PAWS, INC. All Rights Reserved.
TICKLE TICKLE TICKLE
STOP IT, GARFIELD! YOU PLAY TOO ROUGH!
JIM DAVIS 10-17
I'M SORRY I YELLED AT YOU, GARFIELD
CATS HAVE FEELINGS TOO, YOU KNOW

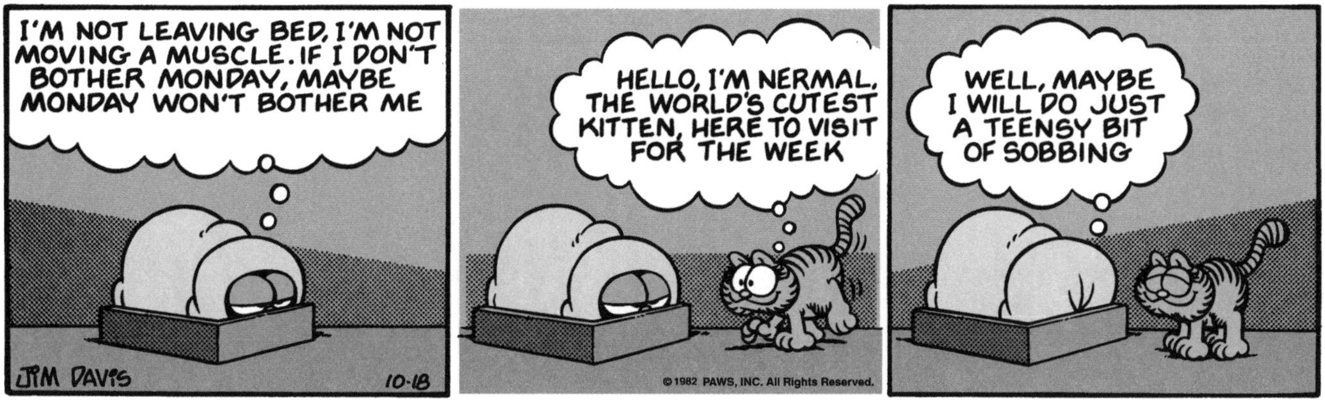
I'M NOT LEAVING BED, I'M NOT MOVING A MUSCLE. IF I DON'T BOTHER MONDAY, MAYBE MONDAY WON'T BOTHER ME
JIM DAVIS
10-18
HELLO, I'M NERMAL, THE WORLD'S CUTEST KITTEN, HERE TO VISIT FOR THE WEEK
© 1982 PAWS, INC. All Rights Reserved.
WELL, MAYBE I WILL DO JUST A TEENSY BIT OF SOBBING

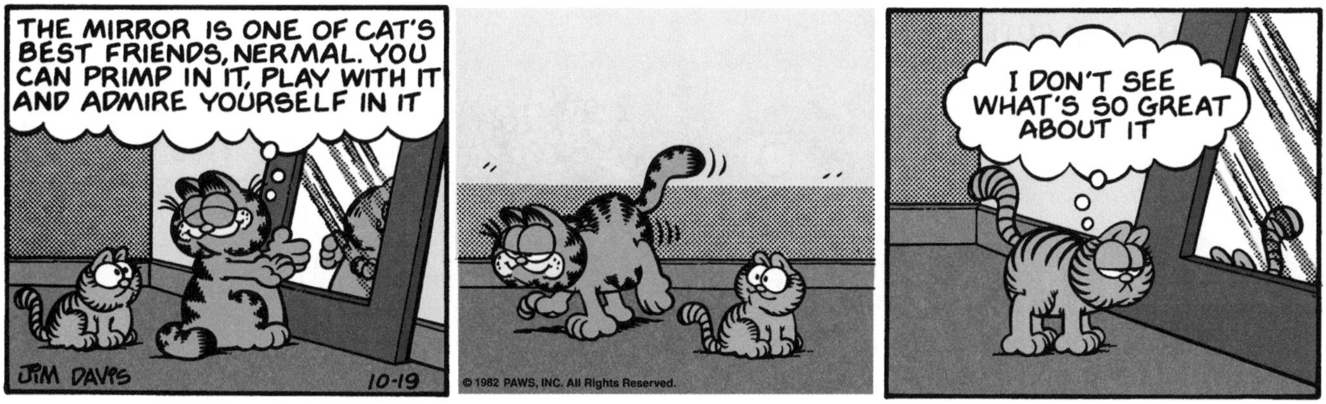
THE MIRROR IS ONE OF CAT'S BEST FRIENDS, NERMAL. YOU CAN PRIMP IN IT, PLAY WITH IT AND ADMIRE YOURSELF IN IT
JIM DAVIS
10-19
© 1982 PAWS, INC. All Rights Reserved.
I DON'T SEE WHAT'S SO GREAT ABOUT IT

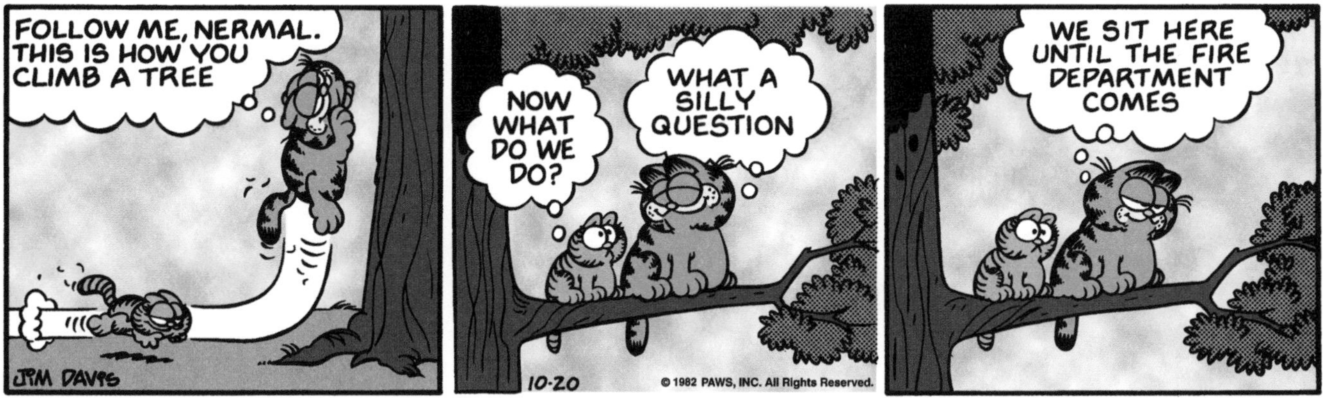
FOLLOW ME, NERMAL. THIS IS HOW YOU CLIMB A TREE
JIM DAVIS
NOW WHAT DO WE DO?
WHAT A SILLY QUESTION
10-20
© 1982 PAWS, INC. All Rights Reserved.
WE SIT HERE UNTIL THE FIRE DEPARTMENT COMES

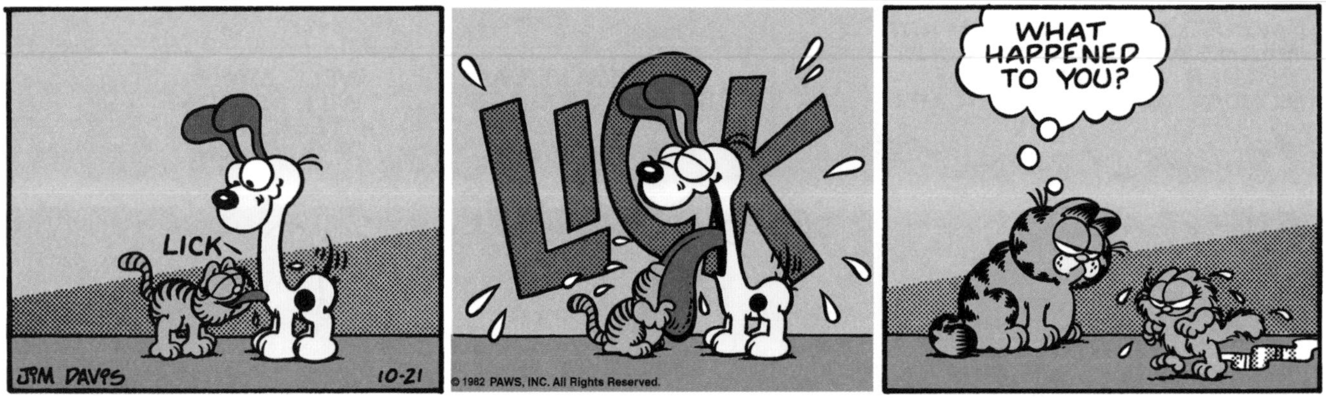
LICK
JIM DAVIS
10-21
LICK
© 1982 PAWS, INC. All Rights Reserved.
WHAT HAPPENED TO YOU?

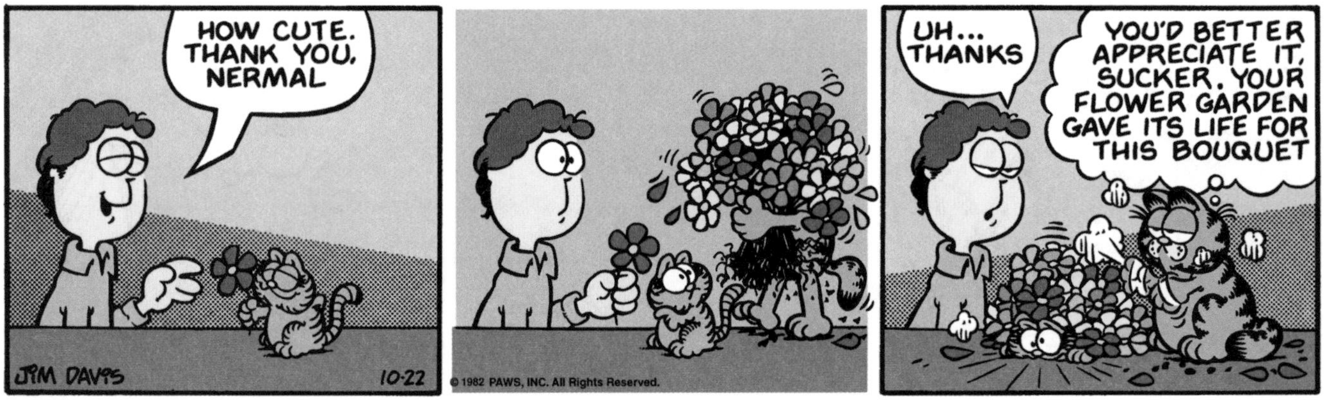
HOW CUTE. THANK YOU, NERMAL
JIM DAVIS
10-22
© 1982 PAWS, INC. All Rights Reserved.
UH... THANKS
YOU'D BETTER APPRECIATE IT, SUCKER. YOUR FLOWER GARDEN GAVE ITS LIFE FOR THIS BOUQUET

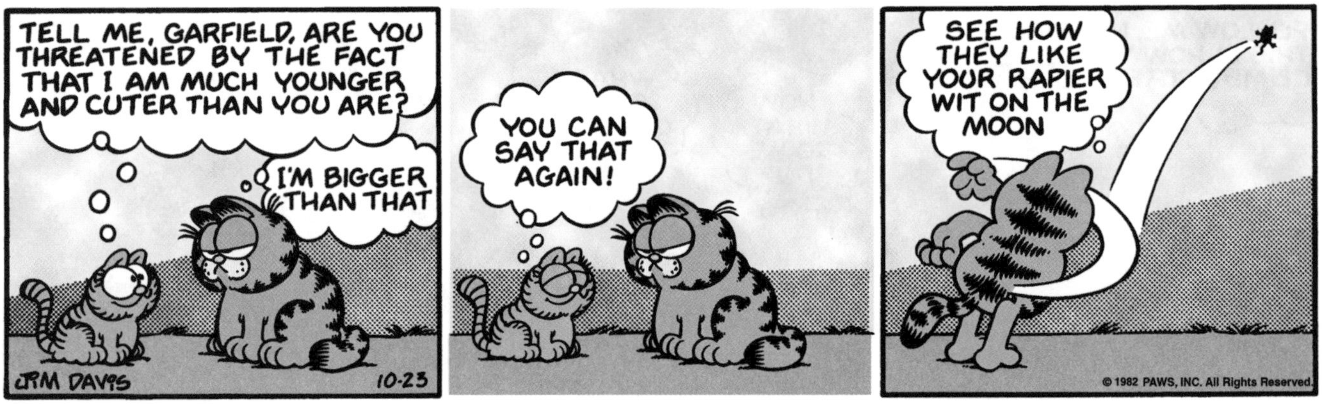
TELL ME, GARFIELD, ARE YOU THREATENED BY THE FACT THAT I AM MUCH YOUNGER AND CUTER THAN YOU ARE?
I'M BIGGER THAN THAT
JIM DAVIS
10-23
YOU CAN SAY THAT AGAIN!
SEE HOW THEY LIKE YOUR RAPIER WIT ON THE MOON
© 1982 PAWS, INC. All Rights Reserved.

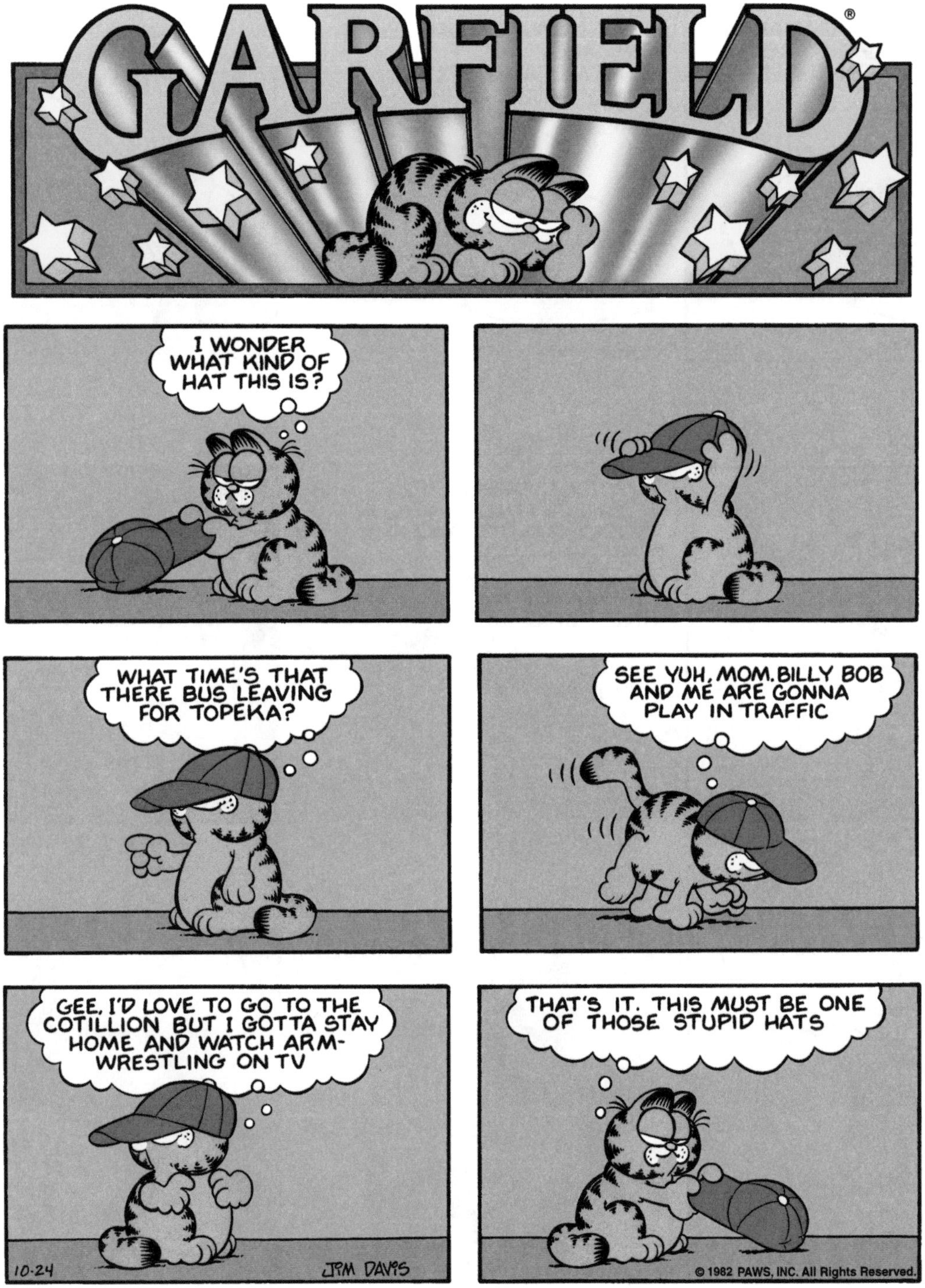
GARFIELD®
I WONDER WHAT KIND OF HAT THIS IS?
WHAT TIME'S THAT THERE BUS LEAVING FOR TOPEKA?
SEE YUH, MOM. BILLY BOB AND ME ARE GONNA PLAY IN TRAFFIC
GEE, I'D LOVE TO GO TO THE COTILLION BUT I GOTTA STAY HOME AND WATCH ARM-WRESTLING ON TV
THAT'S IT. THIS MUST BE ONE OF THOSE STUPID HATS
10-24
JIM DAVIS
© 1982 PAWS, INC. All Rights Reserved.

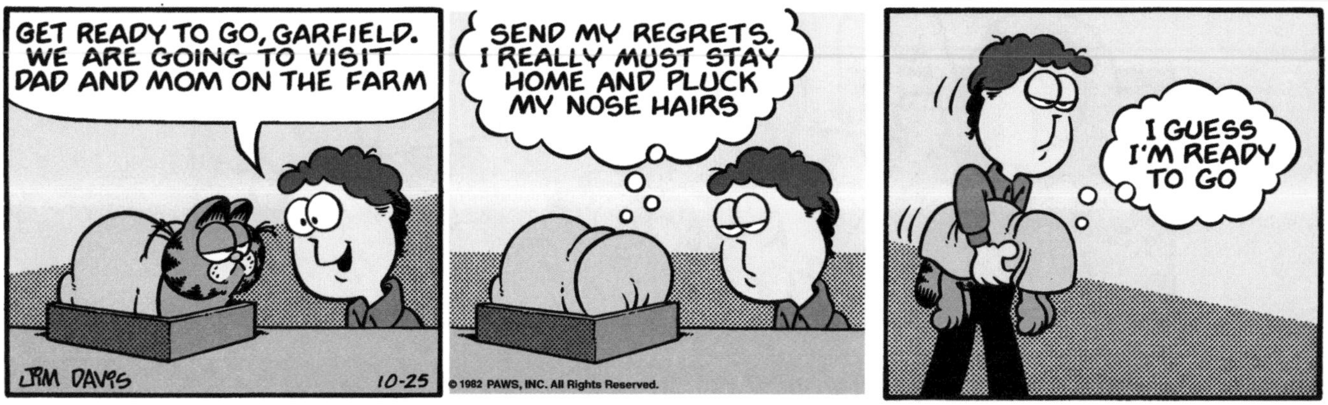
GET READY TO GO, GARFIELD. WE ARE GOING TO VISIT DAD AND MOM ON THE FARM
SEND MY REGRETS. I REALLY MUST STAY HOME AND PLUCK MY NOSE HAIRS
I GUESS I'M READY TO GO
JIM DAVIS
10-25
© 1982 PAWS, INC. All Rights Reserved.

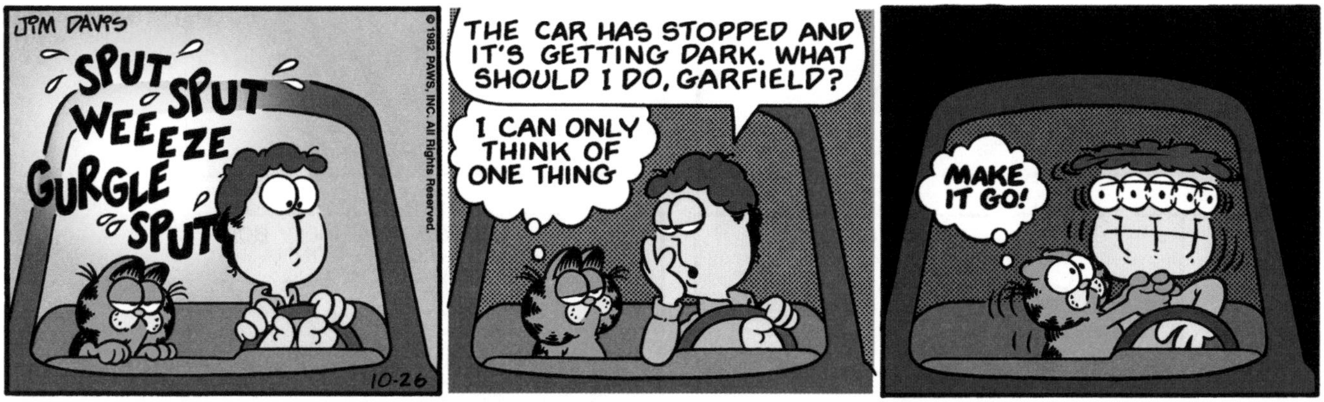
JIM DAVIS
SPUT SPUT
WEEEEZE
GURGLE
SPUT
© 1982 PAWS, INC. All Rights Reserved.
10-26
THE CAR HAS STOPPED AND IT'S GETTING DARK. WHAT SHOULD I DO, GARFIELD?
I CAN ONLY THINK OF ONE THING
MAKE IT GO!

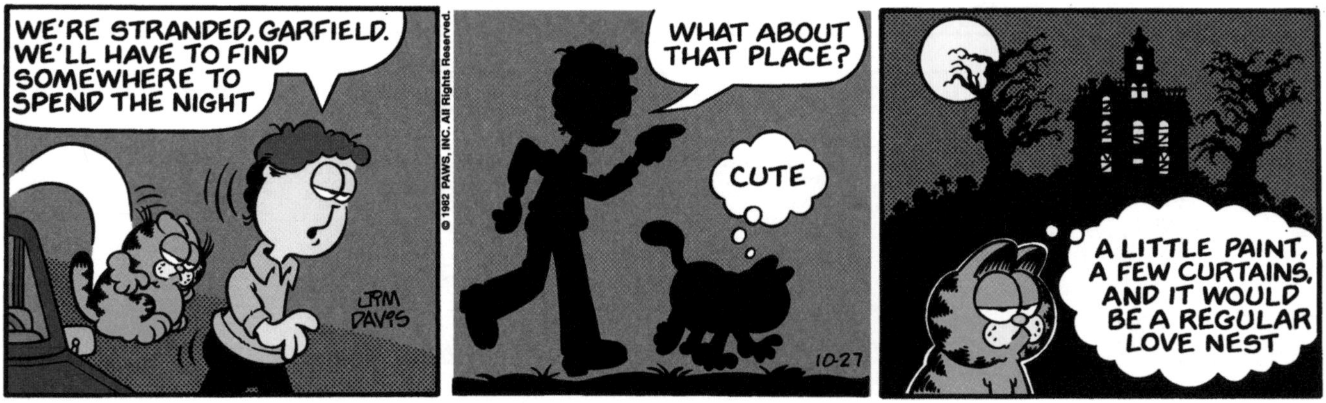
WE'RE STRANDED, GARFIELD. WE'LL HAVE TO FIND SOMEWHERE TO SPEND THE NIGHT
JIM DAVIS
© 1982 PAWS, INC. All Rights Reserved.
WHAT ABOUT THAT PLACE?
CUTE
10-27
A LITTLE PAINT, A FEW CURTAINS, AND IT WOULD BE A REGULAR LOVE NEST

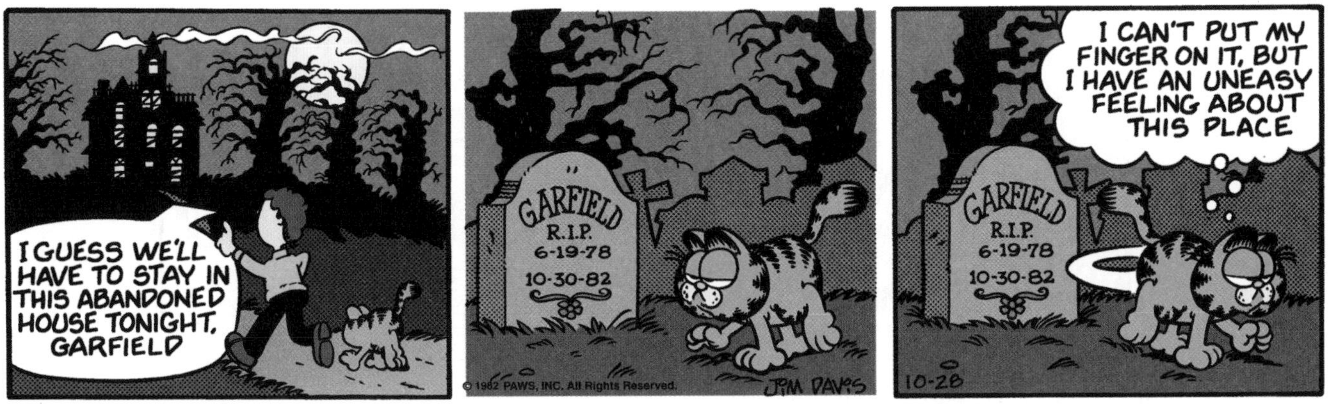
I GUESS WE'LL HAVE TO STAY IN THIS ABANDONED HOUSE TONIGHT, GARFIELD
GARFIELD R.I.P. 6-19-78 10-30-82
© 1982 PAWS, INC. All Rights Reserved.
JIM DAVIS
GARFIELD R.I.P. 6-19-78 10-30-82
I CAN'T PUT MY FINGER ON IT, BUT I HAVE AN UNEASY FEELING ABOUT THIS PLACE
10-28

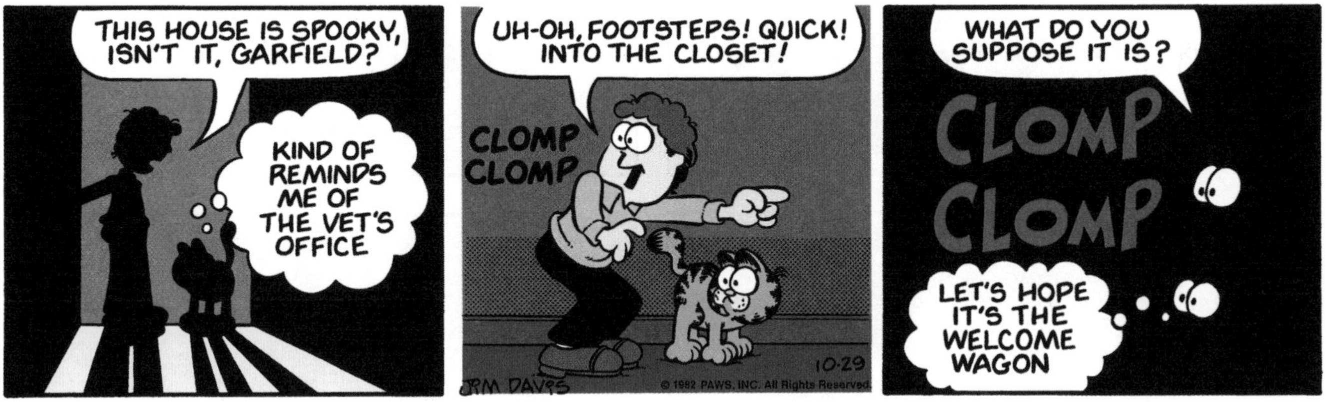
THIS HOUSE IS SPOOKY, ISN'T IT, GARFIELD?
KIND OF REMINDS ME OF THE VET'S OFFICE
UH-OH, FOOTSTEPS! QUICK! INTO THE CLOSET!
CLOMP CLOMP
10-29
JIM DAVIS
© 1982 PAWS, INC. All Rights Reserved.
WHAT DO YOU SUPPOSE IT IS?
CLOMP CLOMP
LET'S HOPE IT'S THE WELCOME WAGON

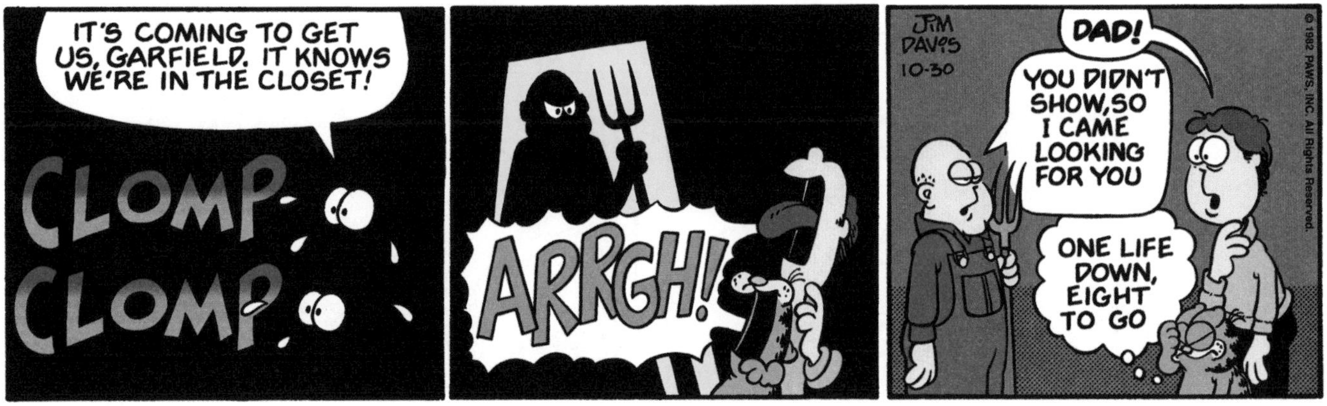
IT'S COMING TO GET US, GARFIELD. IT KNOWS WE'RE IN THE CLOSET!
CLOMP CLOMP
ARRGH!
JIM DAVIS 10-30
DAD!
YOU DIDN'T SHOW, SO I CAME LOOKING FOR YOU
ONE LIFE DOWN, EIGHT TO GO
© 1982 PAWS, INC. All Rights Reserved.

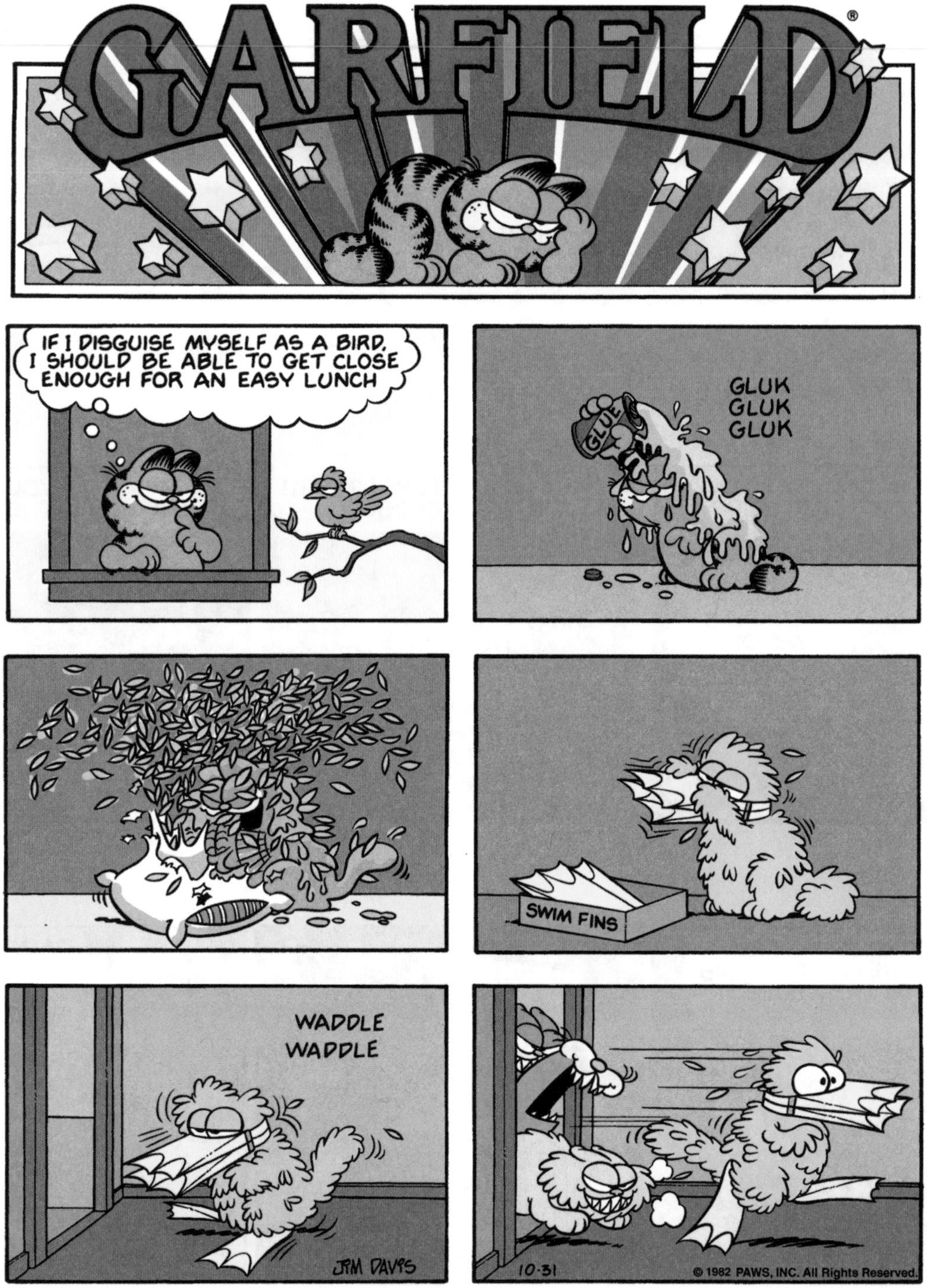
GARFIELD®
IF I DISGUISE MYSELF AS A BIRD, I SHOULD BE ABLE TO GET CLOSE ENOUGH FOR AN EASY LUNCH
GLUK GLUK GLUK
GLUE
SWIM FINS
WADDLE WADDLE
JPM DAVPS
10-31
© 1982 PAWS, INC. All Rights Reserved.

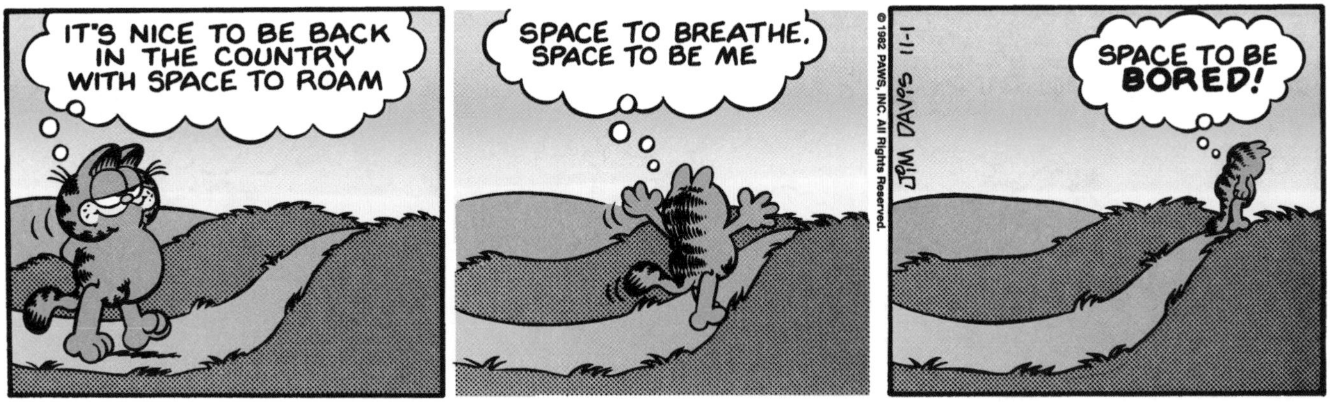
IT'S NICE TO BE BACK IN THE COUNTRY WITH SPACE TO ROAM
SPACE TO BREATHE, SPACE TO BE ME
SPACE TO BE BORED!
JIM DAVIS 11-1
© 1982 PAWS, INC. All Rights Reserved.

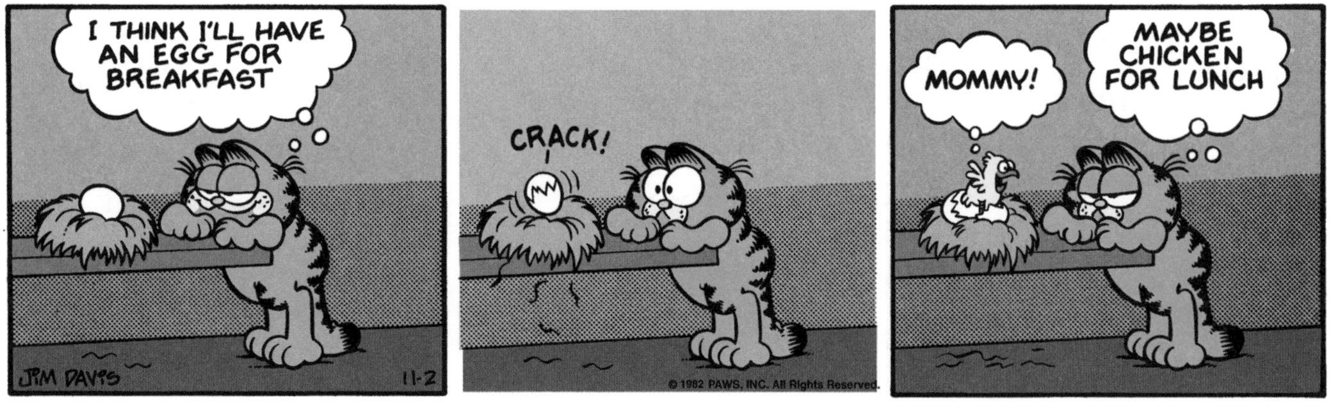
I THINK I'LL HAVE AN EGG FOR BREAKFAST
JIM DAVIS
11-2
CRACK!
© 1982 PAWS, INC. All Rights Reserved.
MOMMY!
MAYBE CHICKEN FOR LUNCH

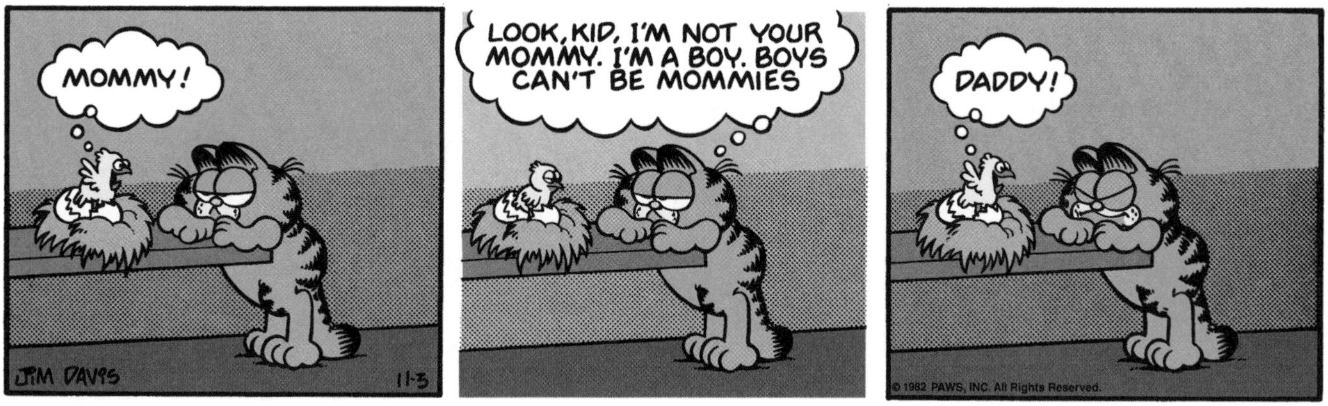
MOMMY!
JIM DAVIS
11-3
LOOK, KID, I'M NOT YOUR MOMMY. I'M A BOY. BOYS CAN'T BE MOMMIES
DADDY!
© 1982 PAWS, INC. All Rights Reserved.

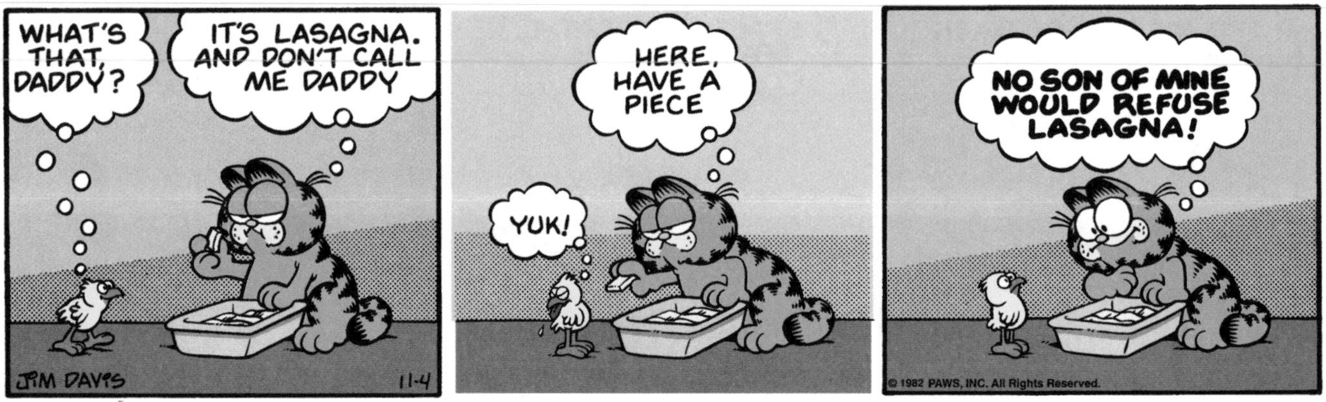
WHAT'S THAT, DADDY?
IT'S LASAGNA. AND DON'T CALL ME DADDY
JIM DAVIS
11-4
HERE, HAVE A PIECE
YUK!
NO SON OF MINE WOULD REFUSE LASAGNA!
© 1982 PAWS, INC. All Rights Reserved.

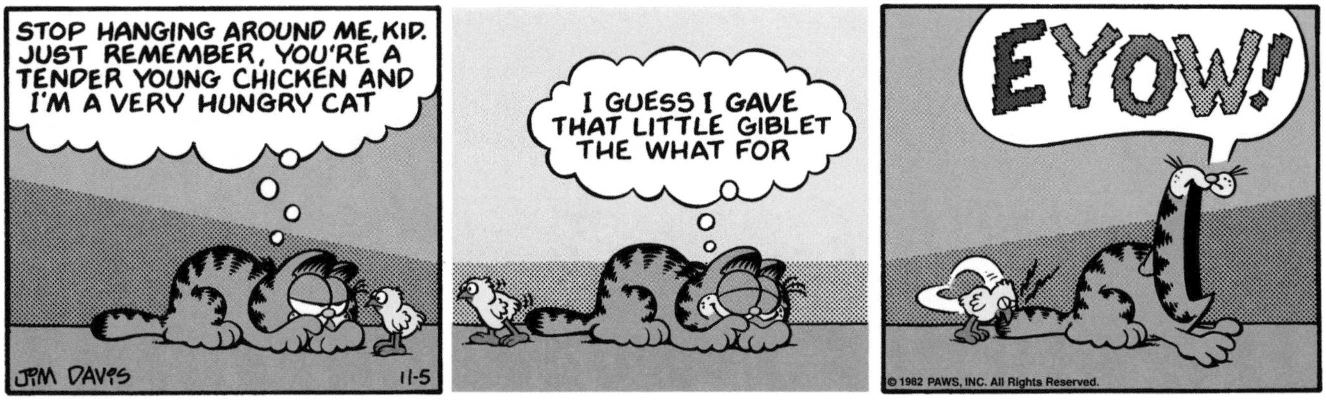
STOP HANGING AROUND ME, KID. JUST REMEMBER, YOU'RE A TENDER YOUNG CHICKEN AND I'M A VERY HUNGRY CAT
JIM DAVIS
11-5
I GUESS I GAVE THAT LITTLE GIBLET THE WHAT FOR
EYOW!
© 1982 PAWS, INC. All Rights Reserved.

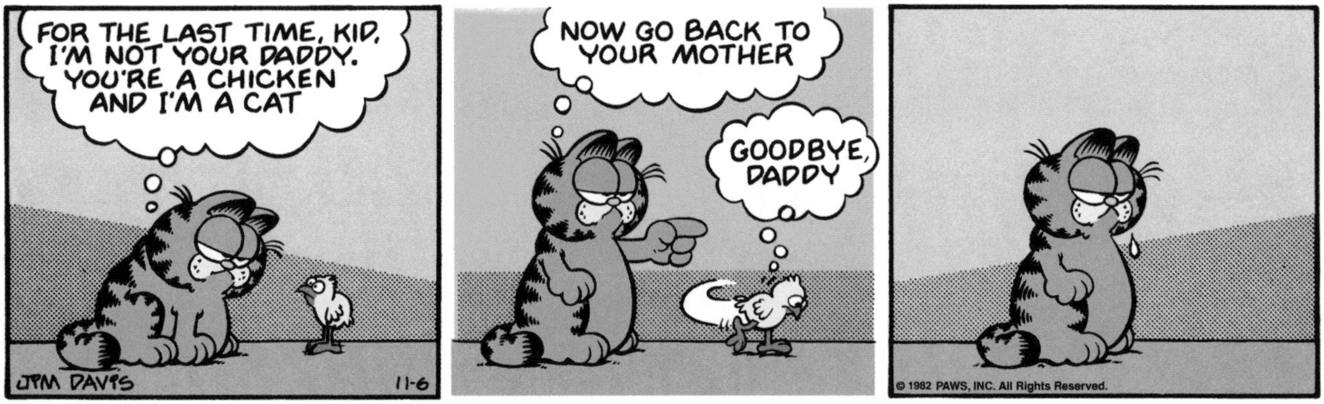
FOR THE LAST TIME, KID, I'M NOT YOUR DADDY. YOU'RE A CHICKEN AND I'M A CAT
JIM DAVIS
11-6
NOW GO BACK TO YOUR MOTHER
GOODBYE, DADDY
© 1982 PAWS, INC. All Rights Reserved.

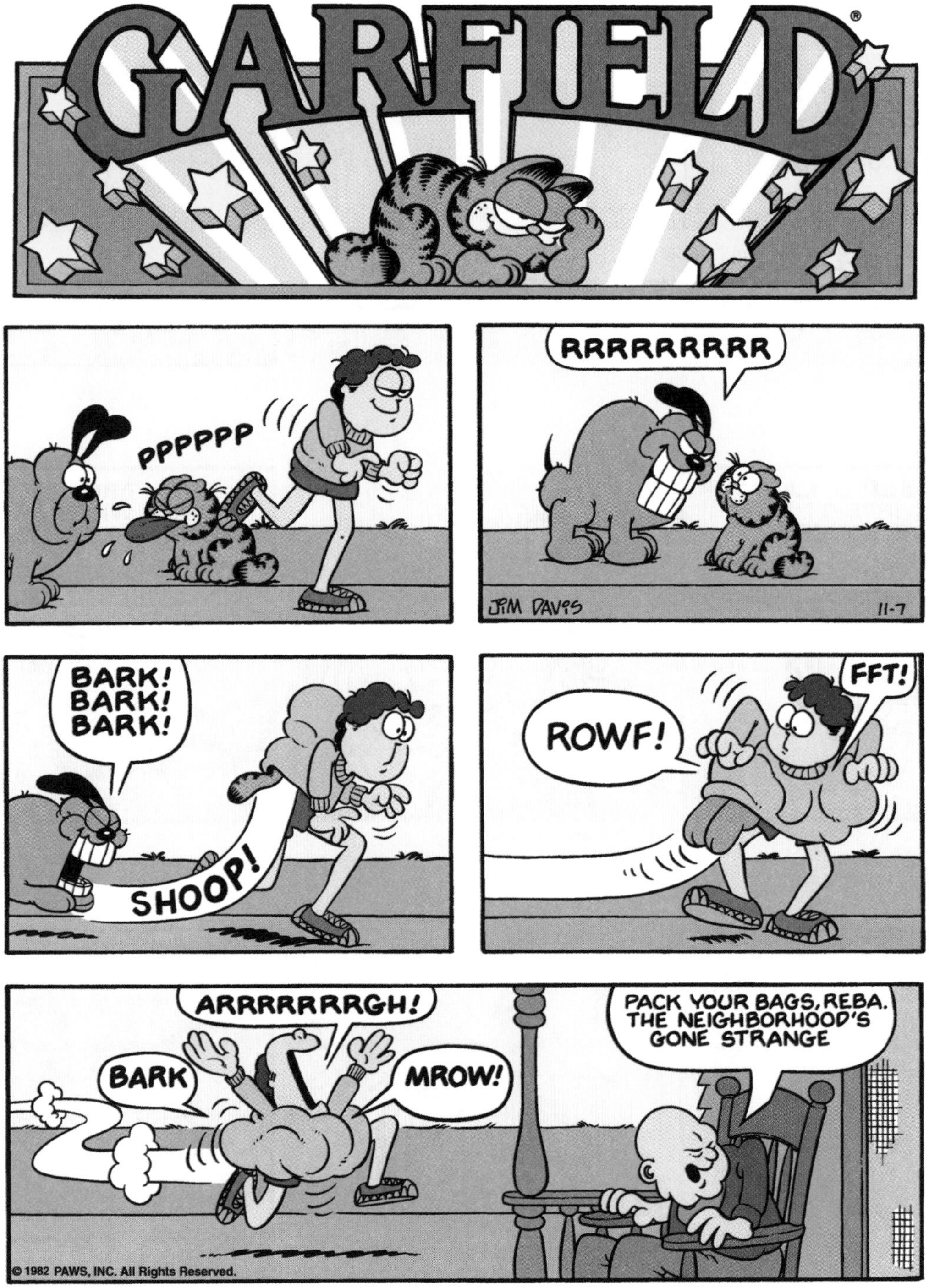
GARFIELD
PPPPPP
RRRRRRRRR
JIM DAVIS
11-7
BARK! BARK! BARK!
SHOOP!
ROWF!
FFT!
ARRRRRRRGH!
BARK
MROW!
PACK YOUR BAGS, REBA. THE NEIGHBORHOOD'S GONE STRANGE

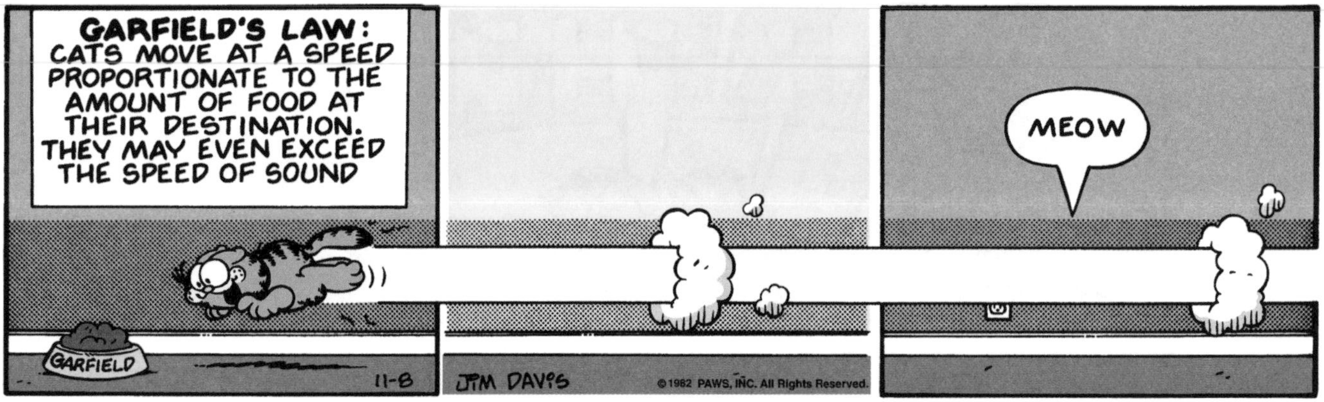
GARFIELD'S LAW:
CATS MOVE AT A SPEED PROPORTIONATE TO THE AMOUNT OF FOOD AT THEIR DESTINATION. THEY MAY EVEN EXCEED THE SPEED OF SOUND
GARFIELD
11-8
JIM DAVIS
© 1982 PAWS, INC. All Rights Reserved.
MEOW

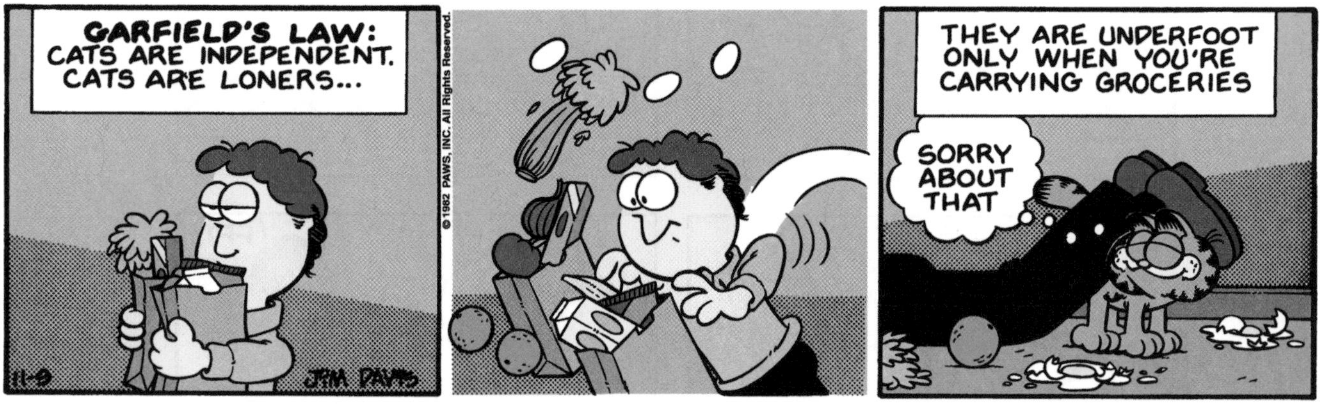
GARFIELD'S LAW:
CATS ARE INDEPENDENT. CATS ARE LONERS...
11-9
JIM DAVIS
© 1982 PAWS, INC. All Rights Reserved.
THEY ARE UNDERFOOT ONLY WHEN YOU'RE CARRYING GROCERIES
SORRY ABOUT THAT

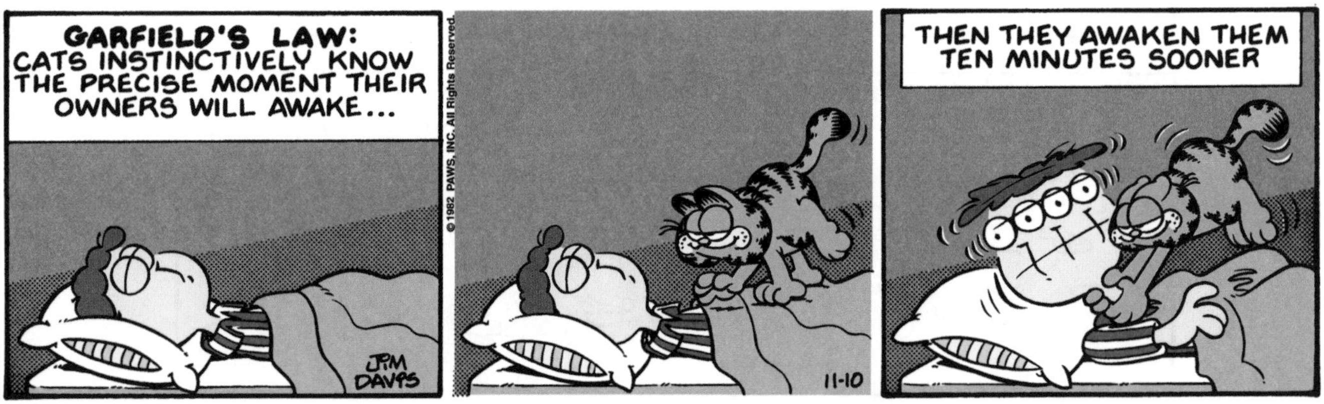
GARFIELD'S LAW:
CATS INSTINCTIVELY KNOW THE PRECISE MOMENT THEIR OWNERS WILL AWAKE...
JIM DAVIS
© 1982 PAWS, INC. All Rights Reserved.
11-10
THEN THEY AWAKEN THEM TEN MINUTES SOONER

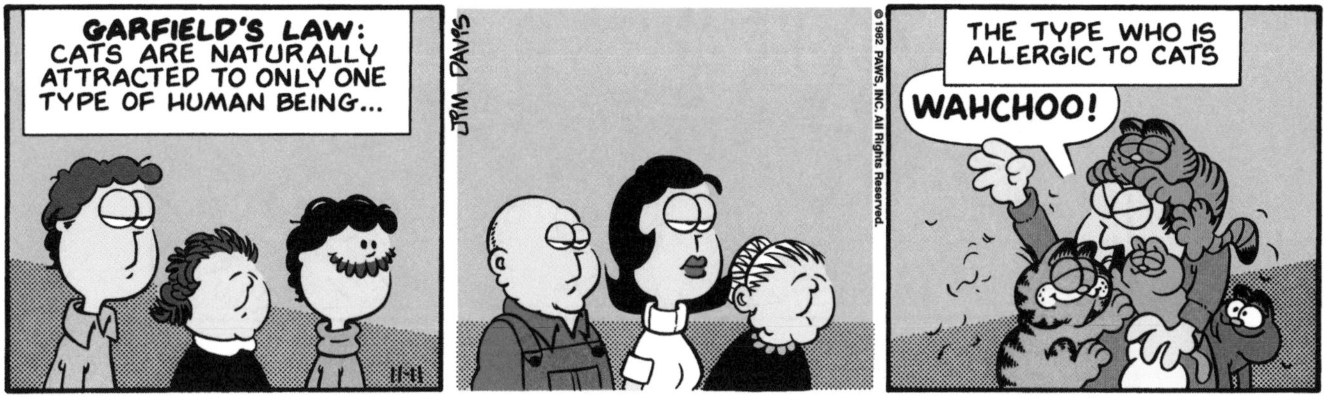
GARFIELD'S LAW: CATS ARE NATURALLY ATTRACTED TO ONLY ONE TYPE OF HUMAN BEING...
11-11
JIM DAVIS
© 1982 PAWS, INC. All Rights Reserved.
THE TYPE WHO IS ALLERGIC TO CATS
WAHCHOO!

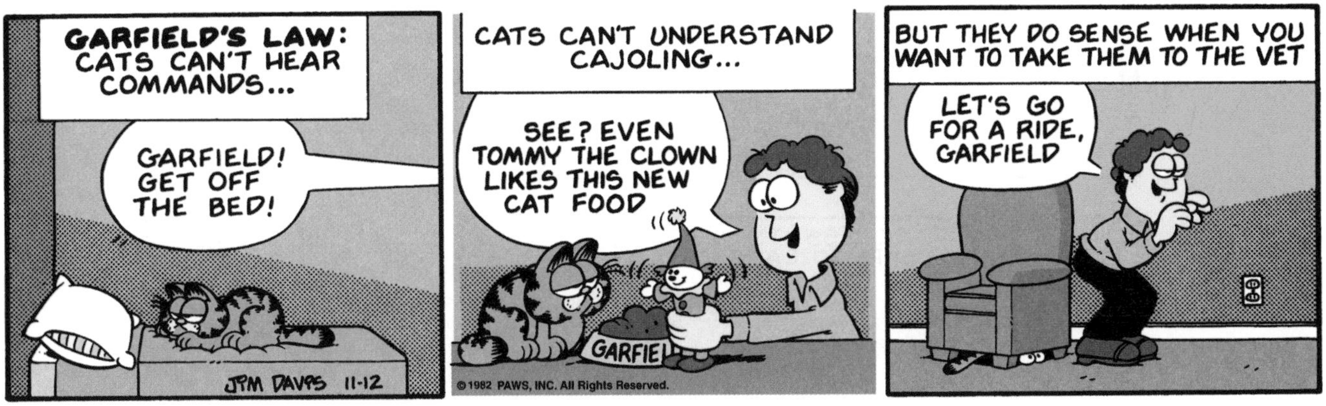
GARFIELD'S LAW: CATS CAN'T HEAR COMMANDS...
GARFIELD! GET OFF THE BED!
JIM DAVIS 11-12
CATS CAN'T UNDERSTAND CAJOLING...
SEE? EVEN TOMMY THE CLOWN LIKES THIS NEW CAT FOOD
GARFIE
© 1982 PAWS, INC. All Rights Reserved.
BUT THEY DO SENSE WHEN YOU WANT TO TAKE THEM TO THE VET
LET'S GO FOR A RIDE, GARFIELD

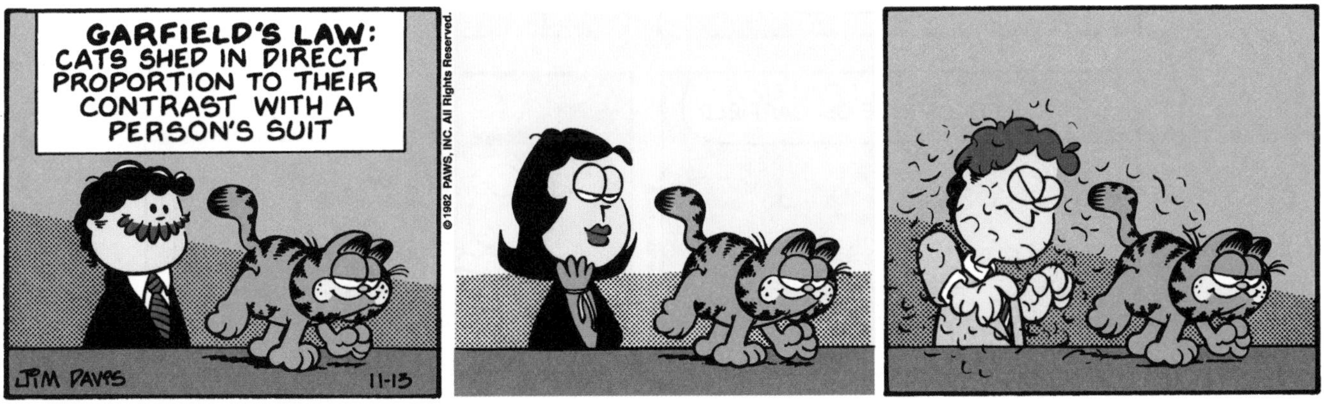
GARFIELD'S LAW: CATS SHED IN DIRECT PROPORTION TO THEIR CONTRAST WITH A PERSON'S SUIT
JIM DAVIS
11-13
© 1982 PAWS, INC. All Rights Reserved.

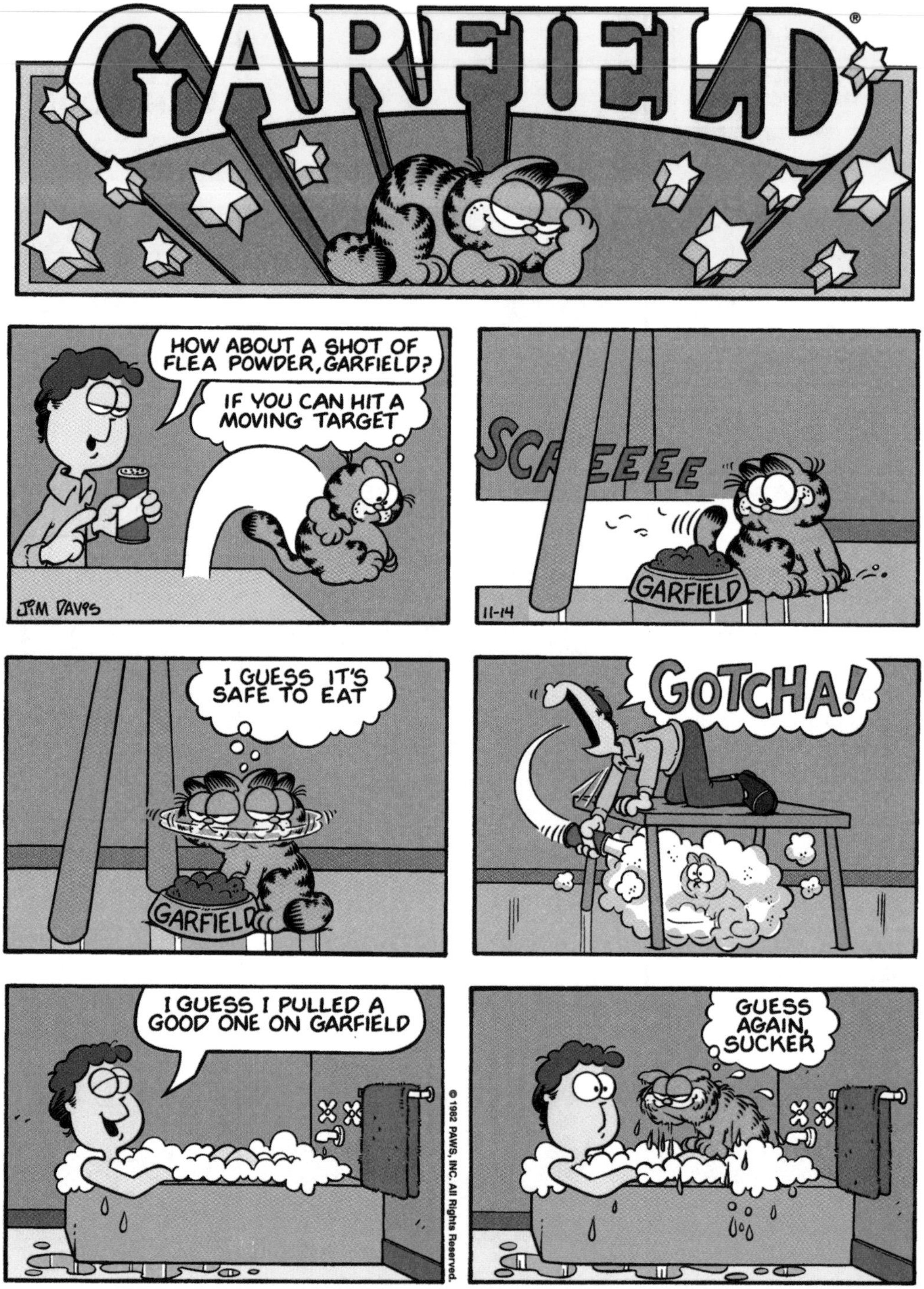
GARFIELD
HOW ABOUT A SHOT OF FLEA POWDER, GARFIELD?
IF YOU CAN HIT A MOVING TARGET
JIM DAVIS
SCREEEEEE
GARFIELD
11-14
I GUESS IT'S SAFE TO EAT
GARFIELD
GOTCHA!
I GUESS I PULLED A GOOD ONE ON GARFIELD
GUESS AGAIN, SUCKER

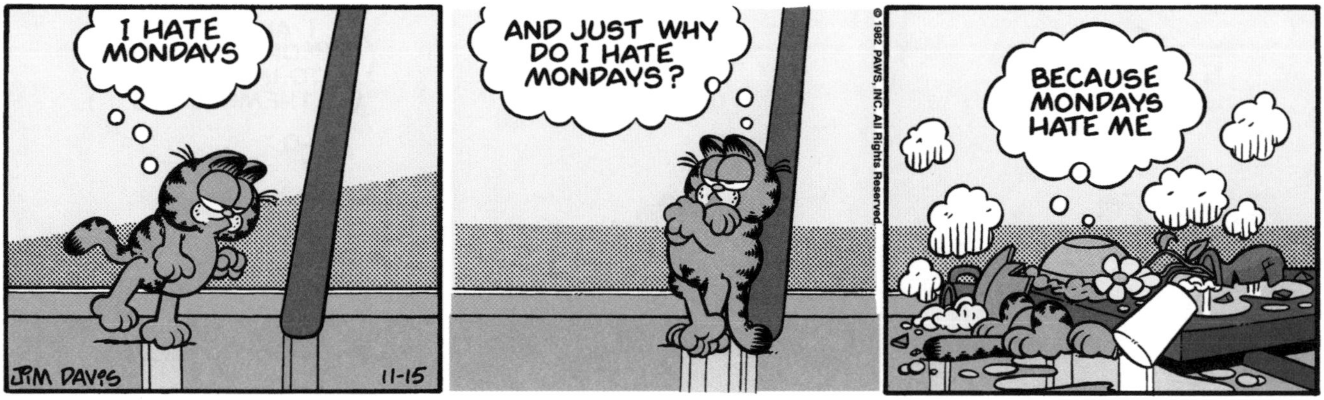
I HATE MONDAYS
JIM DAVIS
11-15
AND JUST WHY DO I HATE MONDAYS?
© 1982 PAWS, INC. All Rights Reserved.
BECAUSE MONDAYS HATE ME

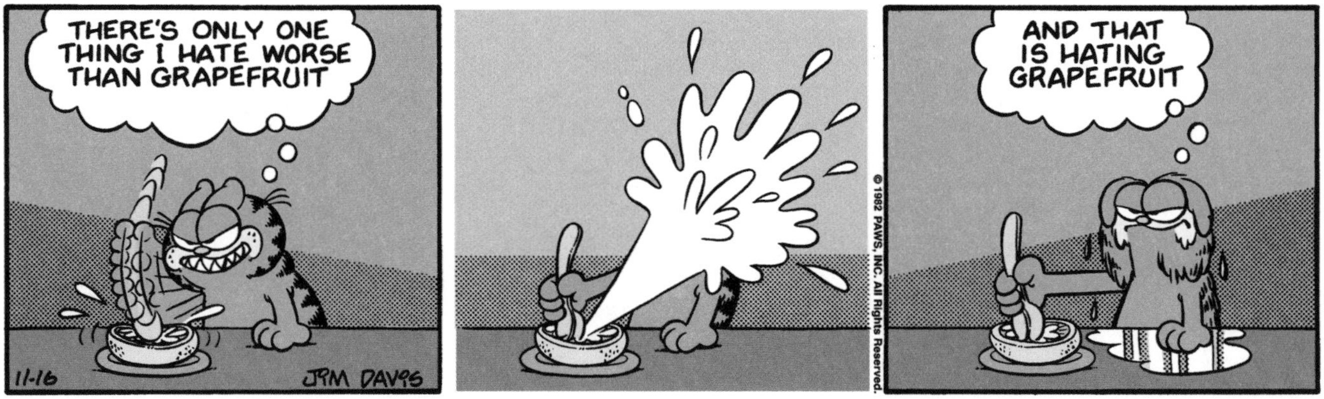
THERE'S ONLY ONE THING I HATE WORSE THAN GRAPEFRUIT
11-16
JIM DAVIS
© 1982 PAWS, INC. All Rights Reserved.
AND THAT IS HATING GRAPEFRUIT

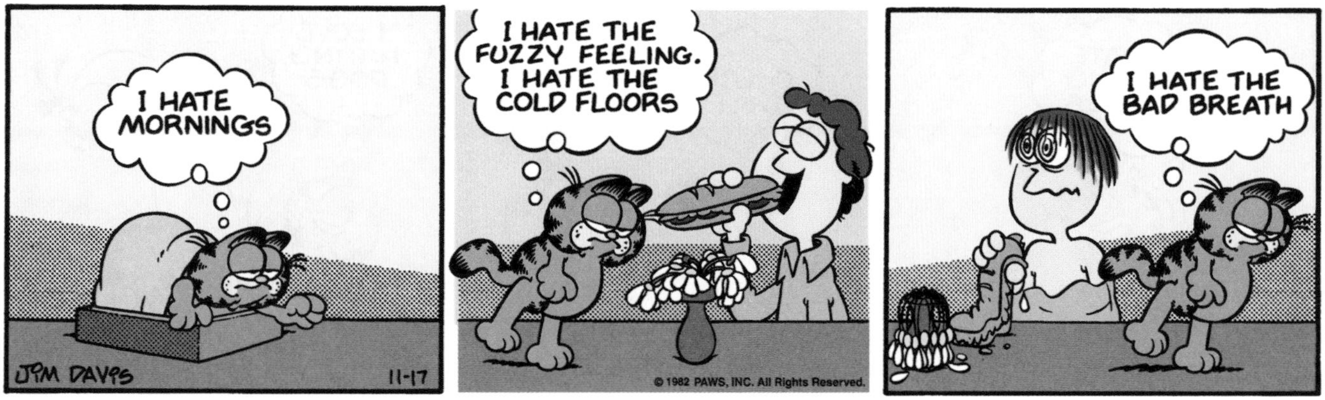
I HATE MORNINGS
JIM DAVIS
11-17
I HATE THE FUZZY FEELING. I HATE THE COLD FLOORS
© 1982 PAWS, INC. All Rights Reserved.
I HATE THE BAD BREATH

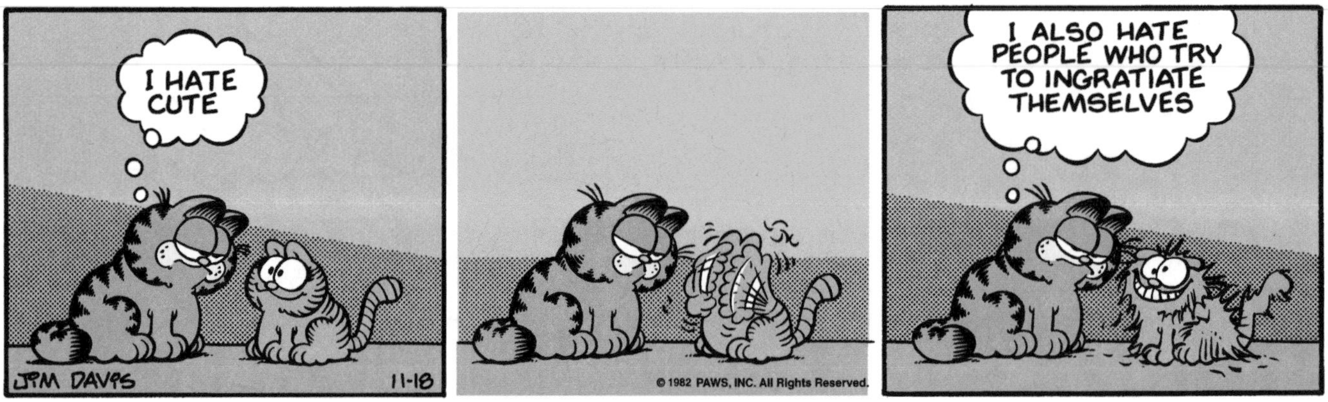
I HATE CUTE
JIM DAVIS
11-18
© 1982 PAWS, INC. All Rights Reserved.
I ALSO HATE PEOPLE WHO TRY TO INGRATIATE THEMSELVES

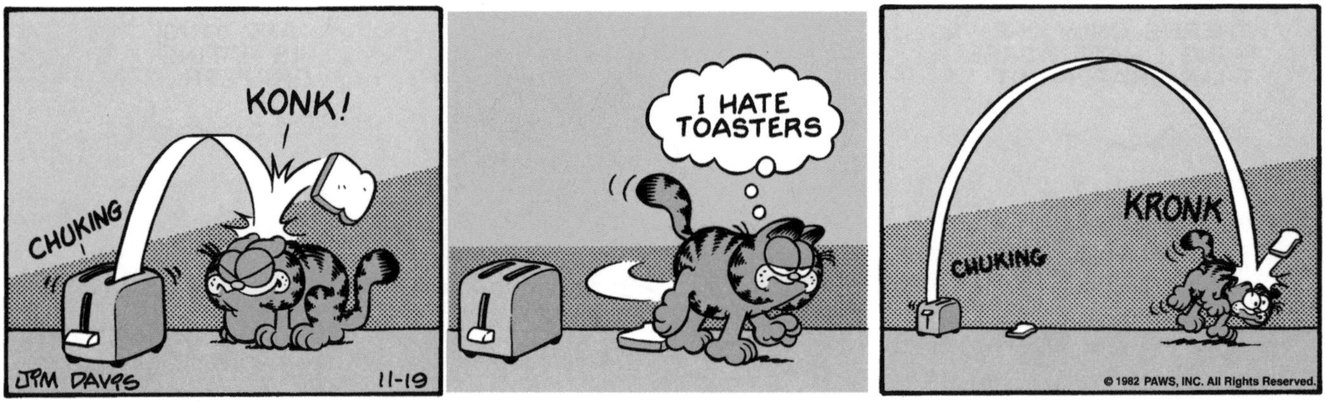
CHUKING
KONK!
JIM DAVIS
11-19
I HATE TOASTERS
CHUKING
KRONK
© 1982 PAWS, INC. All Rights Reserved.

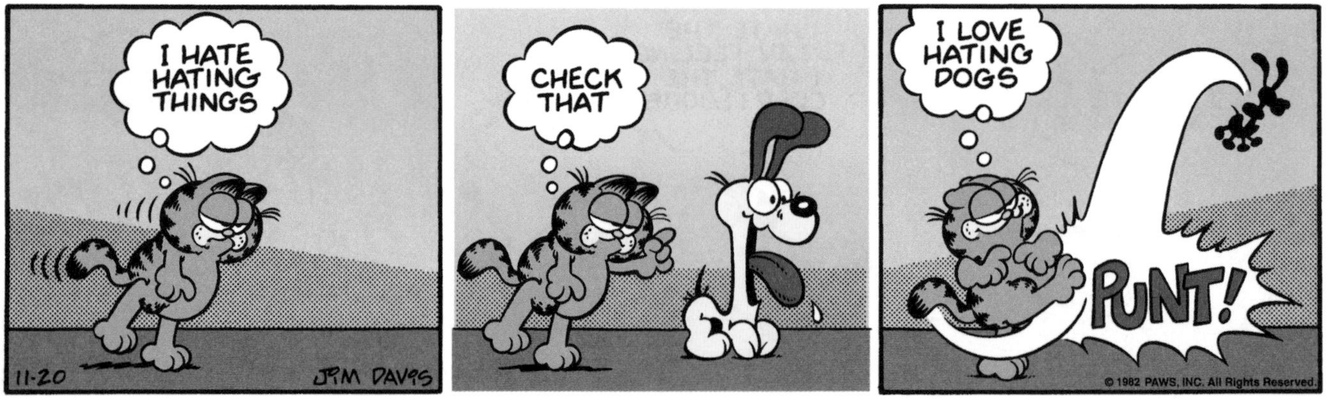
I HATE HATING THINGS
11-20
JIM DAVIS
CHECK THAT
I LOVE HATING DOGS
PUNT!
© 1982 PAWS, INC. All Rights Reserved.

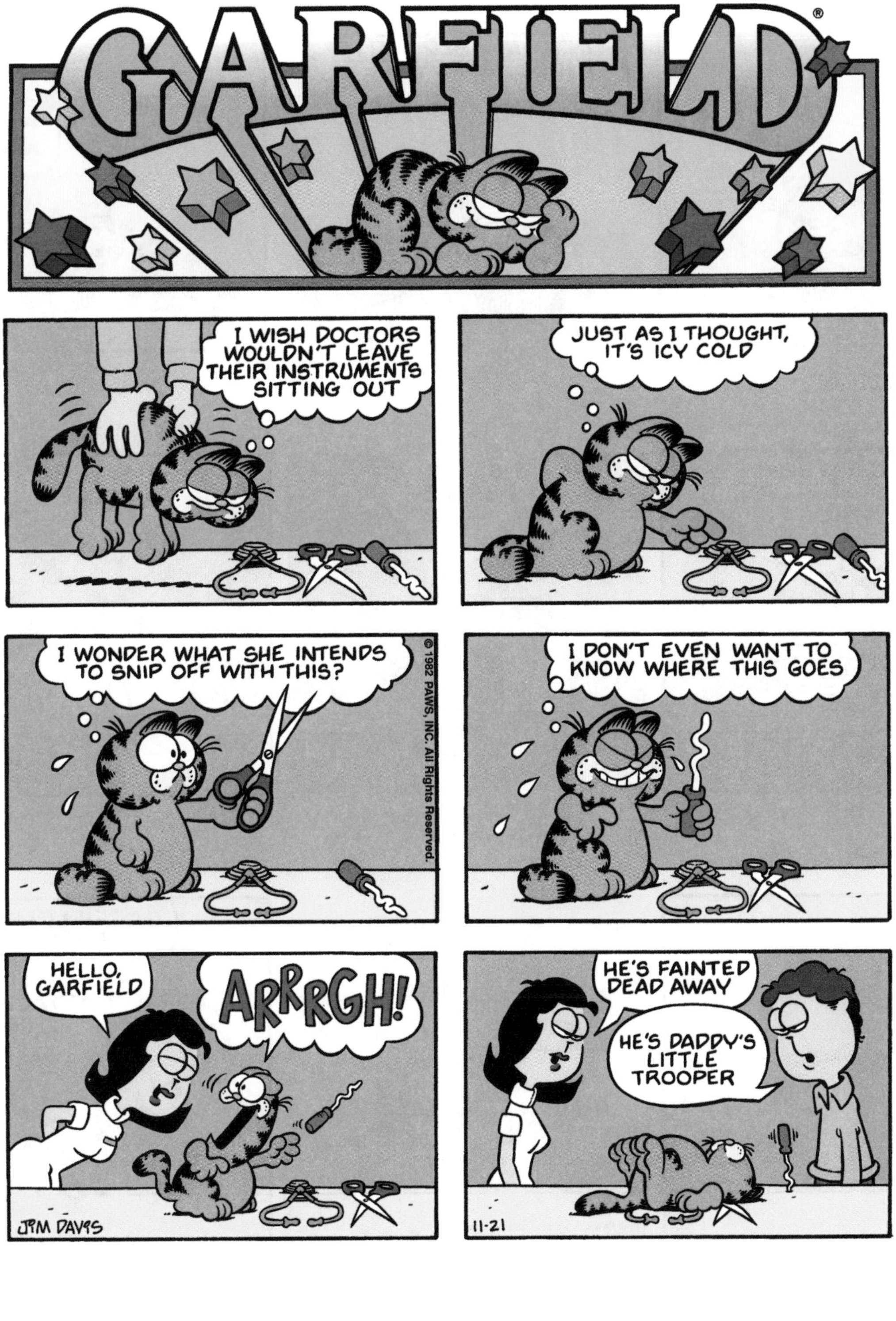
GARFIELD®
I WISH DOCTORS WOULDN'T LEAVE THEIR INSTRUMENTS SITTING OUT
JUST AS I THOUGHT, IT'S ICY COLD
I WONDER WHAT SHE INTENDS TO SNIP OFF WITH THIS?
© 1982 PAWS, INC. All Rights Reserved.
I DON'T EVEN WANT TO KNOW WHERE THIS GOES
HELLO, GARFIELD
ARRRGH!
JIM DAVIS
HE'S FAINTED DEAD AWAY
HE'S DADDY'S LITTLE TROOPER
11-21

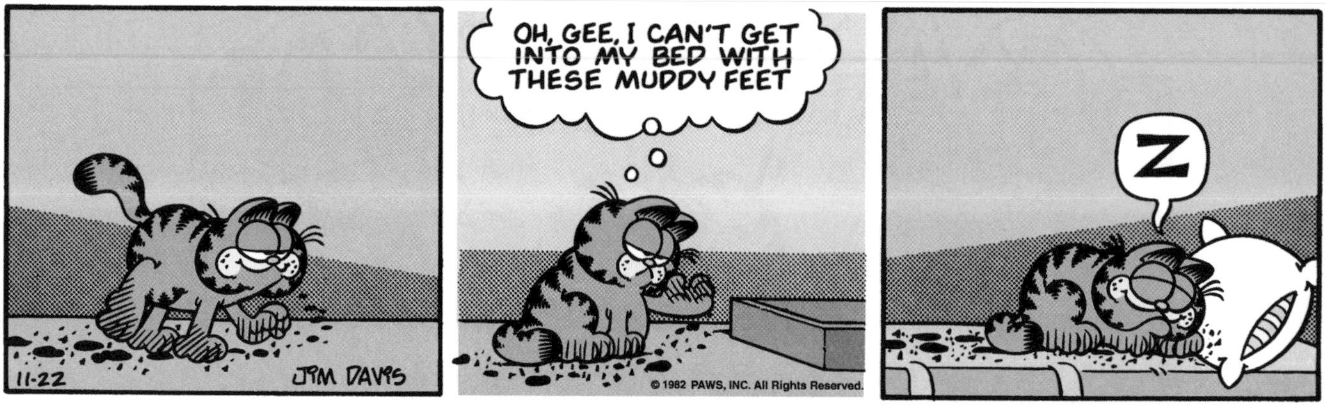
11-22
JIM DAVIS
OH, GEE, I CAN'T GET INTO MY BED WITH THESE MUDDY FEET
© 1982 PAWS, INC. All Rights Reserved.
Z

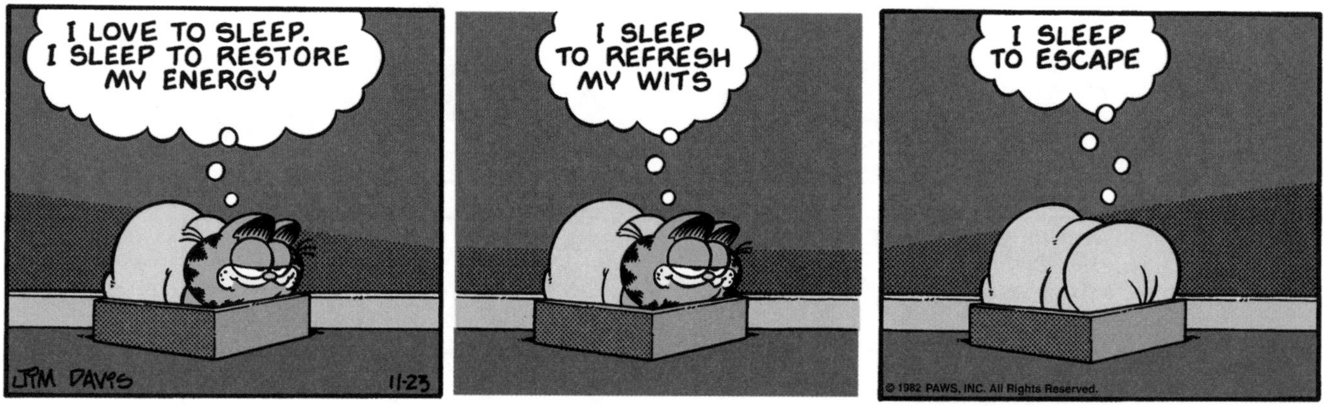
I LOVE TO SLEEP. I SLEEP TO RESTORE MY ENERGY
JIM DAVIS
11-23
I SLEEP TO REFRESH MY WITS
I SLEEP TO ESCAPE
© 1982 PAWS, INC. All Rights Reserved.

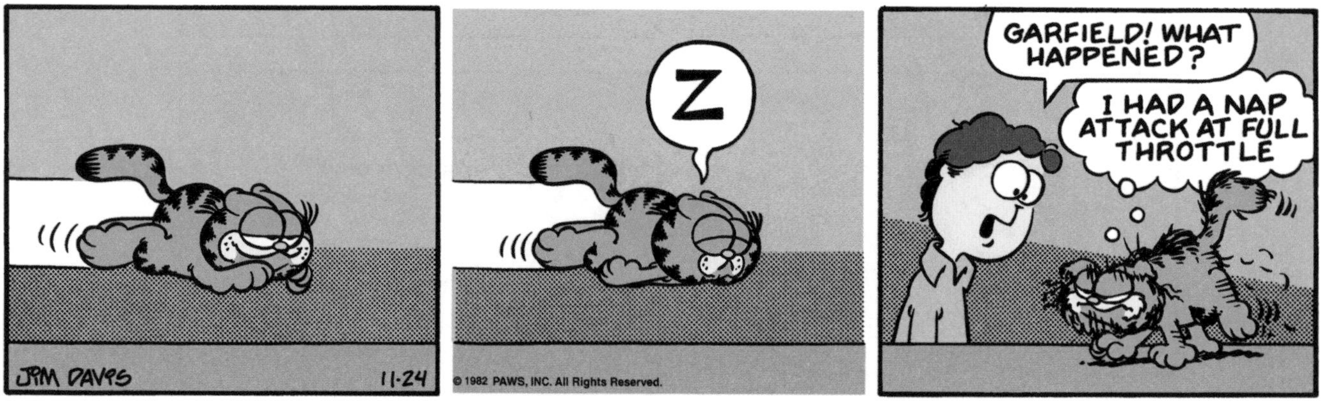
JIM DAVIS
11-24
Z
© 1982 PAWS, INC. All Rights Reserved.
GARFIELD! WHAT HAPPENED?
I HAD A NAP ATTACK AT FULL THROTTLE

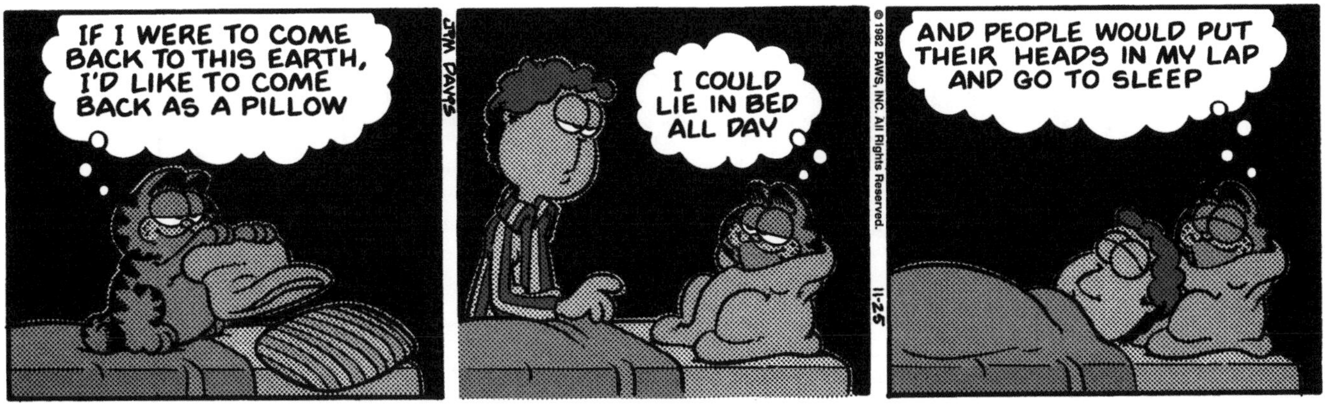
IF I WERE TO COME BACK TO THIS EARTH, I'D LIKE TO COME BACK AS A PILLOW
JIM DAVIS
I COULD LIE IN BED ALL DAY
© 1982 PAWS, INC. All Rights Reserved.
11-25
AND PEOPLE WOULD PUT THEIR HEADS IN MY LAP AND GO TO SLEEP

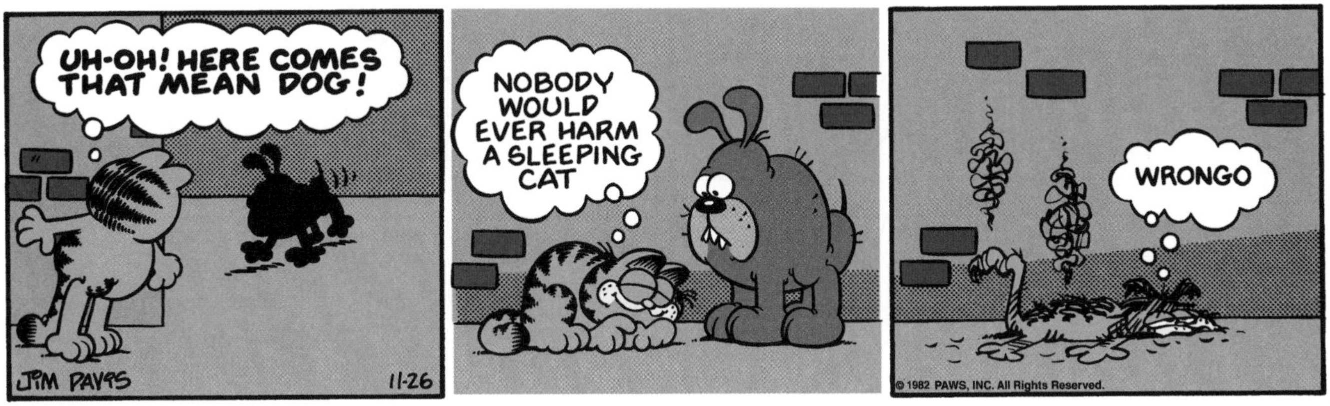
UH-OH! HERE COMES THAT MEAN DOG!
JIM DAVIS
11-26
NOBODY WOULD EVER HARM A SLEEPING CAT
WRONGO
© 1982 PAWS, INC. All Rights Reserved.

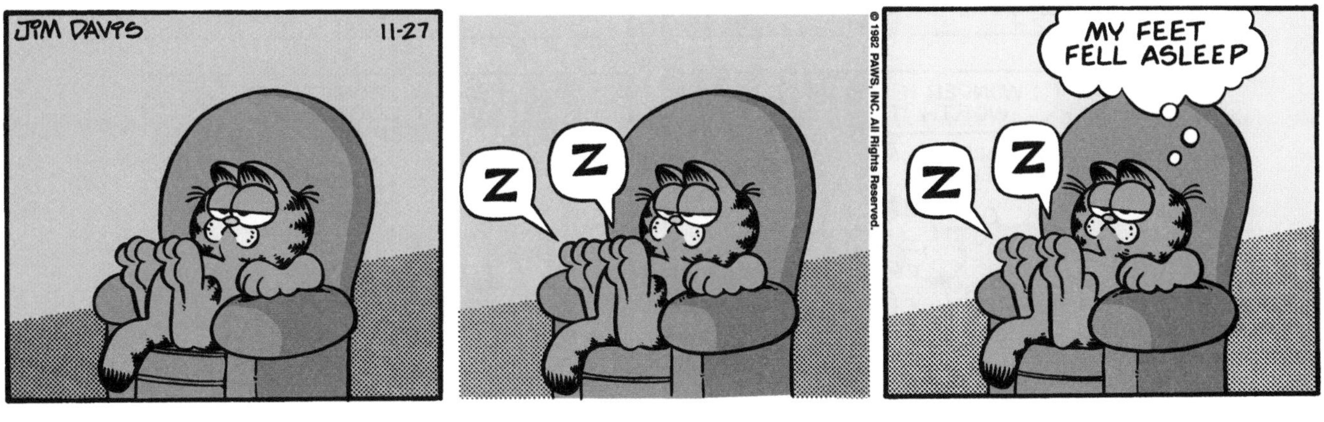
JIM DAVIS
11-27
Z
Z
© 1982 PAWS, INC. All Rights Reserved.
Z
Z
MY FEET FELL ASLEEP

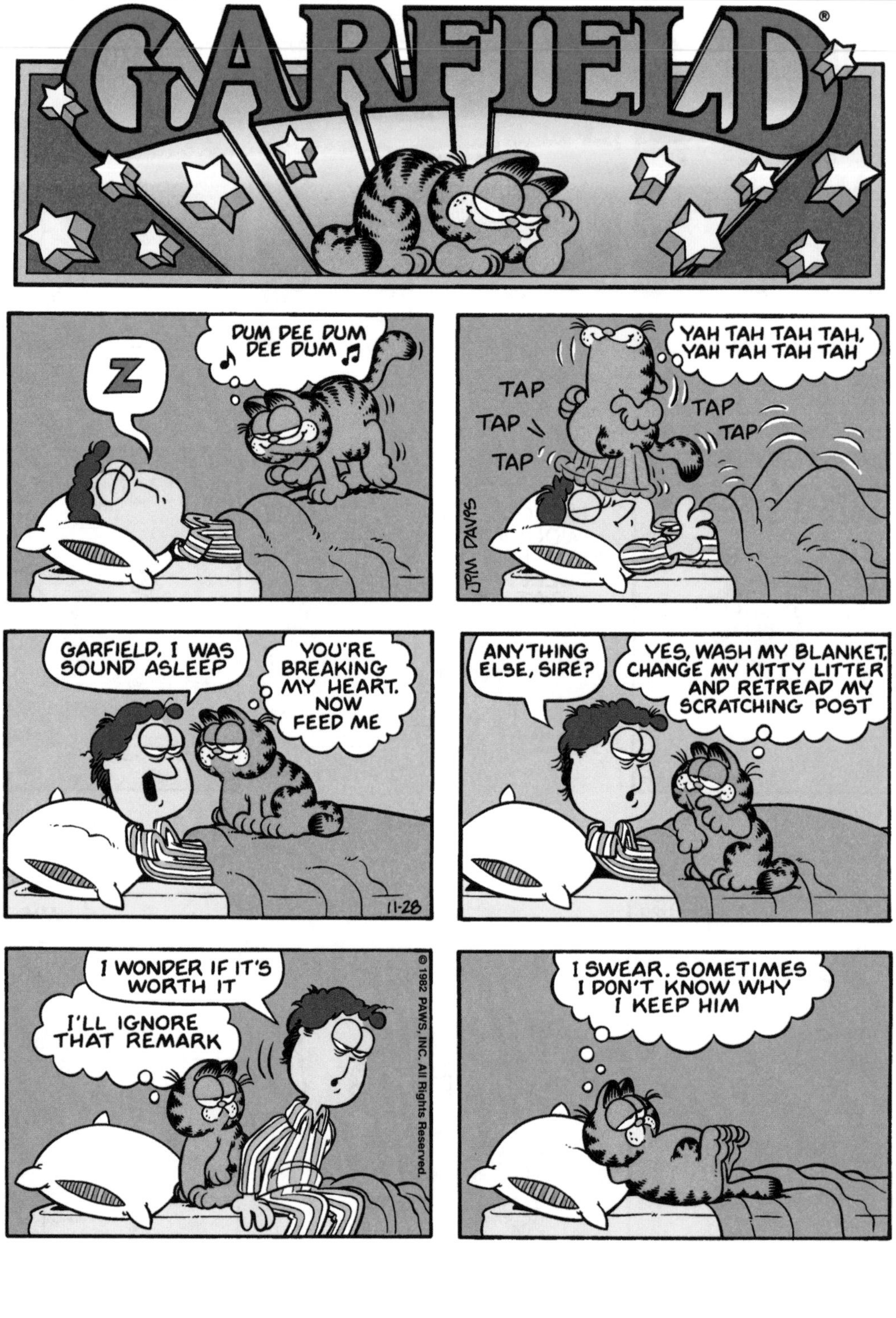
GARFIELD®
Z
DUM DEE DUM DEE DUM
YAH TAH TAH TAH, YAH TAH TAH TAH
TAP
TAP
TAP
TAP
TAP
TAP
JIM DAVIS
GARFIELD, I WAS SOUND ASLEEP
YOU'RE BREAKING MY HEART. NOW FEED ME
11-28
ANYTHING ELSE, SIRE?
YES, WASH MY BLANKET, CHANGE MY KITTY LITTER AND RETREAD MY SCRATCHING POST
I WONDER IF IT'S WORTH IT
I'LL IGNORE THAT REMARK
© 1982 PAWS, INC. All Rights Reserved.
I SWEAR. SOMETIMES I DON'T KNOW WHY I KEEP HIM

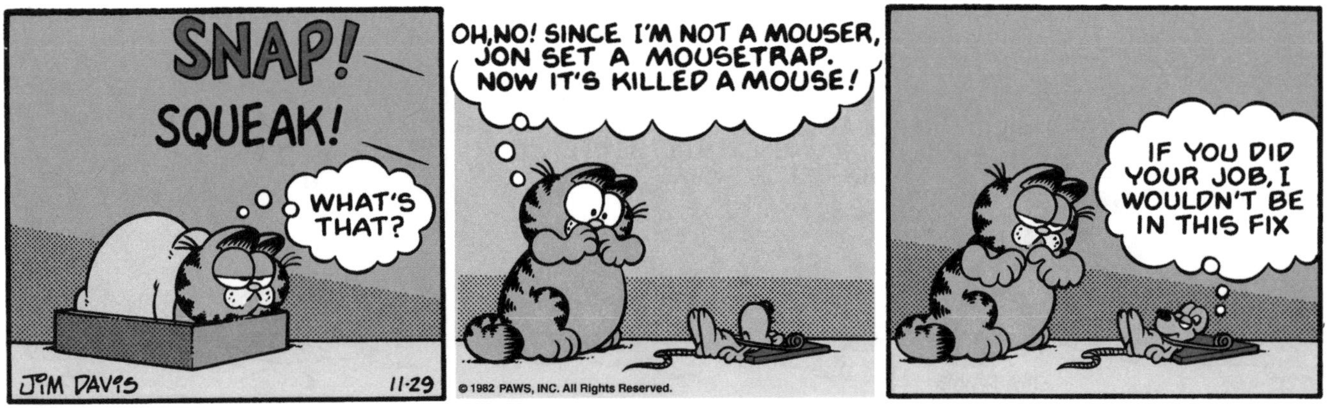
SNAP!
SQUEAK!
WHAT'S THAT?
JIM DAVIS
11-29
OH, NO! SINCE I'M NOT A MOUSER, JON SET A MOUSETRAP. NOW IT'S KILLED A MOUSE!
© 1982 PAWS, INC. All Rights Reserved.
IF YOU DID YOUR JOB, I WOULDN'T BE IN THIS FIX

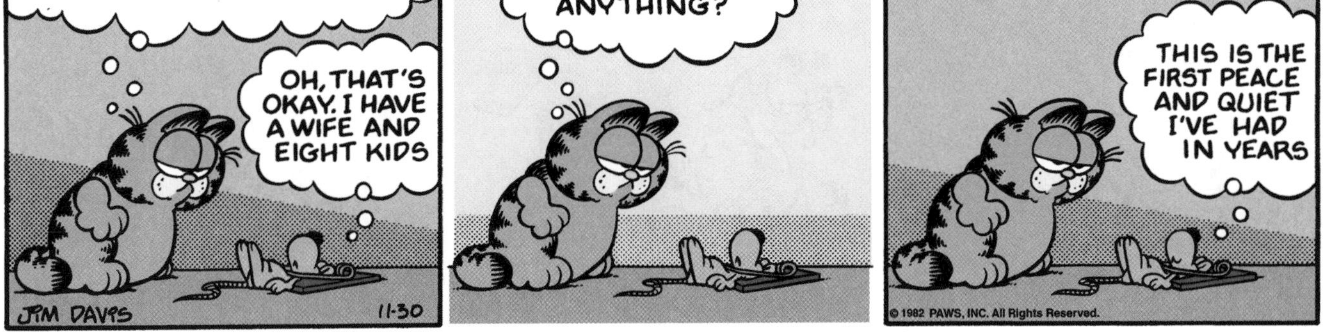
I'M SORRY YOU GOT CAUGHT IN THAT MOUSETRAP, MOUSE
OH, THAT'S OKAY. I HAVE A WIFE AND EIGHT KIDS
JIM DAVIS
11-30
WHAT DOES THAT HAVE TO DO WITH ANYTHING?
THIS IS THE FIRST PEACE AND QUIET I'VE HAD IN YEARS
© 1982 PAWS, INC. All Rights Reserved.

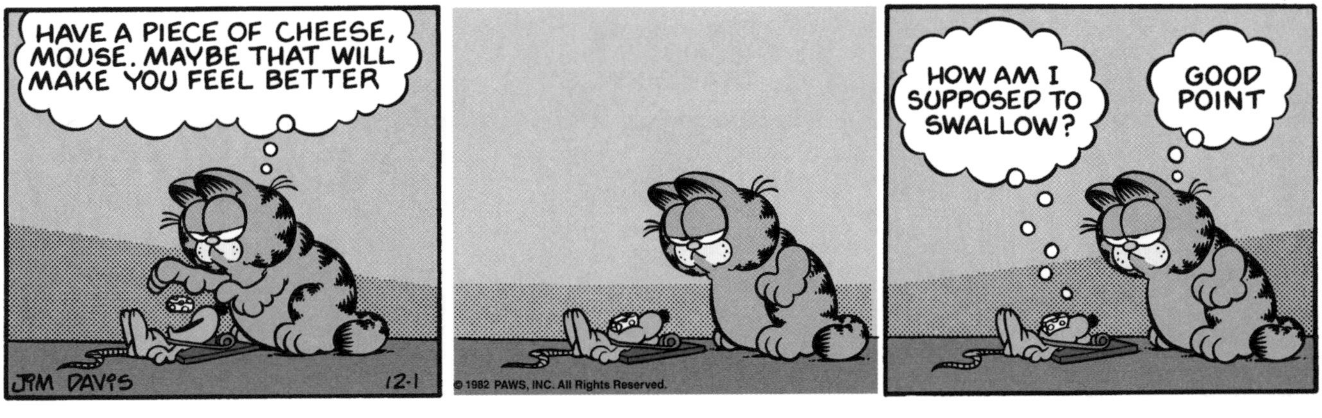
HAVE A PIECE OF CHEESE, MOUSE. MAYBE THAT WILL MAKE YOU FEEL BETTER
JIM DAVIS
12-1
© 1982 PAWS, INC. All Rights Reserved.
HOW AM I SUPPOSED TO SWALLOW?
GOOD POINT

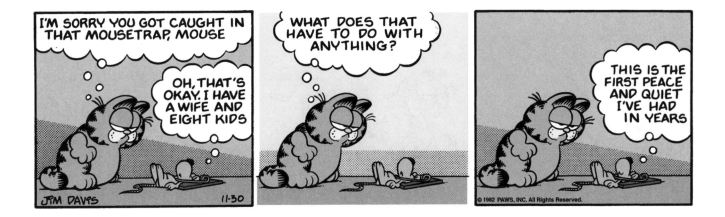

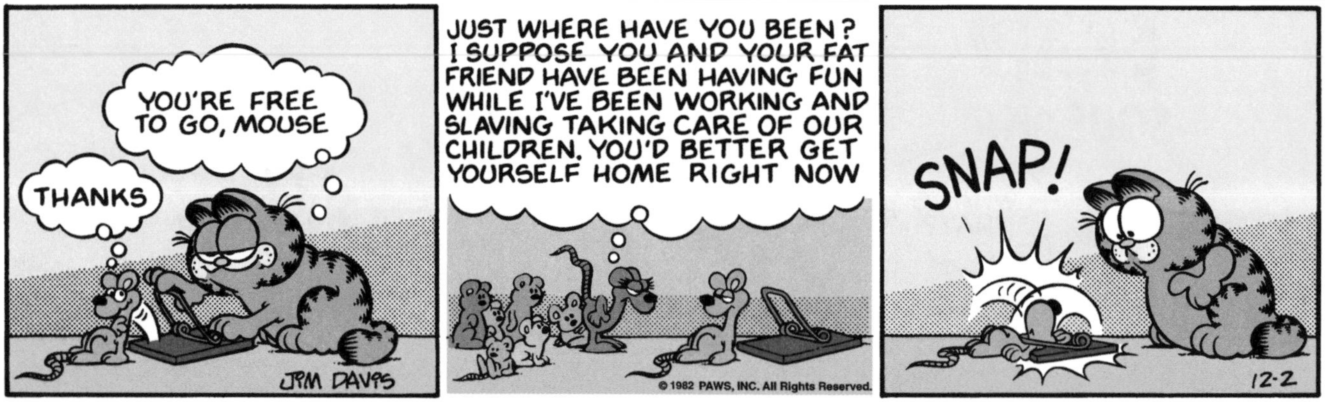
YOU'RE FREE TO GO, MOUSE
THANKS
JIM DAVIS
JUST WHERE HAVE YOU BEEN? I SUPPOSE YOU AND YOUR FAT FRIEND HAVE BEEN HAVING FUN WHILE I'VE BEEN WORKING AND SLAVING TAKING CARE OF OUR CHILDREN. YOU'D BETTER GET YOURSELF HOME RIGHT NOW
© 1982 PAWS, INC. All Rights Reserved.
SNAP!
12-2

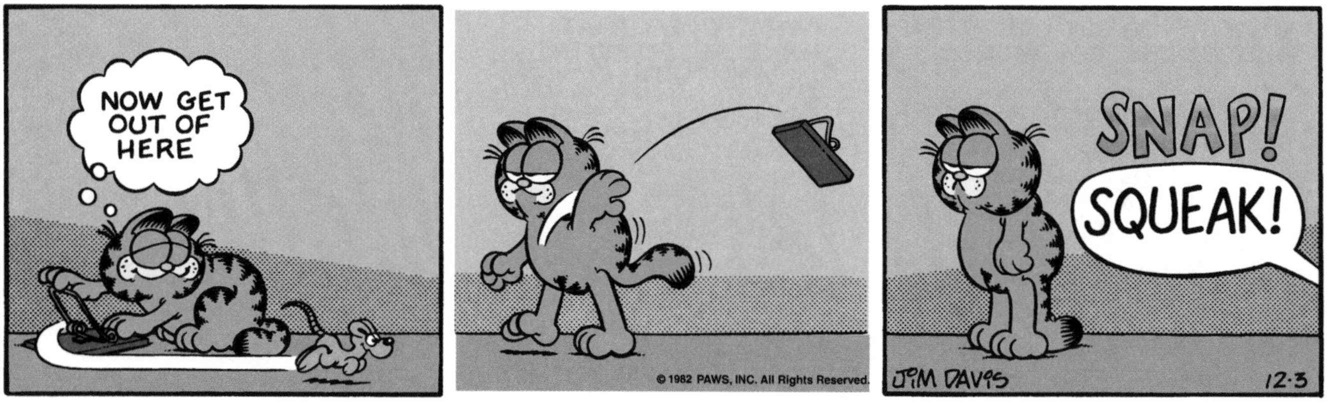
NOW GET OUT OF HERE
© 1982 PAWS, INC. All Rights Reserved.
SNAP!
SQUEAK!
JIM DAVIS
12-3

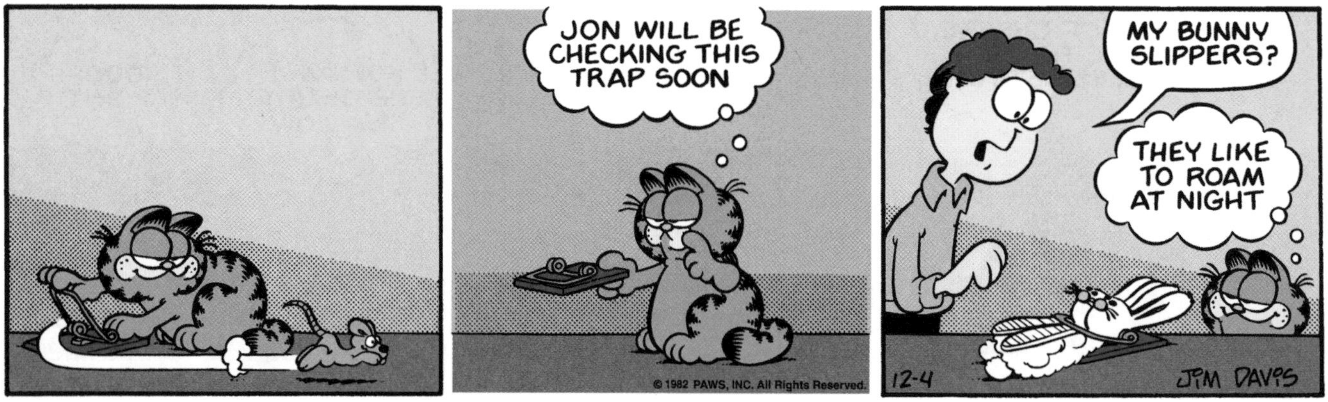
JON WILL BE CHECKING THIS TRAP SOON
© 1982 PAWS, INC. All Rights Reserved.
MY BUNNY SLIPPERS?
THEY LIKE TO ROAM AT NIGHT
12-4
JIM DAVIS

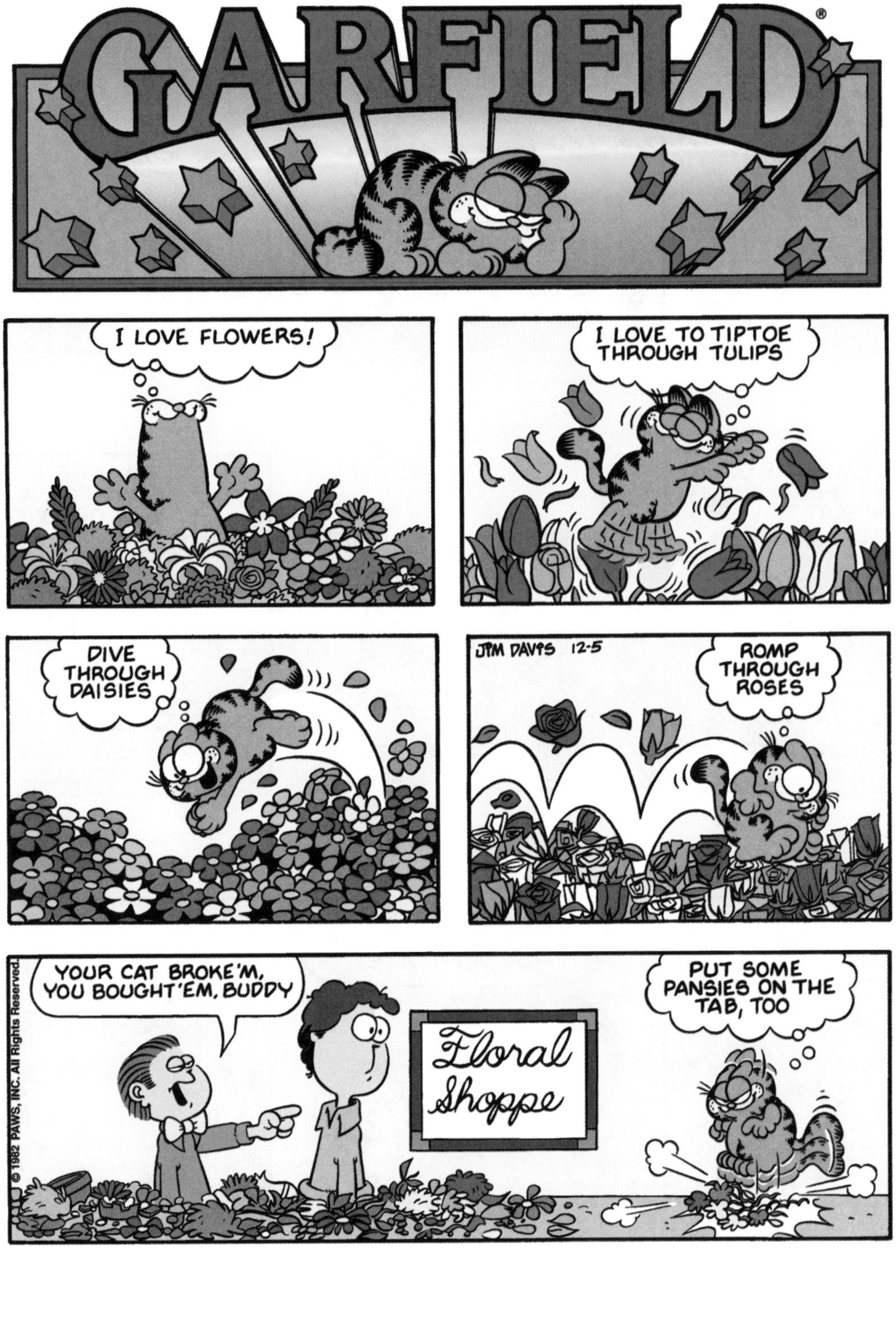
GARFIELD®
I LOVE FLOWERS!
I LOVE TO TIPTOE THROUGH TULIPS
DIVE THROUGH DAISIES
JIM DAVIS 12-5
ROMP THROUGH ROSES
YOUR CAT BROKE'M, YOU BOUGHT'EM, BUDDY
Floral Shoppe
PUT SOME PANSIES ON THE TAB, TOO
© 1982 PAWS, INC. All Rights Reserved.

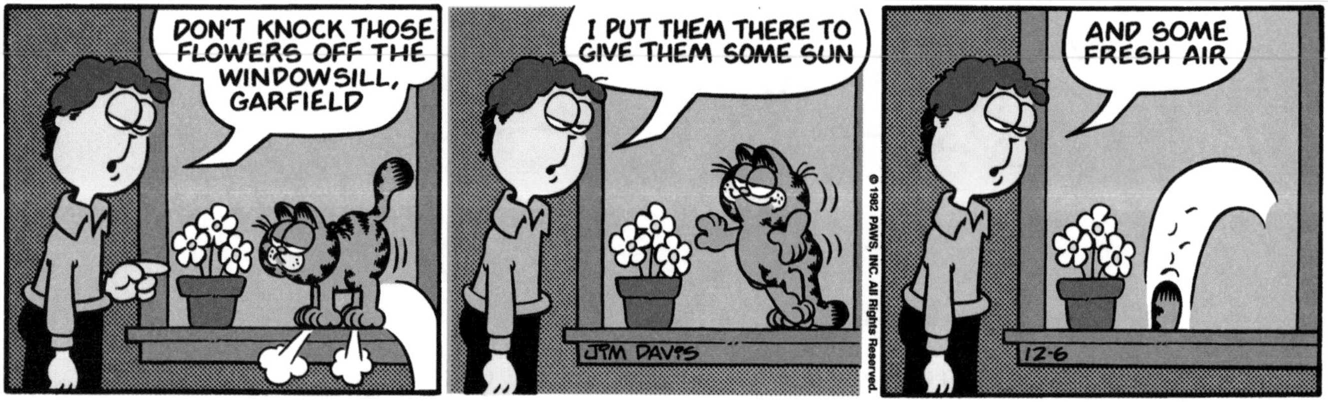
DON'T KNOCK THOSE FLOWERS OFF THE WINDOWSILL, GARFIELD
I PUT THEM THERE TO GIVE THEM SOME SUN
AND SOME FRESH AIR
JIM DAVIS
© 1982 PAWS, INC. All Rights Reserved.
12-6

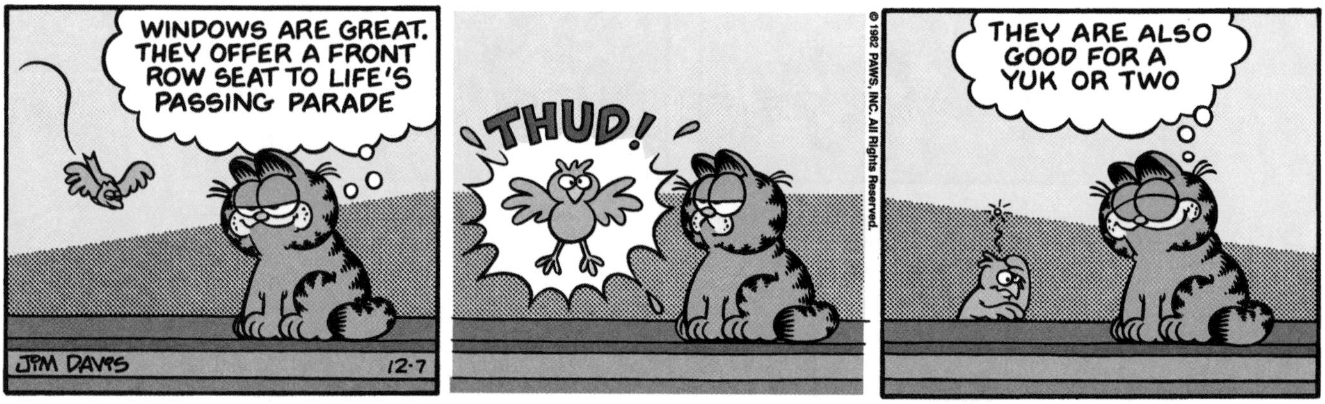
WINDOWS ARE GREAT. THEY OFFER A FRONT ROW SEAT TO LIFE'S PASSING PARADE
JIM DAVIS
12-7
THUD!
© 1982 PAWS, INC. All Rights Reserved.
THEY ARE ALSO GOOD FOR A YUK OR TWO

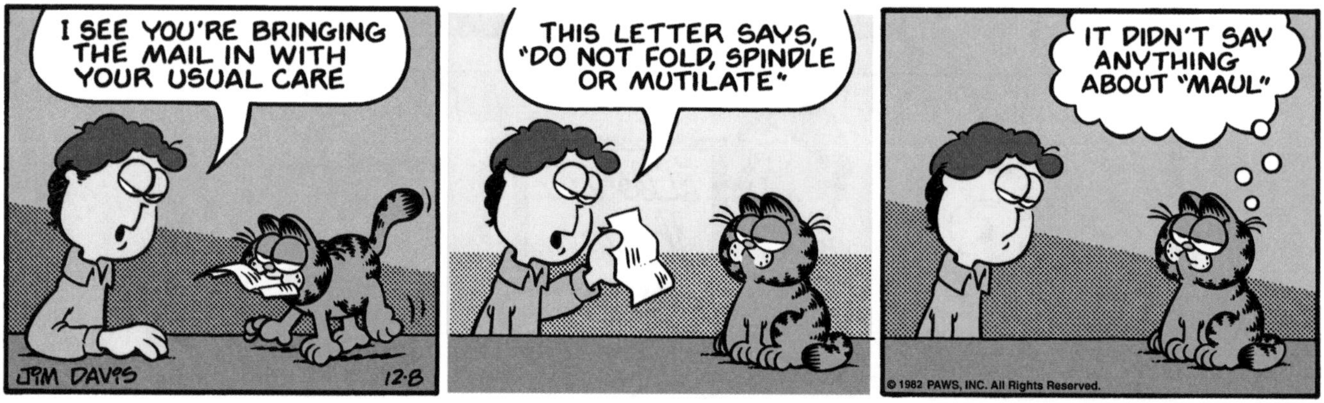
I SEE YOU'RE BRINGING THE MAIL IN WITH YOUR USUAL CARE
JIM DAVIS
12-8
THIS LETTER SAYS, "DO NOT FOLD, SPINDLE OR MUTILATE"
IT DIDN'T SAY ANYTHING ABOUT "MAUL"
© 1982 PAWS, INC. All Rights Reserved.

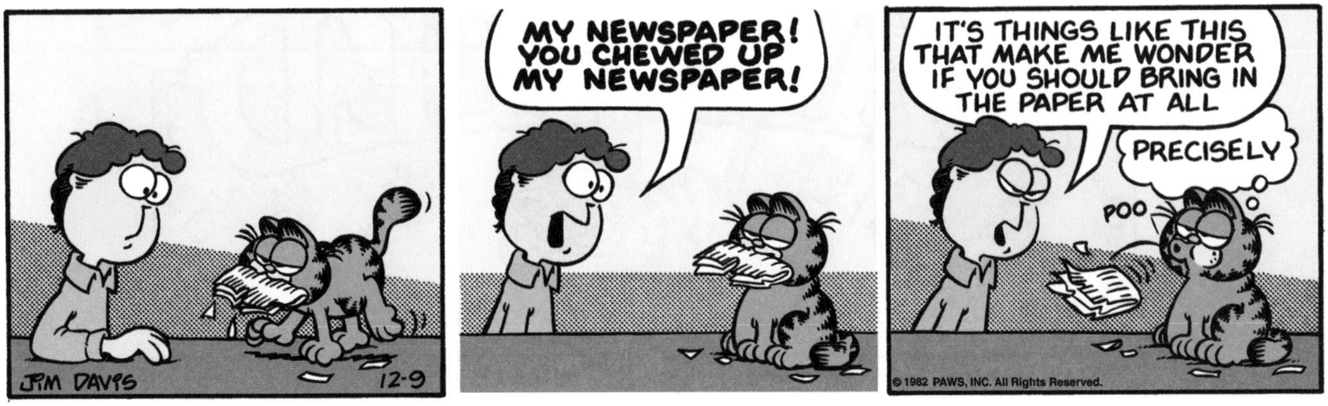
JIM DAVIS 12-9
MY NEWSPAPER! YOU CHEWED UP MY NEWSPAPER!
IT'S THINGS LIKE THIS THAT MAKE ME WONDER IF YOU SHOULD BRING IN THE PAPER AT ALL
PRECISELY
POO
© 1982 PAWS, INC. All Rights Reserved.

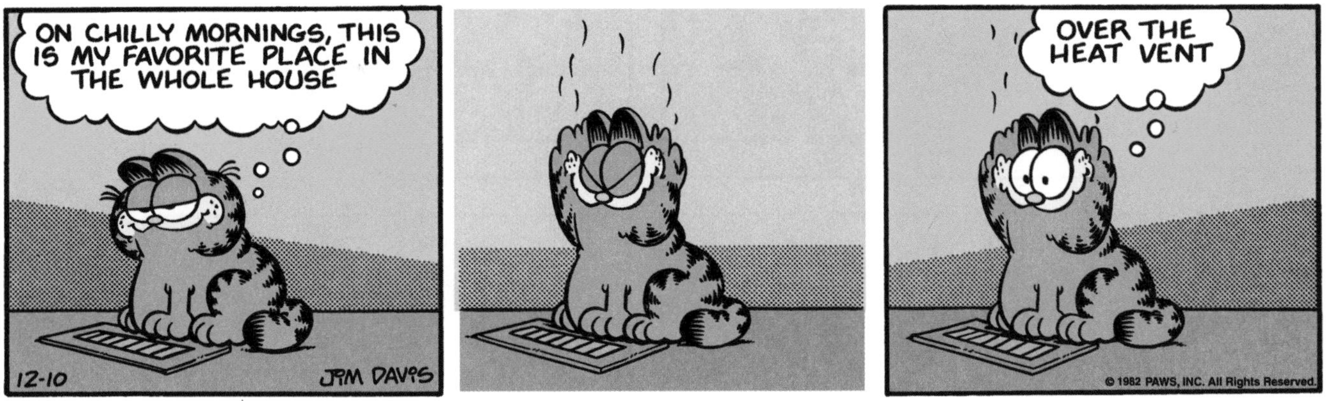
ON CHILLY MORNINGS, THIS IS MY FAVORITE PLACE IN THE WHOLE HOUSE
12-10 JIM DAVIS
OVER THE HEAT VENT
© 1982 PAWS, INC. All Rights Reserved.

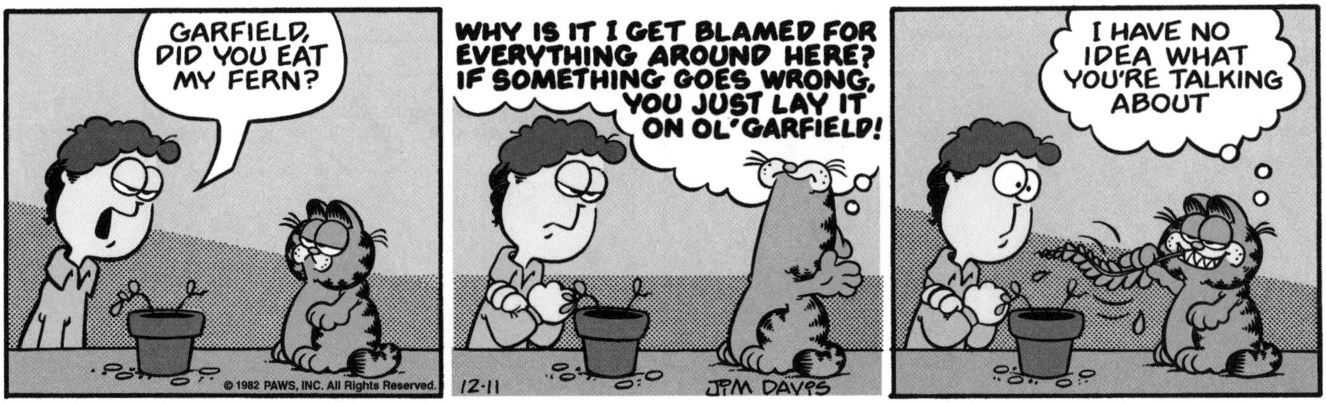
GARFIELD, DID YOU EAT MY FERN?
© 1982 PAWS, INC. All Rights Reserved.
WHY IS IT I GET BLAMED FOR EVERYTHING AROUND HERE? IF SOMETHING GOES WRONG, YOU JUST LAY IT ON OL' GARFIELD!
12-11 JIM DAVIS
I HAVE NO IDEA WHAT YOU'RE TALKING ABOUT

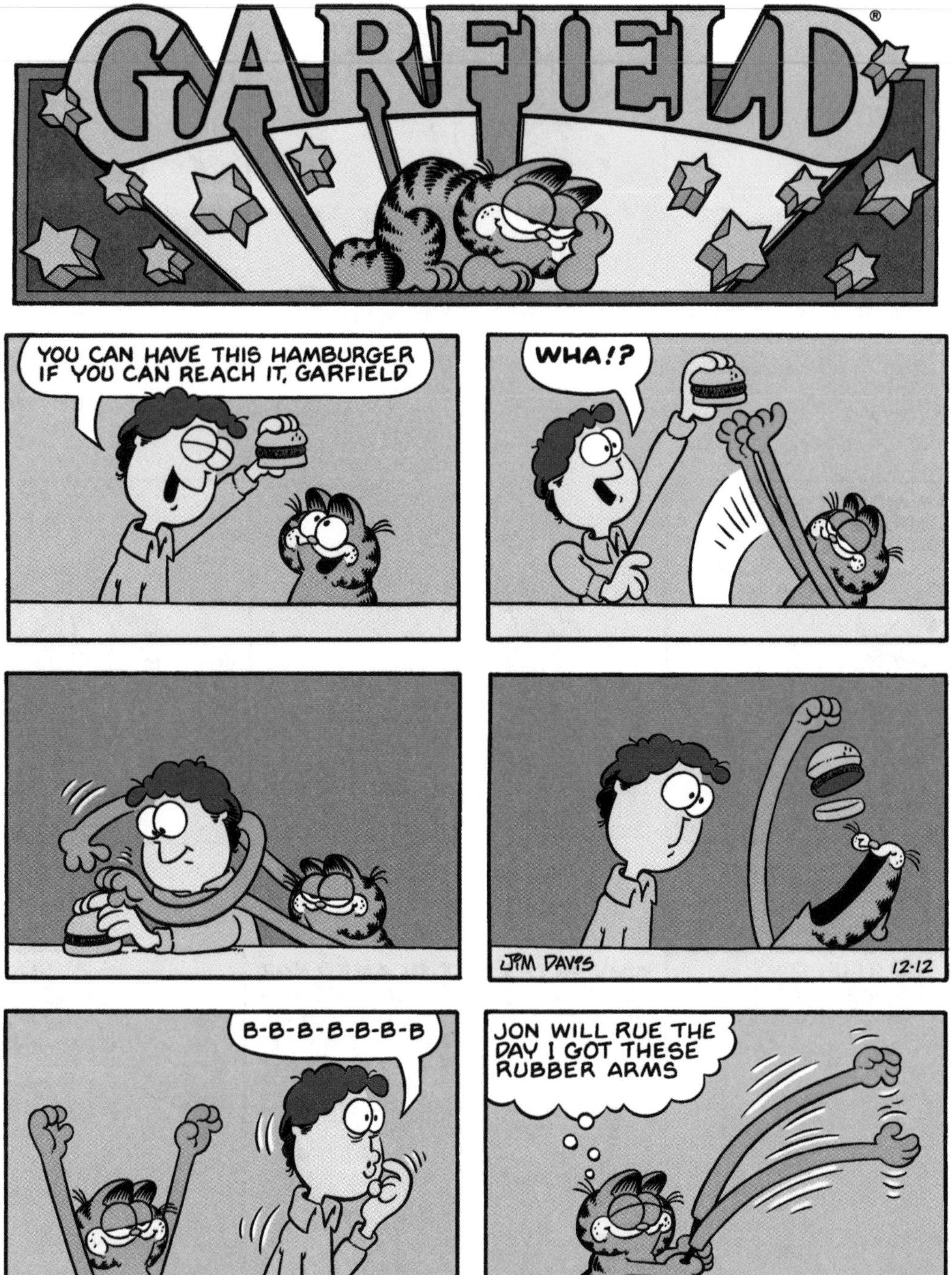
GARFIELD®
YOU CAN HAVE THIS HAMBURGER IF YOU CAN REACH IT, GARFIELD
WHA!?
JIM DAVIS
12-12
B-B-B-B-B-B-B
JON WILL RUE THE DAY I GOT THESE RUBBER ARMS
© 1982 PAWS, INC. All Rights Reserved.

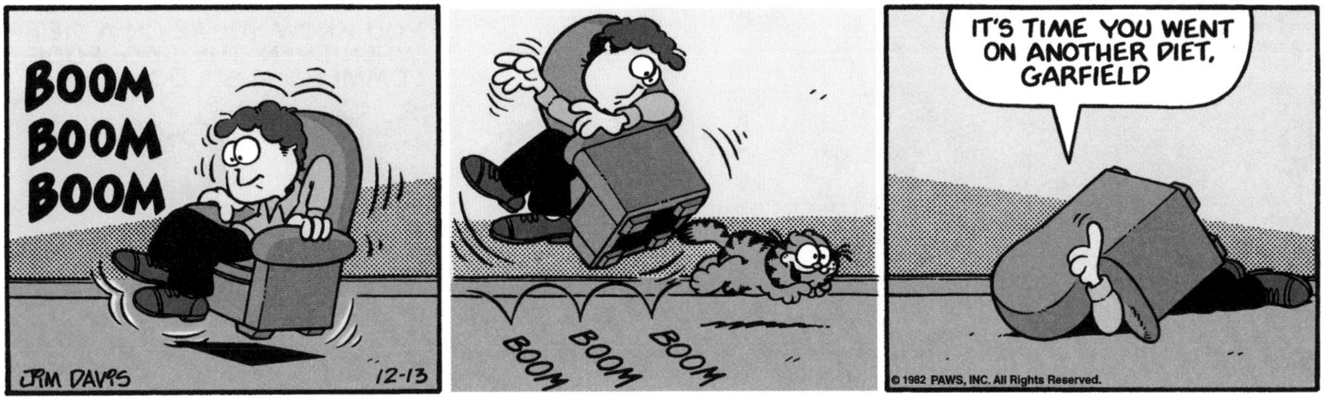
BOOM
BOOM
BOOM
JIM DAVIS
12-13
BOOM BOOM BOOM
IT'S TIME YOU WENT ON ANOTHER DIET, GARFIELD
© 1982 PAWS, INC. All Rights Reserved.

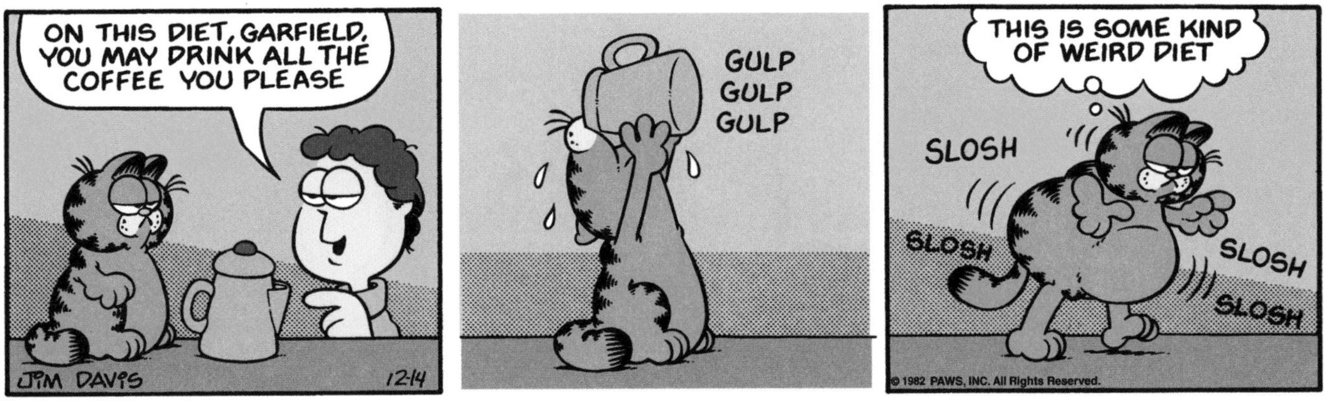
ON THIS DIET, GARFIELD, YOU MAY DRINK ALL THE COFFEE YOU PLEASE
JIM DAVIS
12-14
GULP
GULP
GULP
THIS IS SOME KIND OF WEIRD DIET
SLOSH
SLOSH
SLOSH
SLOSH
© 1982 PAWS, INC. All Rights Reserved.

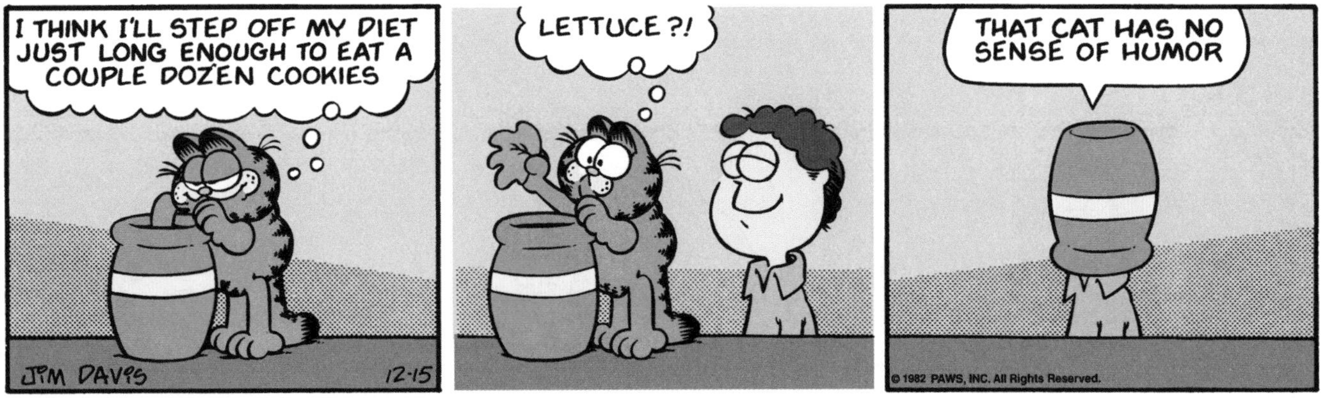
I THINK I'LL STEP OFF MY DIET JUST LONG ENOUGH TO EAT A COUPLE DOZEN COOKIES
JIM DAVIS
12-15
LETTUCE ?!
THAT CAT HAS NO SENSE OF HUMOR
© 1982 PAWS, INC. All Rights Reserved.

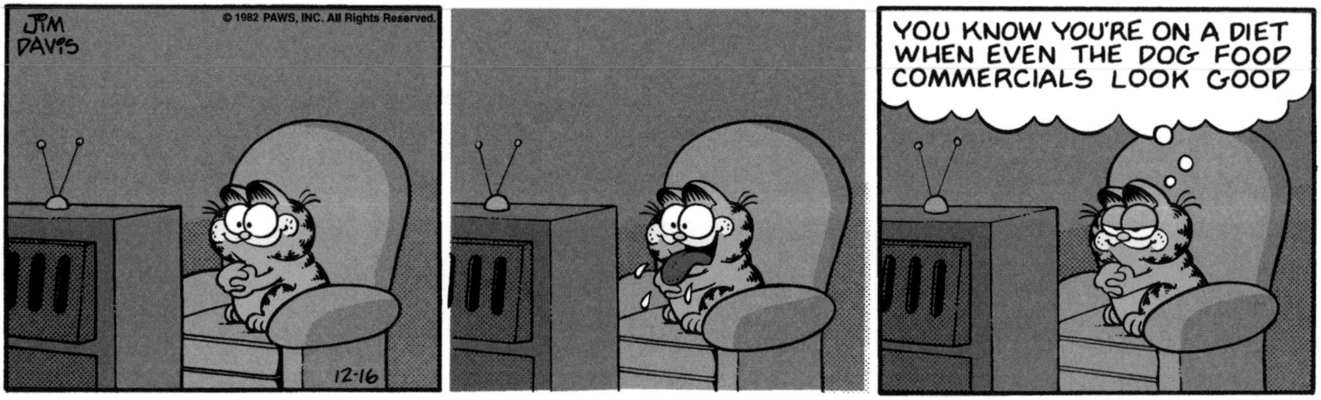
JIM DAVIS
© 1982 PAWS, INC. All Rights Reserved.
12-16
YOU KNOW YOU'RE ON A DIET WHEN EVEN THE DOG FOOD COMMERCIALS LOOK GOOD

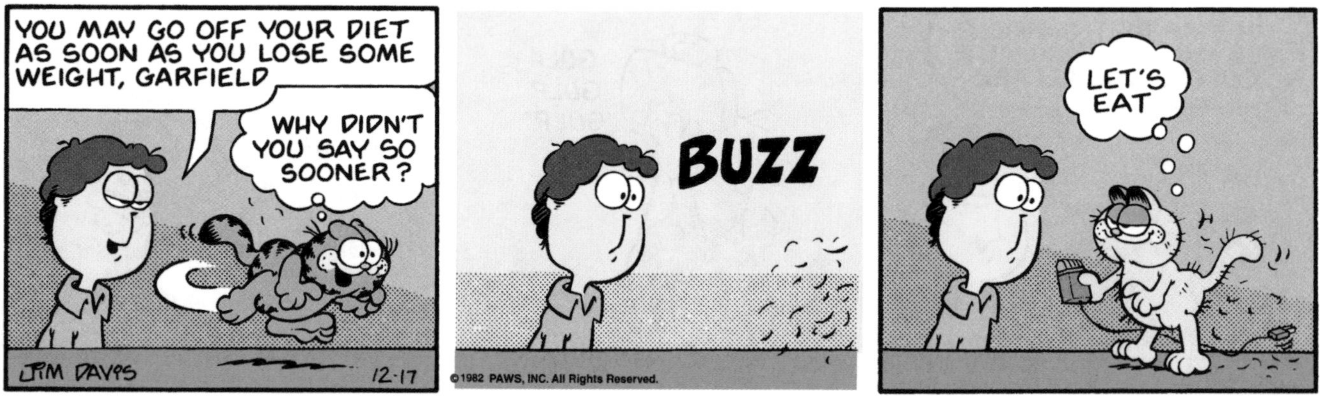
YOU MAY GO OFF YOUR DIET AS SOON AS YOU LOSE SOME WEIGHT, GARFIELD
WHY DIDN'T YOU SAY SO SOONER?
JIM DAVIS
12-17
BUZZ
©1982 PAWS, INC. All Rights Reserved.
LET'S EAT

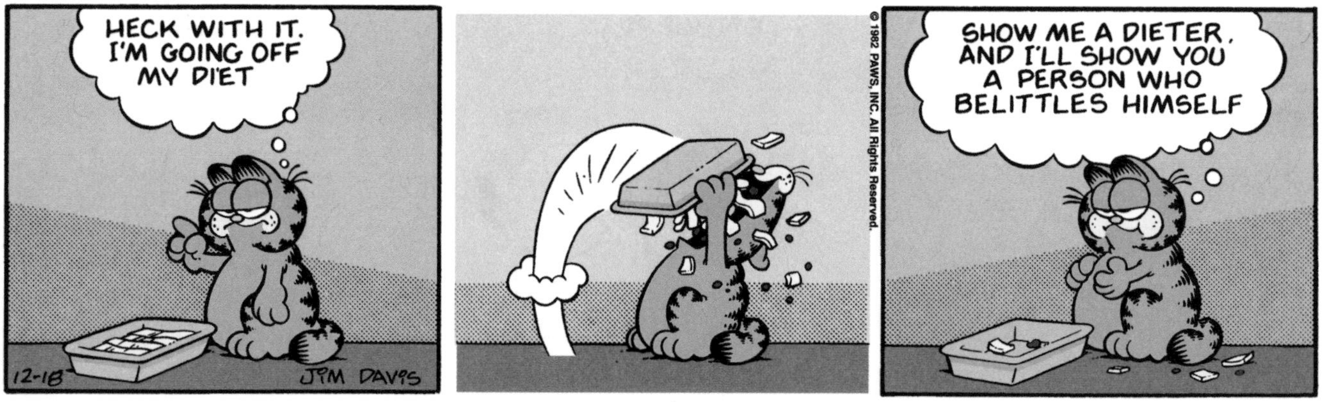
HECK WITH IT. I'M GOING OFF MY DIET
12-18
JIM DAVIS
© 1982 PAWS, INC. All Rights Reserved.
SHOW ME A DIETER, AND I'LL SHOW YOU A PERSON WHO BELITTLES HIMSELF

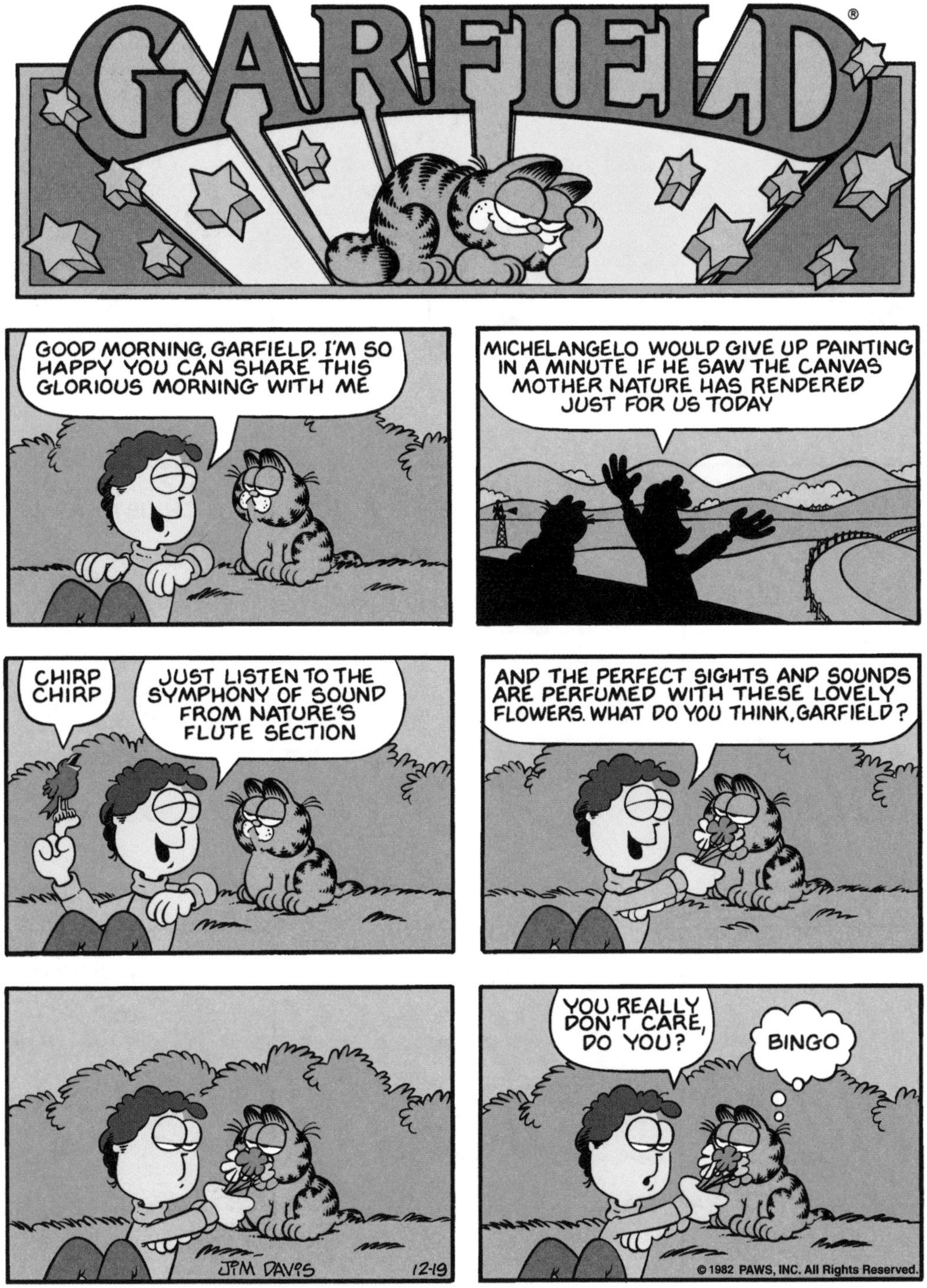
GARFIELD®
GOOD MORNING, GARFIELD. I'M SO HAPPY YOU CAN SHARE THIS GLORIOUS MORNING WITH ME
MICHELANGELO WOULD GIVE UP PAINTING IN A MINUTE IF HE SAW THE CANVAS MOTHER NATURE HAS RENDERED JUST FOR US TODAY
CHIRP CHIRP
JUST LISTEN TO THE SYMPHONY OF SOUND FROM NATURE'S FLUTE SECTION
AND THE PERFECT SIGHTS AND SOUNDS ARE PERFUMED WITH THESE LOVELY FLOWERS. WHAT DO YOU THINK, GARFIELD?
JIM DAVIS
12-19
YOU REALLY DON'T CARE, DO YOU?
BINGO
© 1982 PAWS, INC. All Rights Reserved.

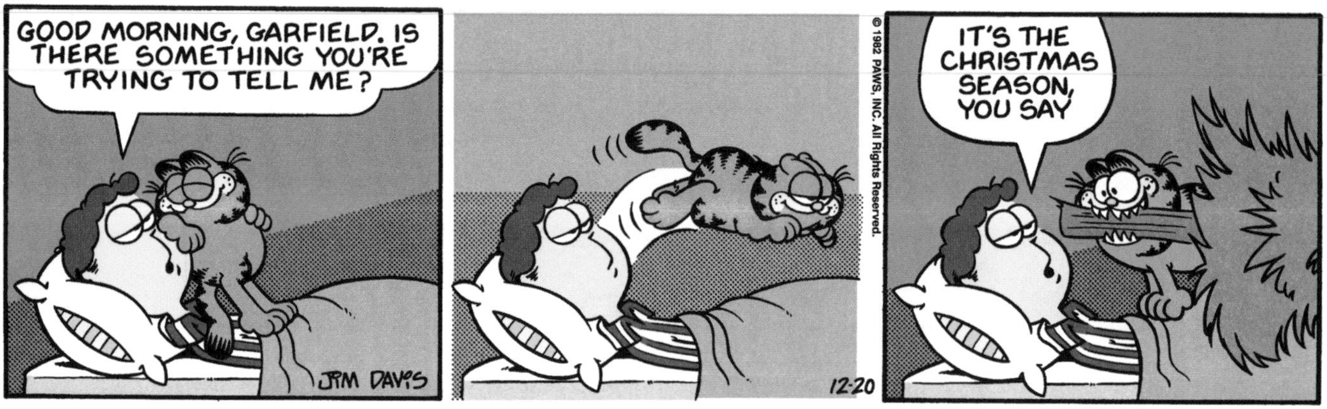
GOOD MORNING, GARFIELD. IS THERE SOMETHING YOU'RE TRYING TO TELL ME?
JIM DAVIS
© 1982 PAWS, INC. All Rights Reserved.
12-20
IT'S THE CHRISTMAS SEASON, YOU SAY

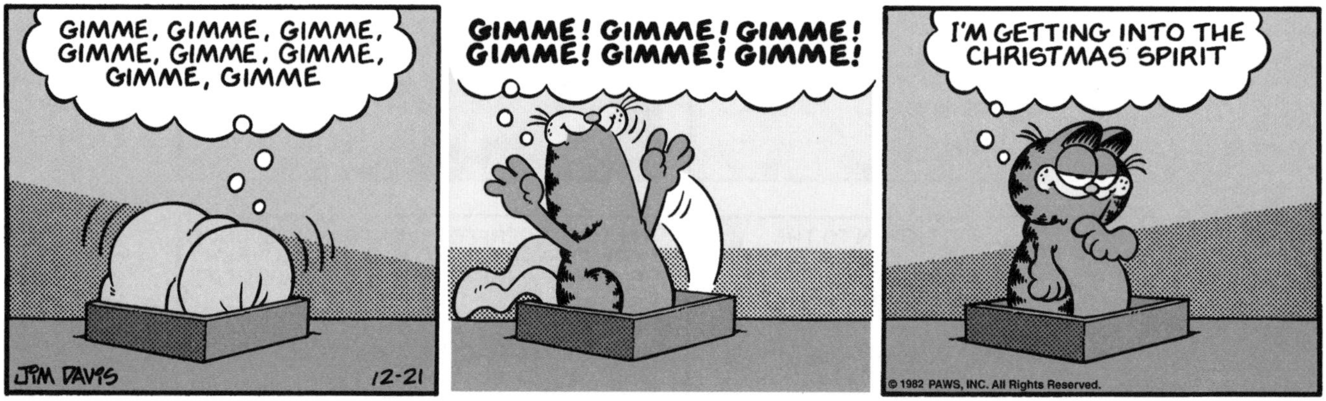
GIMME, GIMME, GIMME, GIMME, GIMME, GIMME, GIMME, GIMME, GIMME
JIM DAVIS
12-21
GIMME! GIMME! GIMME! GIMME! GIMME! GIMME!
I'M GETTING INTO THE CHRISTMAS SPIRIT
© 1982 PAWS, INC. All Rights Reserved.

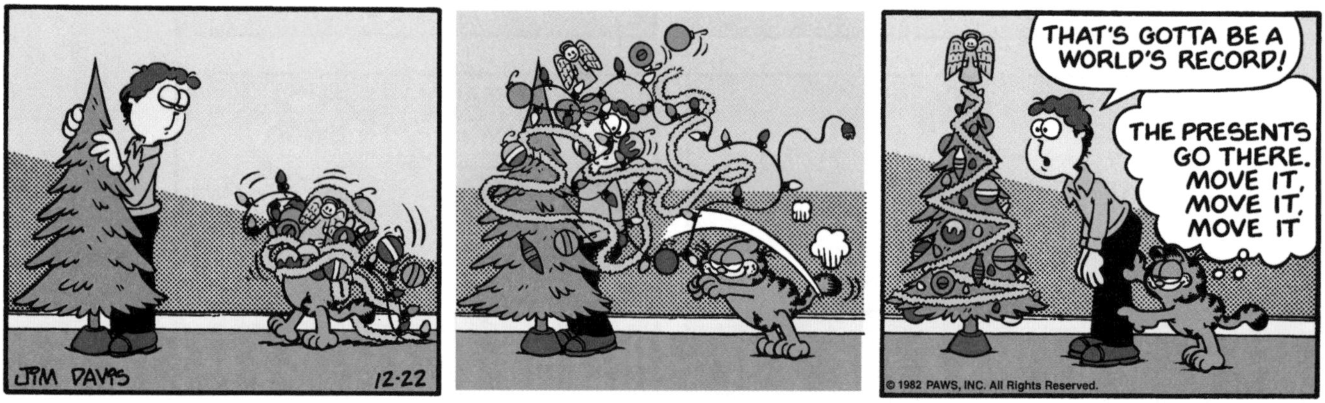
JIM DAVIS
12-22
THAT'S GOTTA BE A WORLD'S RECORD!
THE PRESENTS GO THERE. MOVE IT, MOVE IT, MOVE IT
© 1982 PAWS, INC. All Rights Reserved.

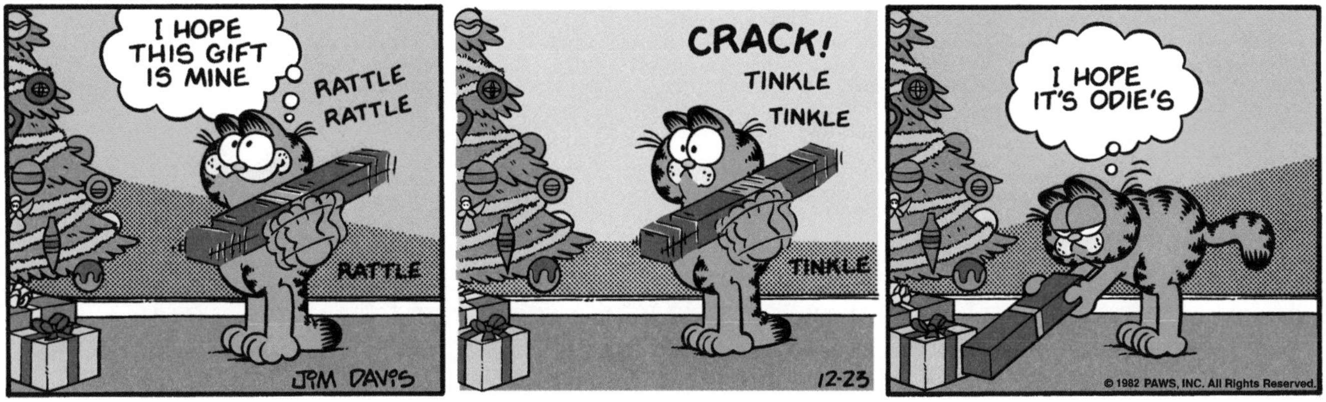
I HOPE THIS GIFT IS MINE
RATTLE RATTLE
RATTLE
JIM DAVIS
CRACK!
TINKLE
TINKLE
TINKLE
12-23
I HOPE IT'S ODIE'S
© 1982 PAWS, INC. All Rights Reserved.

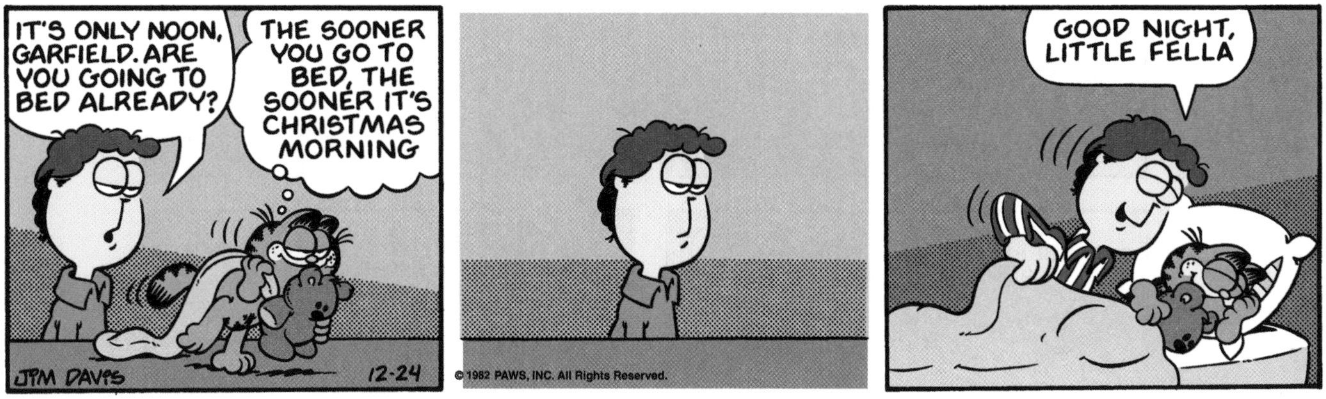
IT'S ONLY NOON, GARFIELD. ARE YOU GOING TO BED ALREADY?
THE SOONER YOU GO TO BED, THE SOONER IT'S CHRISTMAS MORNING
JIM DAVIS
12-24
© 1982 PAWS, INC. All Rights Reserved.
GOOD NIGHT, LITTLE FELLA

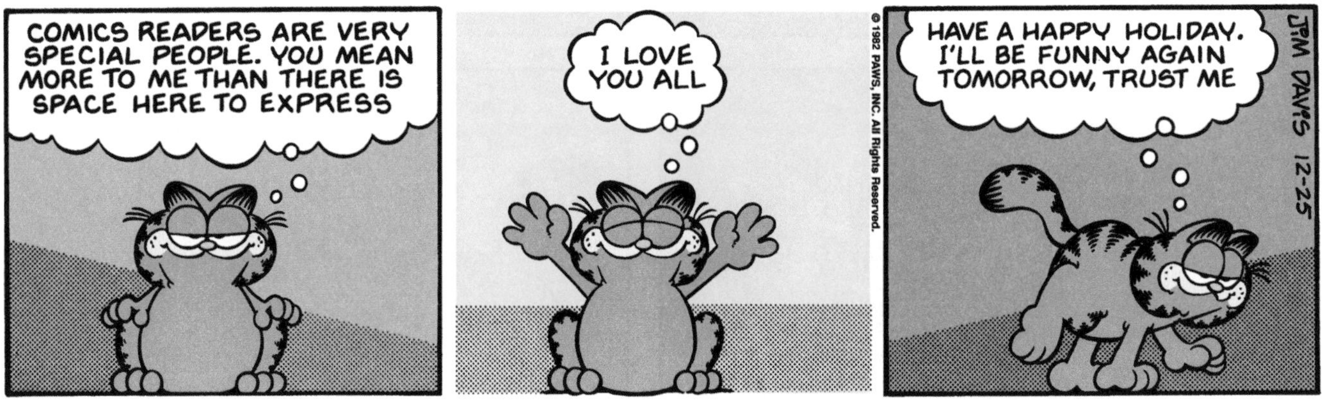
COMICS READERS ARE VERY SPECIAL PEOPLE. YOU MEAN MORE TO ME THAN THERE IS SPACE HERE TO EXPRESS
I LOVE YOU ALL
© 1982 PAWS, INC. All Rights Reserved.
HAVE A HAPPY HOLIDAY. I'LL BE FUNNY AGAIN TOMORROW, TRUST ME
JIM DAVIS
12-25

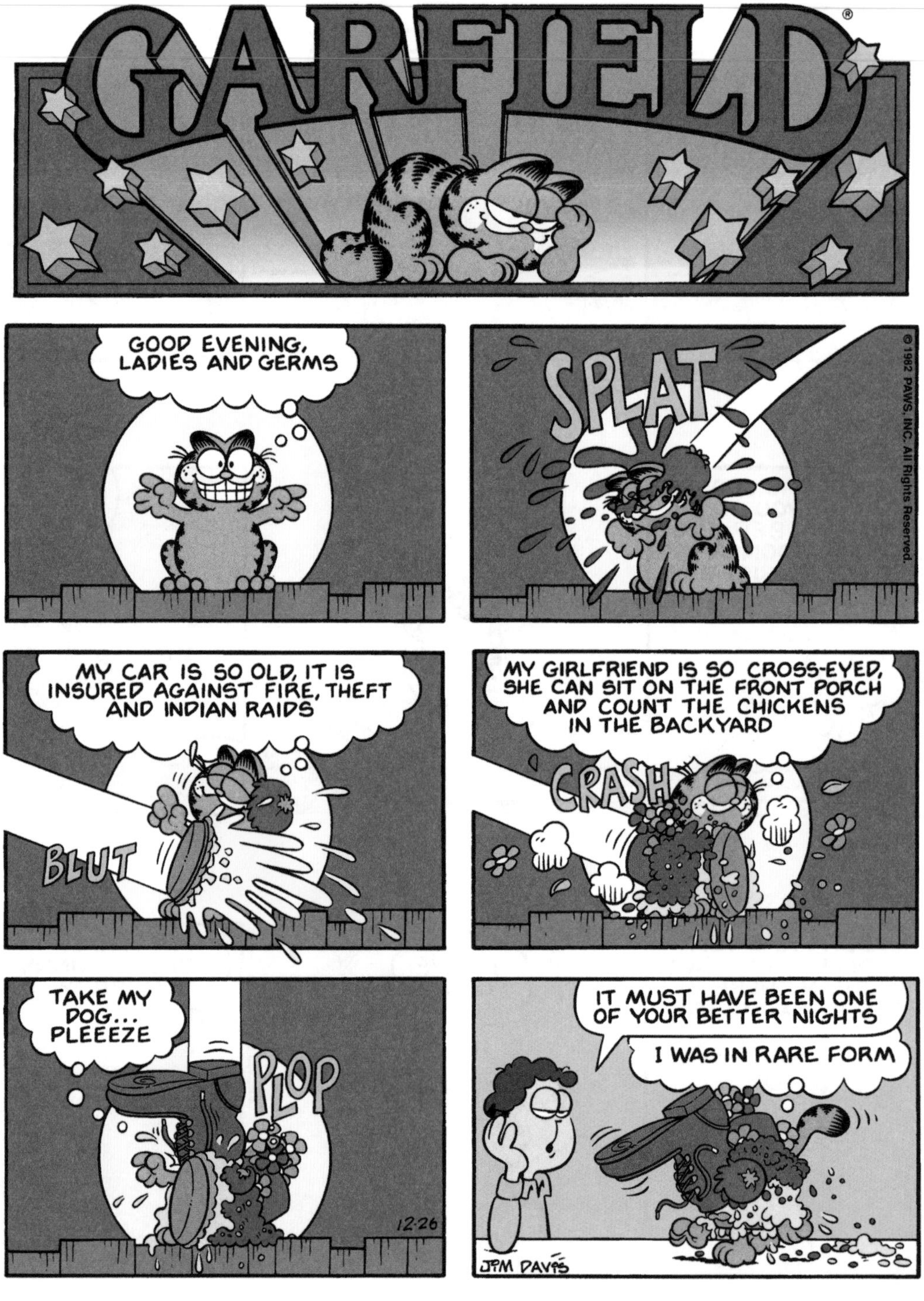
GARFIELD®
GOOD EVENING, LADIES AND GERMS
SPLAT
© 1982 PAWS, INC. All Rights Reserved.
MY CAR IS SO OLD, IT IS INSURED AGAINST FIRE, THEFT AND INDIAN RAIDS
BLUT
MY GIRLFRIEND IS SO CROSS-EYED, SHE CAN SIT ON THE FRONT PORCH AND COUNT THE CHICKENS IN THE BACKYARD
CRASH
TAKE MY DOG... PLEEEZE
PLOP
12-26
IT MUST HAVE BEEN ONE OF YOUR BETTER NIGHTS
I WAS IN RARE FORM
JIM DAVIS

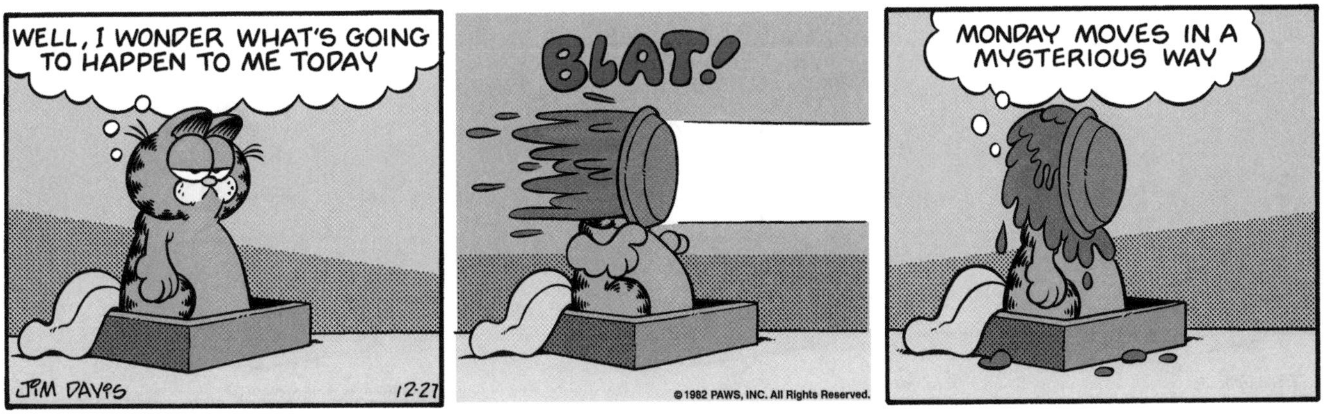
WELL, I WONDER WHAT'S GOING TO HAPPEN TO ME TODAY
JIM DAVIS
12-27
BLAT!
© 1982 PAWS, INC. All Rights Reserved.
MONDAY MOVES IN A MYSTERIOUS WAY

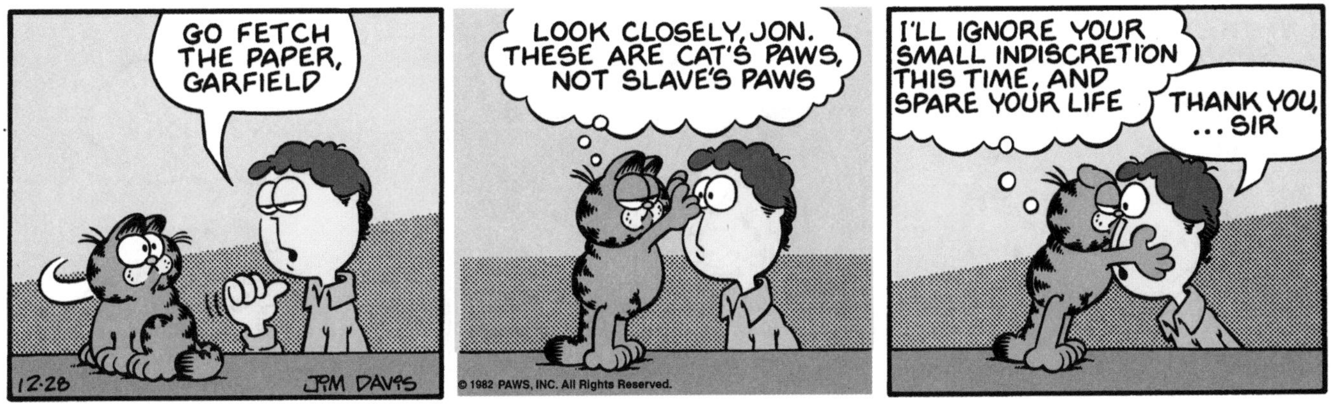
GO FETCH THE PAPER, GARFIELD
12-28
JIM DAVIS
LOOK CLOSELY, JON. THESE ARE CAT'S PAWS, NOT SLAVE'S PAWS
© 1982 PAWS, INC. All Rights Reserved.
I'LL IGNORE YOUR SMALL INDISCRETION THIS TIME, AND SPARE YOUR LIFE
THANK YOU, ... SIR

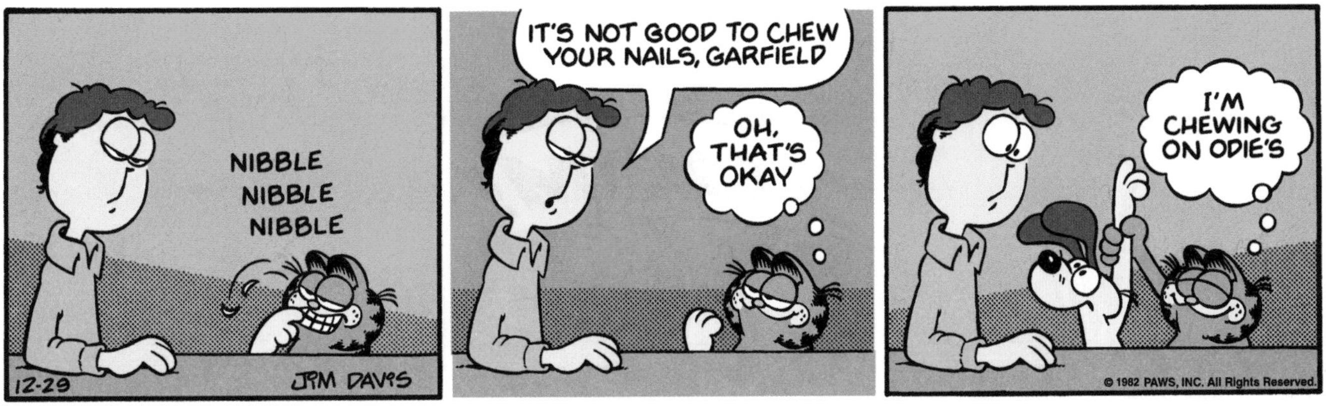
NIBBLE NIBBLE NIBBLE
12-29
JIM DAVIS
IT'S NOT GOOD TO CHEW YOUR NAILS, GARFIELD
OH, THAT'S OKAY
I'M CHEWING ON ODIE'S
© 1982 PAWS, INC. All Rights Reserved.

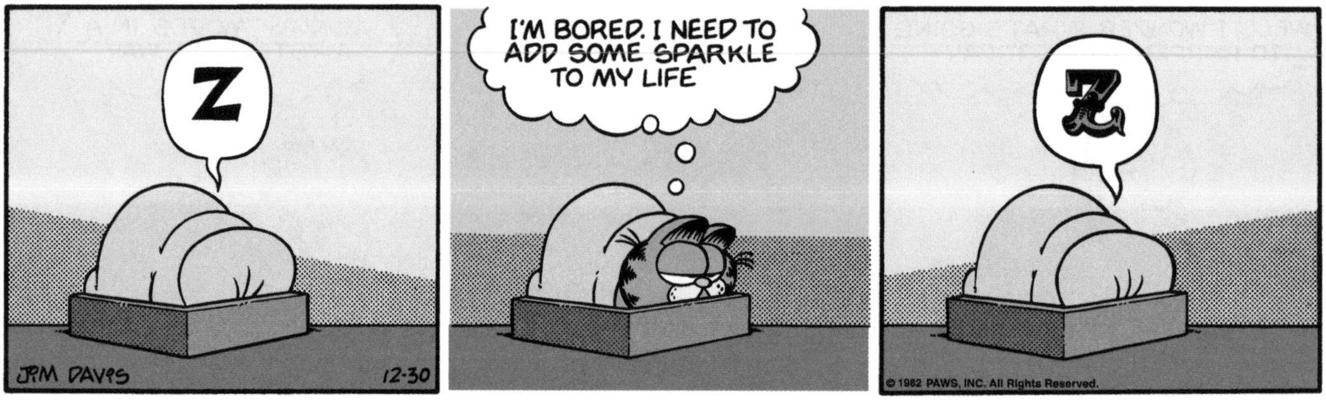
Z
I'M BORED. I NEED TO ADD SOME SPARKLE TO MY LIFE
Z
JIM DAVIS
12-30
© 1982 PAWS, INC. All Rights Reserved.

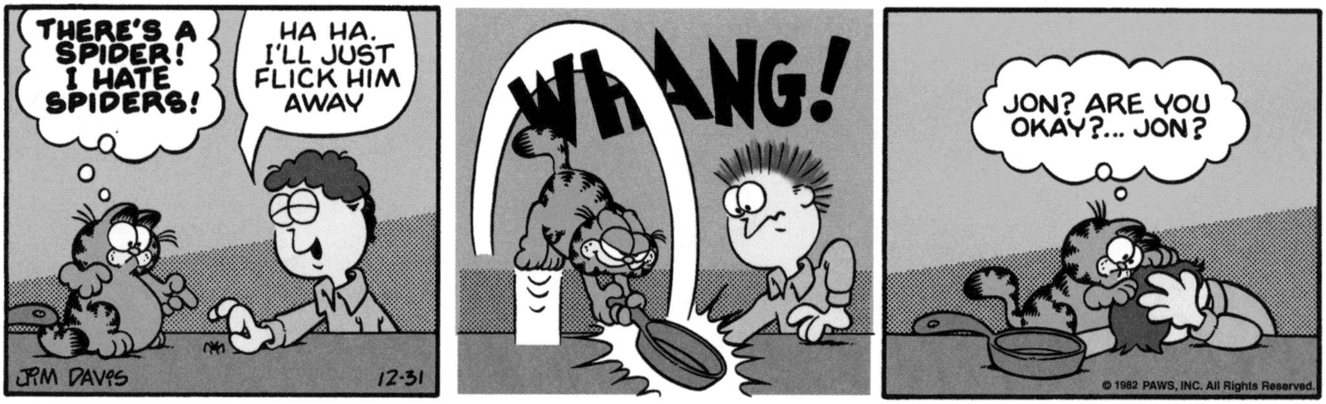
THERE'S A SPIDER! I HATE SPIDERS!
HA HA. I'LL JUST FLICK HIM AWAY
WHANG!
JON? ARE YOU OKAY?... JON?
JIM DAVIS
12-31
© 1982 PAWS, INC. All Rights Reserved.

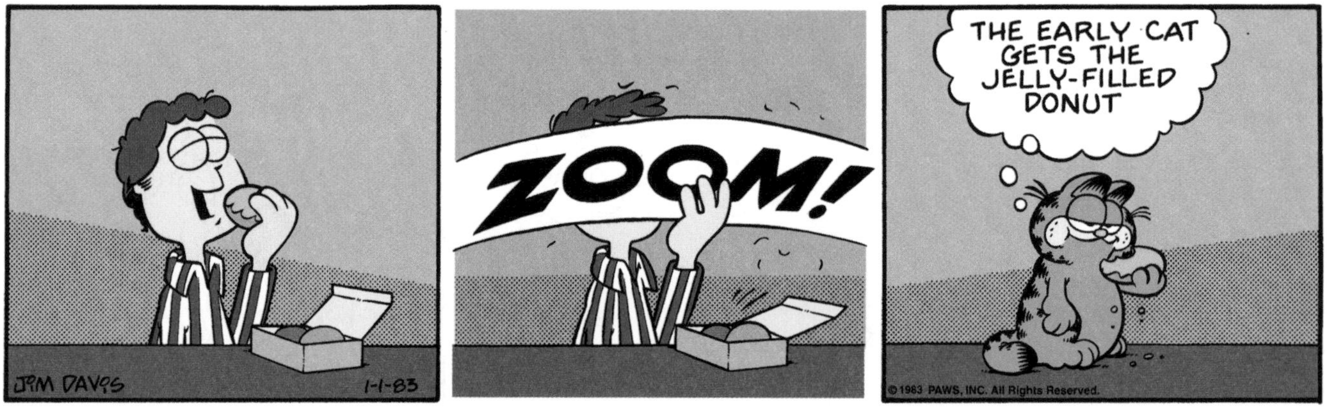
ZOOM!
THE EARLY CAT GETS THE JELLY-FILLED DONUT
JIM DAVIS
1-1-83
© 1983 PAWS, INC. All Rights Reserved.

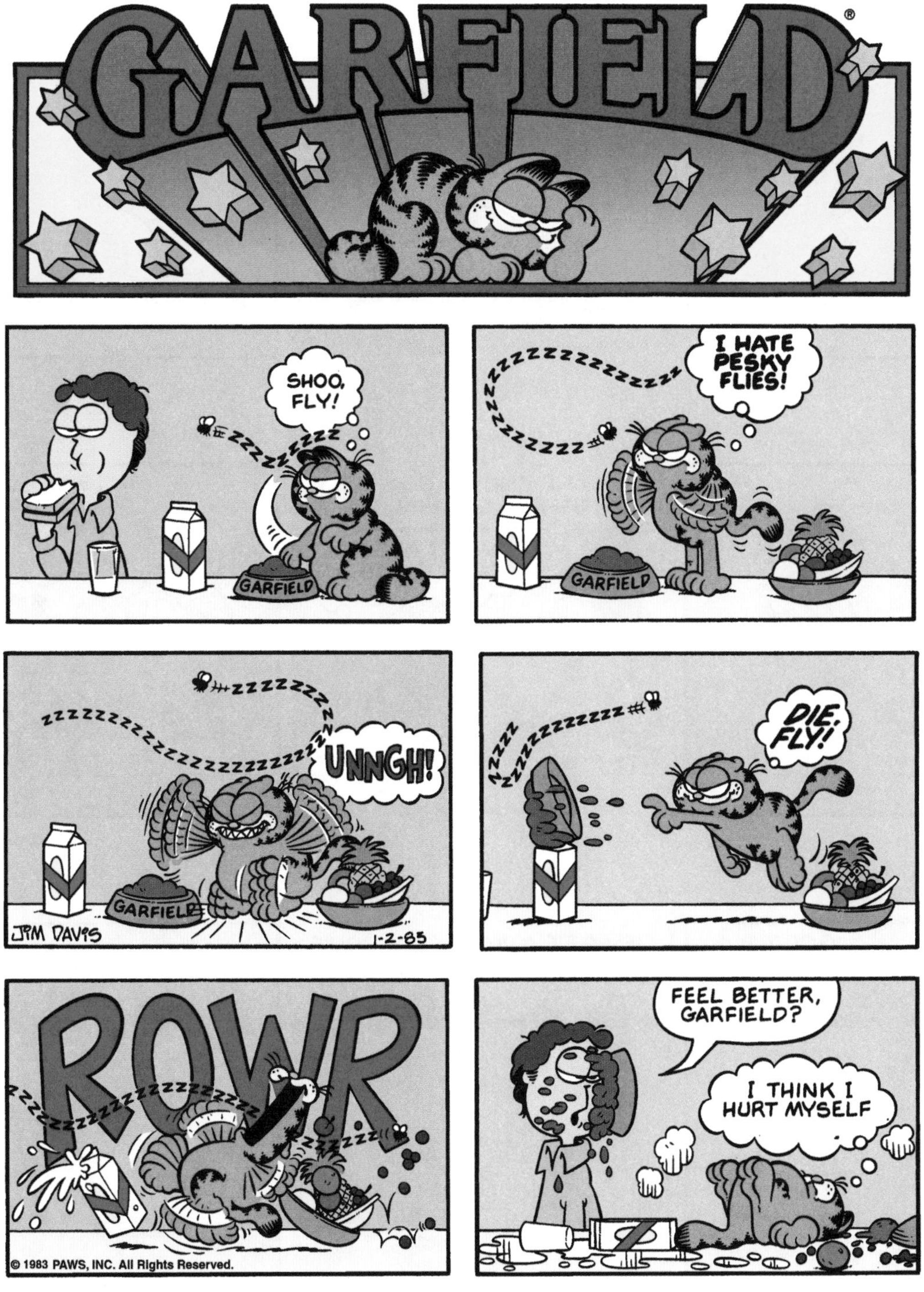
GARFIELD®
SHOO, FLY!
I HATE PESKY FLIES!
UNNGH!
JIM DAVIS
1-2-83
DIE, FLY!
ROWR
© 1983 PAWS, INC. All Rights Reserved.
FEEL BETTER, GARFIELD?
I THINK I HURT MYSELF

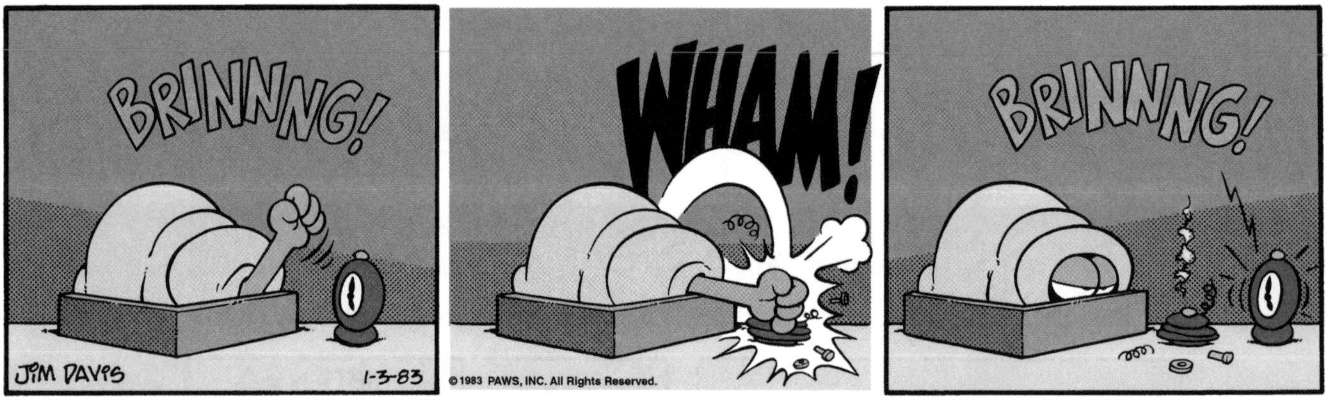
BRINNNG!
JIM DAVIS
1-3-83
WHAM!
© 1983 PAWS, INC. All Rights Reserved.
BRINNNG!

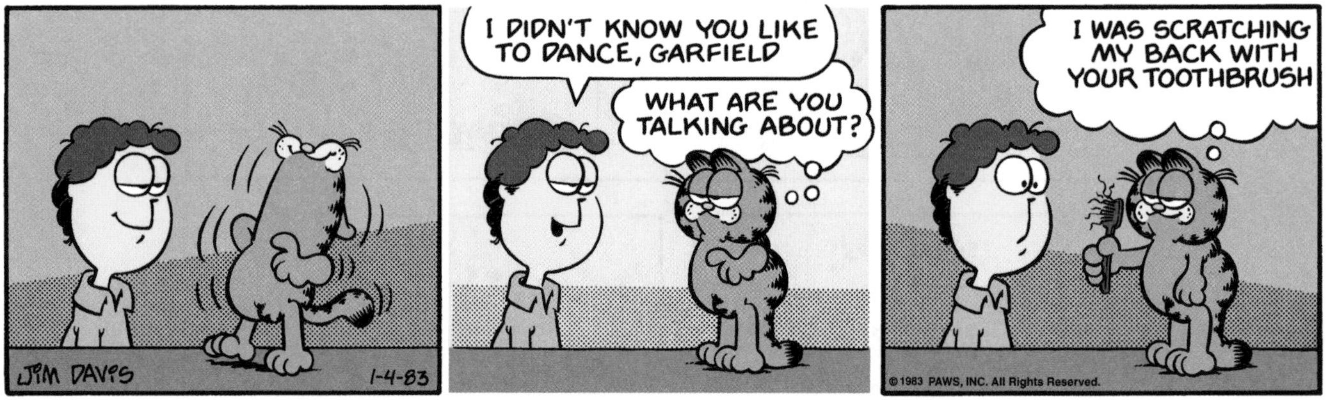
JIM DAVIS
1-4-83
I DIDN'T KNOW YOU LIKE TO DANCE, GARFIELD
WHAT ARE YOU TALKING ABOUT?
I WAS SCRATCHING MY BACK WITH YOUR TOOTHBRUSH
© 1983 PAWS, INC. All Rights Reserved.

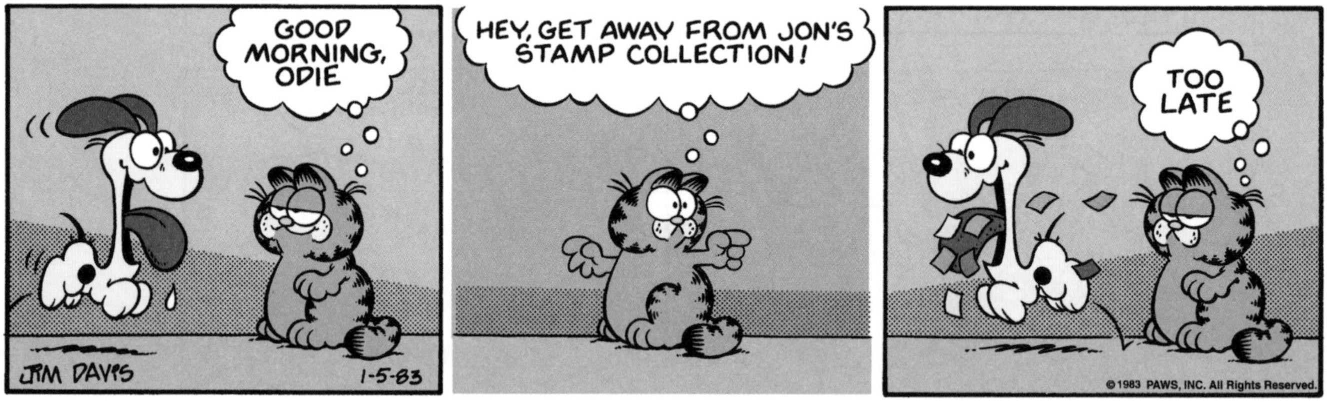
GOOD MORNING, ODIE
JIM DAVIS
1-5-83
HEY, GET AWAY FROM JON'S STAMP COLLECTION!
TOO LATE
© 1983 PAWS, INC. All Rights Reserved.

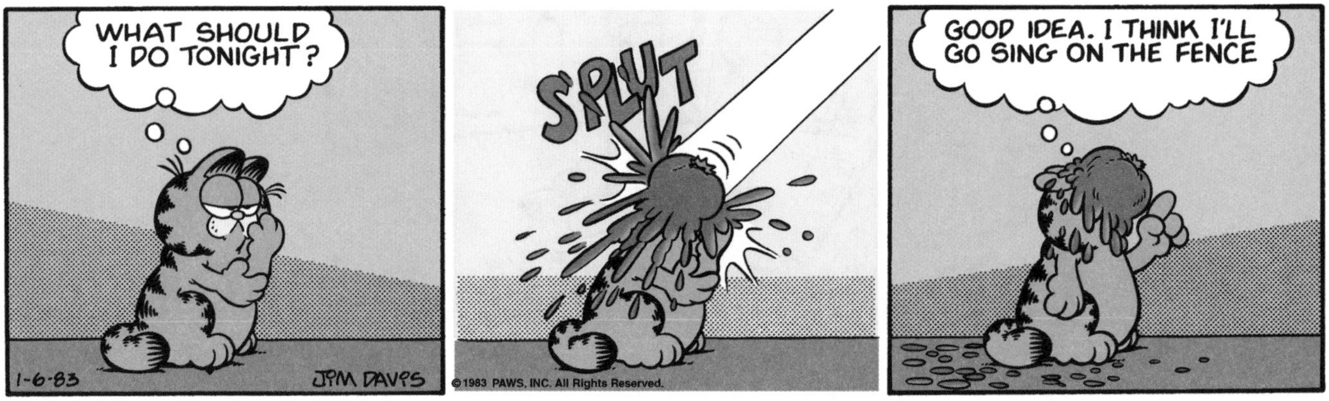
WHAT SHOULD I DO TONIGHT?
1-6-83
JIM DAVIS
SPLUT
© 1983 PAWS, INC. All Rights Reserved.
GOOD IDEA. I THINK I'LL GO SING ON THE FENCE

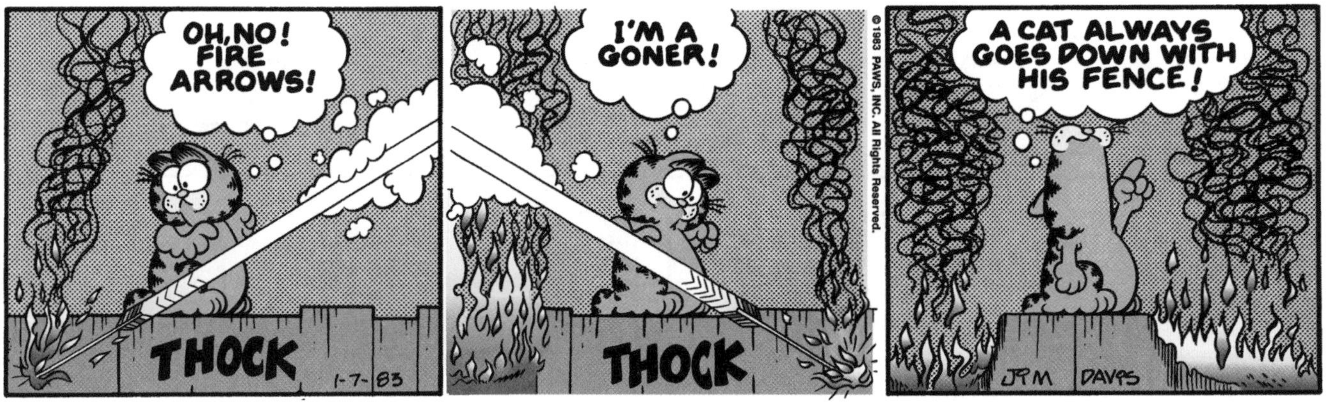
OH, NO! FIRE ARROWS!
THOCK
1-7-83
I'M A GONER!
THOCK
© 1983 PAWS, INC. All Rights Reserved.
A CAT ALWAYS GOES DOWN WITH HIS FENCE!
JIM DAVIS

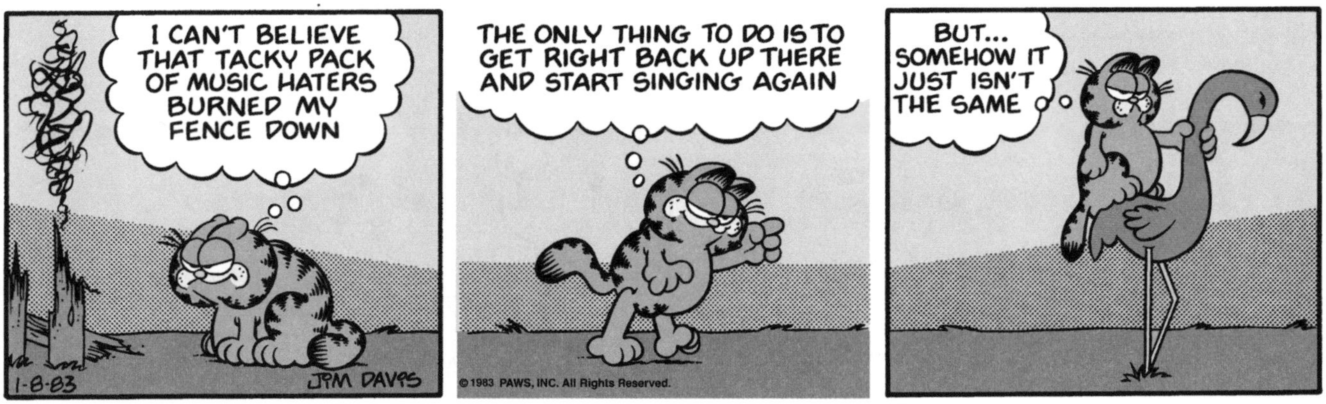
I CAN'T BELIEVE THAT TACKY PACK OF MUSIC HATERS BURNED MY FENCE DOWN
1-8-83
JIM DAVIS
THE ONLY THING TO DO IS TO GET RIGHT BACK UP THERE AND START SINGING AGAIN
© 1983 PAWS, INC. All Rights Reserved.
BUT... SOMEHOW IT JUST ISN'T THE SAME

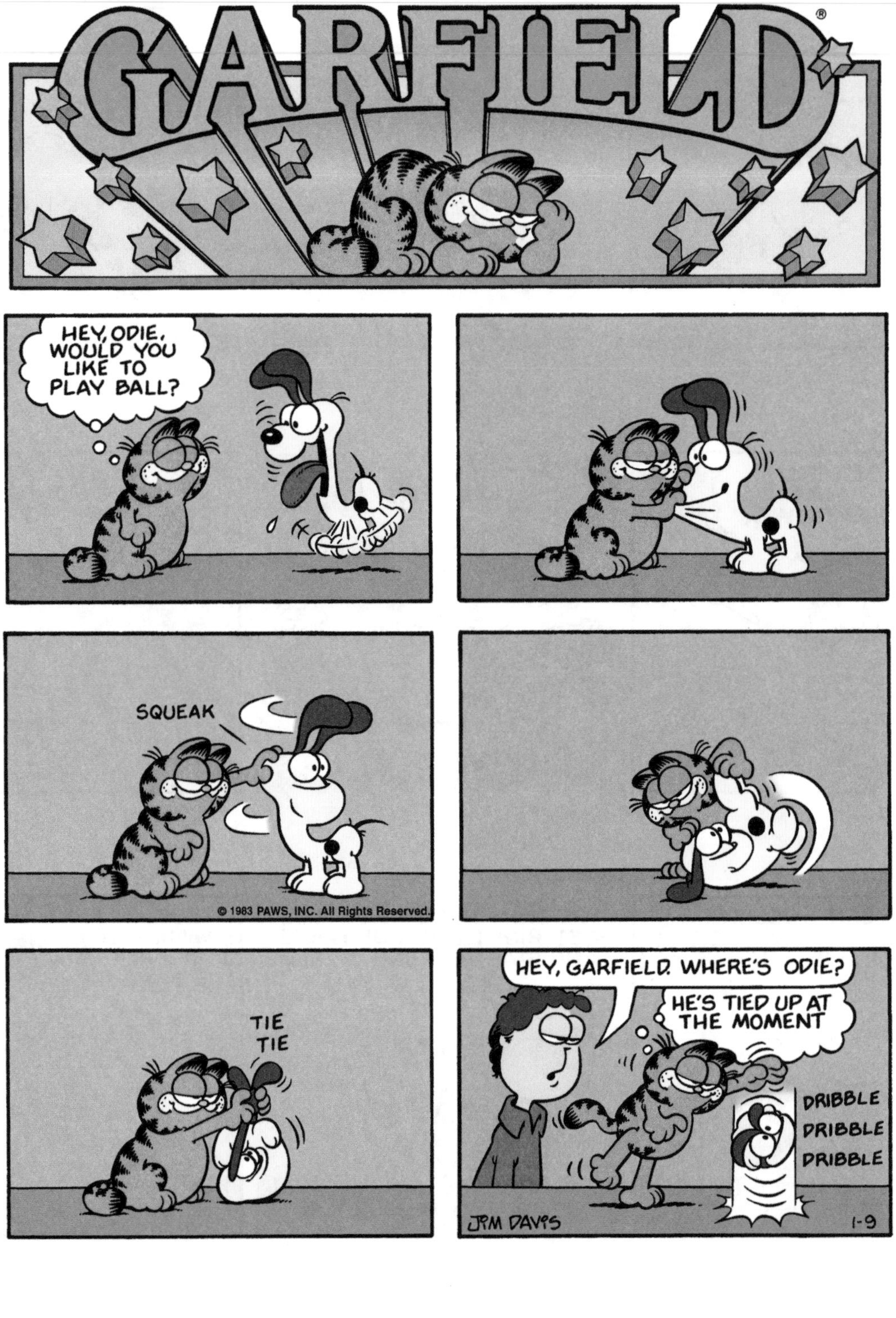

GARFIELD®
HEY, ODIE, WOULD YOU LIKE TO PLAY BALL?
SQUEAK
© 1983 PAWS, INC. All Rights Reserved.
TIE TIE
HEY, GARFIELD. WHERE'S ODIE?
HE'S TIED UP AT THE MOMENT
DRIBBLE DRIBBLE DRIBBLE
JIM DAVIS
1-9

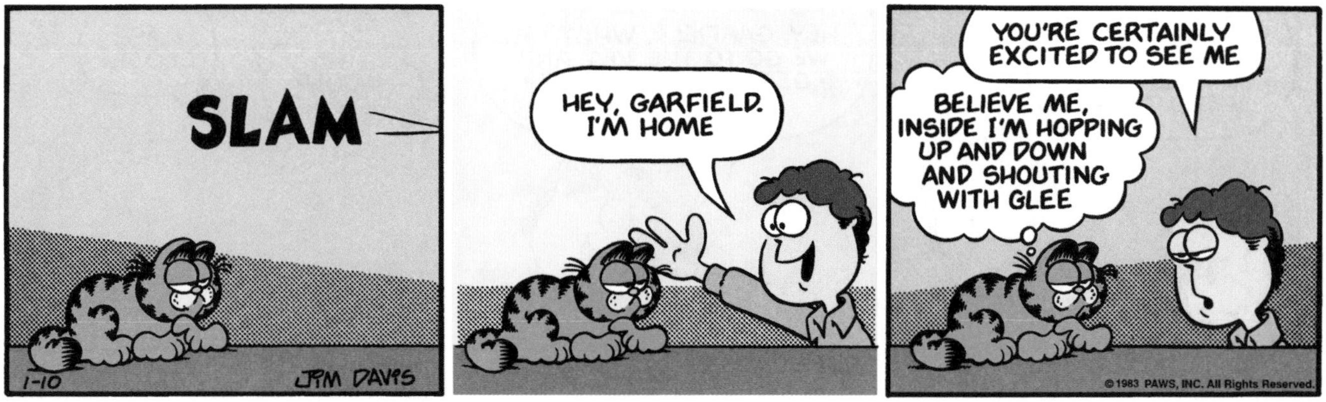
SLAM
1-10
JIM DAVIS
HEY, GARFIELD. I'M HOME
YOU'RE CERTAINLY EXCITED TO SEE ME
BELIEVE ME, INSIDE I'M HOPPING UP AND DOWN AND SHOUTING WITH GLEE
© 1983 PAWS, INC. All Rights Reserved.

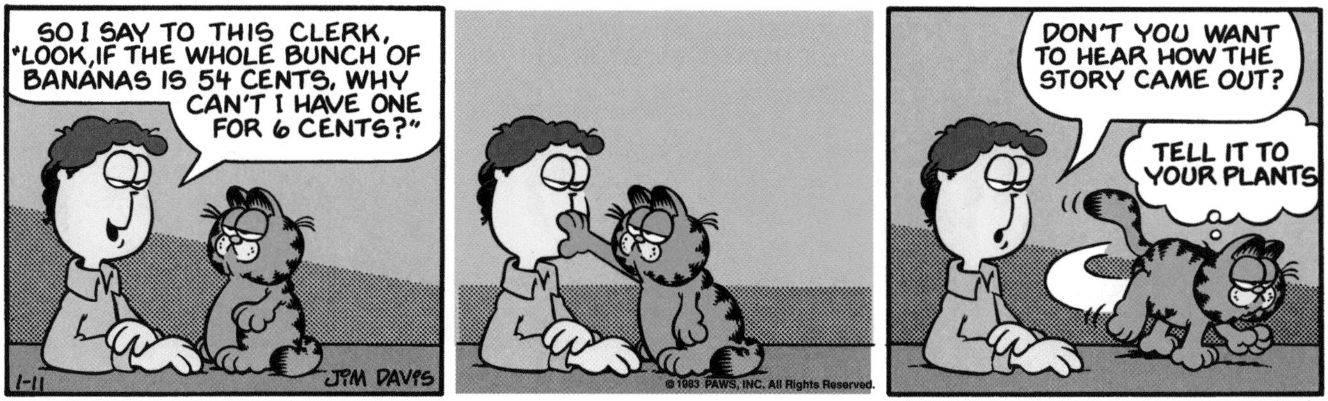
SO I SAY TO THIS CLERK, "LOOK, IF THE WHOLE BUNCH OF BANANAS IS 54 CENTS, WHY CAN'T I HAVE ONE FOR 6 CENTS?"
1-11
JIM DAVIS
© 1983 PAWS, INC. All Rights Reserved.
DON'T YOU WANT TO HEAR HOW THE STORY CAME OUT?
TELL IT TO YOUR PLANTS

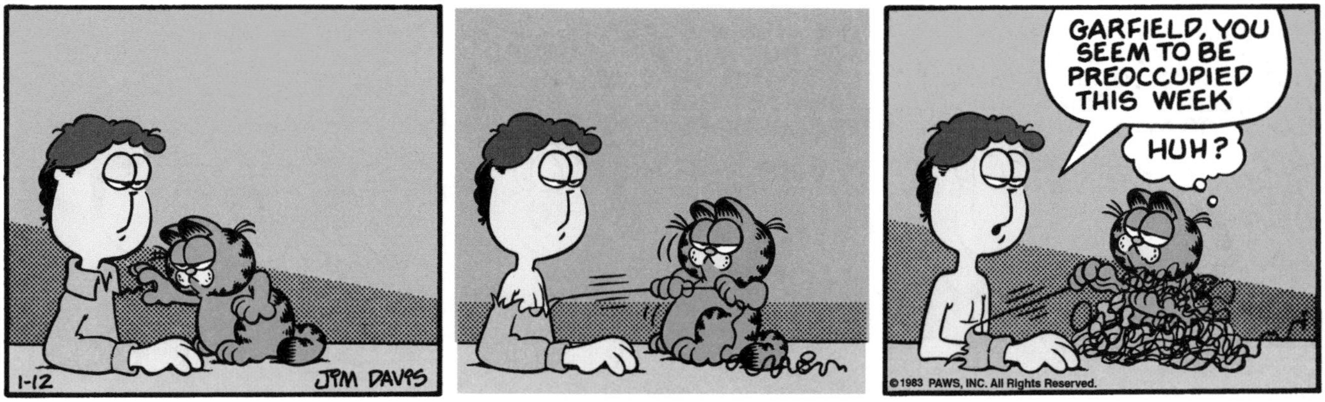
1-12
JIM DAVIS
GARFIELD, YOU SEEM TO BE PREOCCUPIED THIS WEEK
HUH?
© 1983 PAWS, INC. All Rights Reserved.

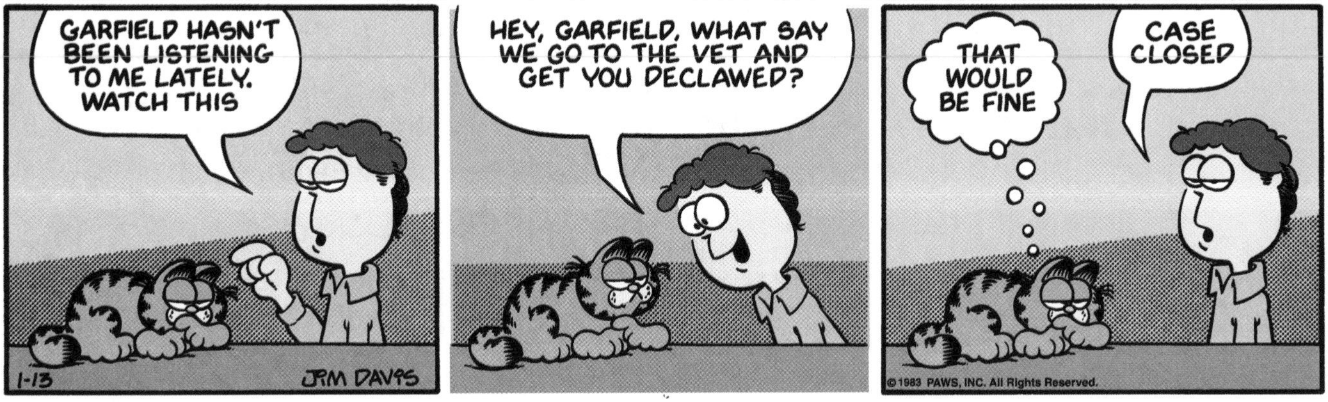
GARFIELD HASN'T BEEN LISTENING TO ME LATELY. WATCH THIS
1-13
JIM DAVIS
HEY, GARFIELD, WHAT SAY WE GO TO THE VET AND GET YOU DECLAWED?
THAT WOULD BE FINE
CASE CLOSED
©1983 PAWS, INC. All Rights Reserved.

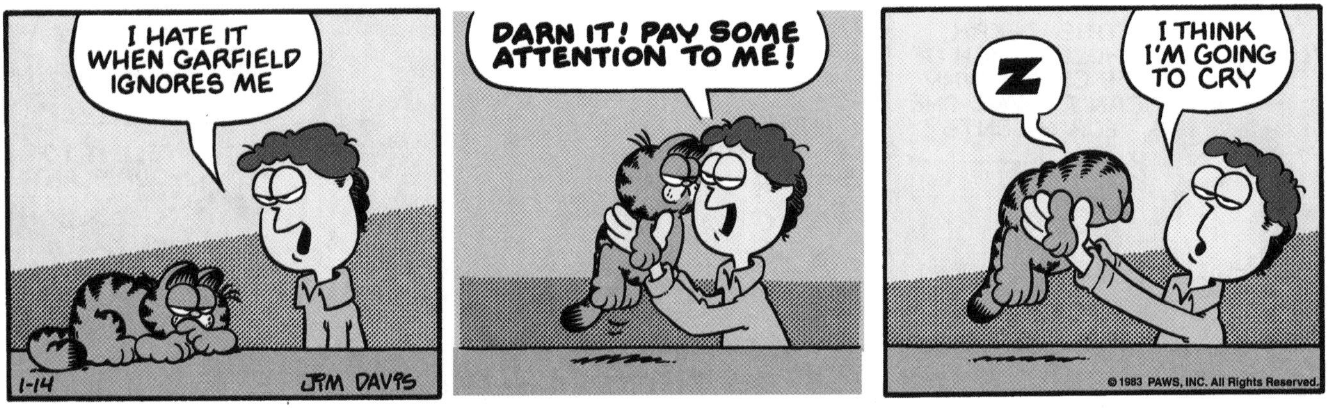
I HATE IT WHEN GARFIELD IGNORES ME
1-14
JIM DAVIS
DARN IT! PAY SOME ATTENTION TO ME!
Z
I THINK I'M GOING TO CRY
©1983 PAWS, INC. All Rights Reserved.

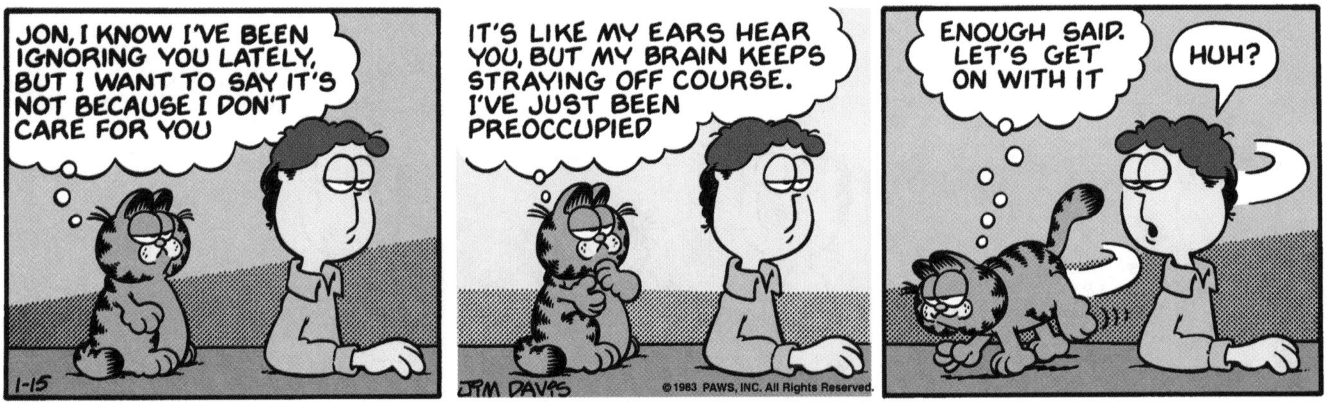
JON, I KNOW I'VE BEEN IGNORING YOU LATELY, BUT I WANT TO SAY IT'S NOT BECAUSE I DON'T CARE FOR YOU
1-15
IT'S LIKE MY EARS HEAR YOU, BUT MY BRAIN KEEPS STRAYING OFF COURSE. I'VE JUST BEEN PREOCCUPIED
JIM DAVIS
©1983 PAWS, INC. All Rights Reserved.
ENOUGH SAID. LET'S GET ON WITH IT
HUH?

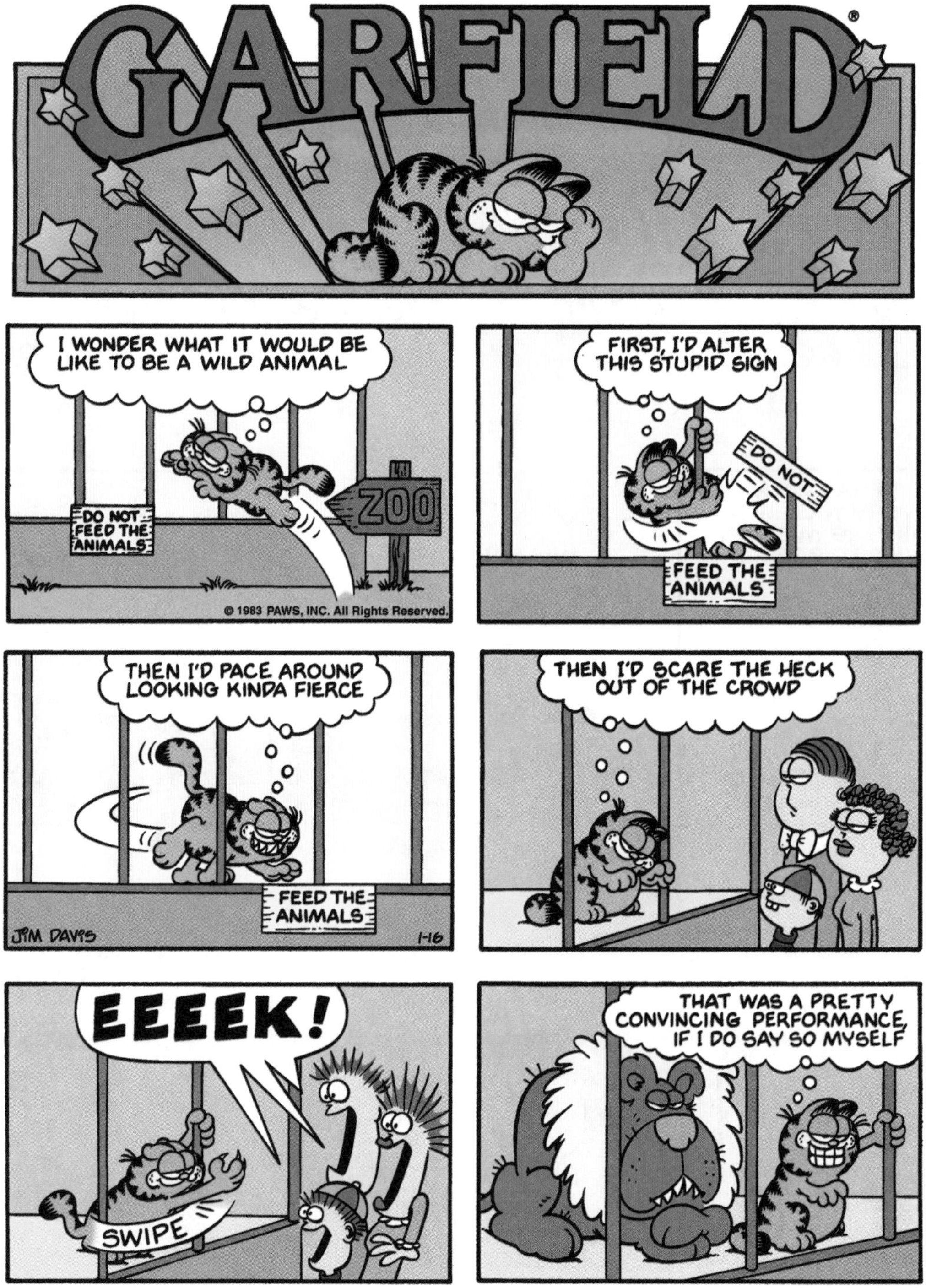
GARFIELD®
I WONDER WHAT IT WOULD BE LIKE TO BE A WILD ANIMAL
DO NOT FEED THE ANIMALS
ZOO
© 1983 PAWS, INC. All Rights Reserved.
FIRST, I'D ALTER THIS STUPID SIGN
DO NOT
FEED THE ANIMALS
THEN I'D PACE AROUND LOOKING KINDA FIERCE
FEED THE ANIMALS
JIM DAVIS
1-16
THEN I'D SCARE THE HECK OUT OF THE CROWD
EEEEK!
SWIPE
THAT WAS A PRETTY CONVINCING PERFORMANCE, IF I DO SAY SO MYSELF

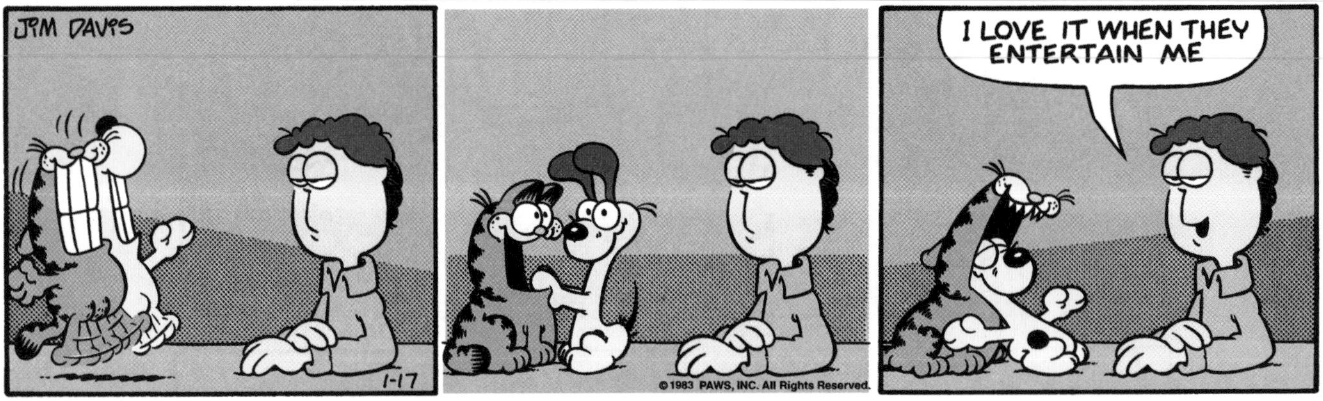
JIM DAVIS
1-17
©1983 PAWS, INC. All Rights Reserved.
I LOVE IT WHEN THEY ENTERTAIN ME

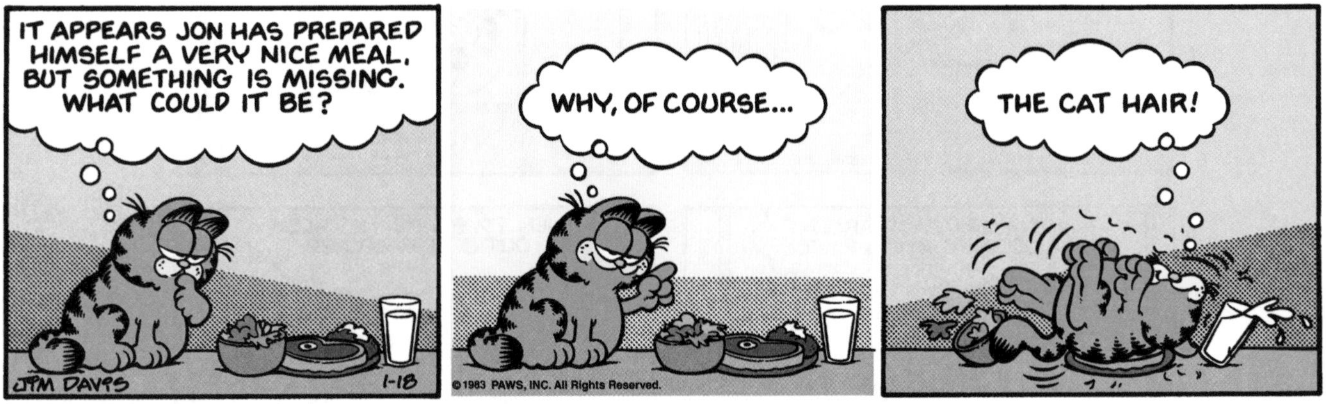
IT APPEARS JON HAS PREPARED HIMSELF A VERY NICE MEAL. BUT SOMETHING IS MISSING. WHAT COULD IT BE?
JIM DAVIS
1-18
WHY, OF COURSE...
©1983 PAWS, INC. All Rights Reserved.
THE CAT HAIR!

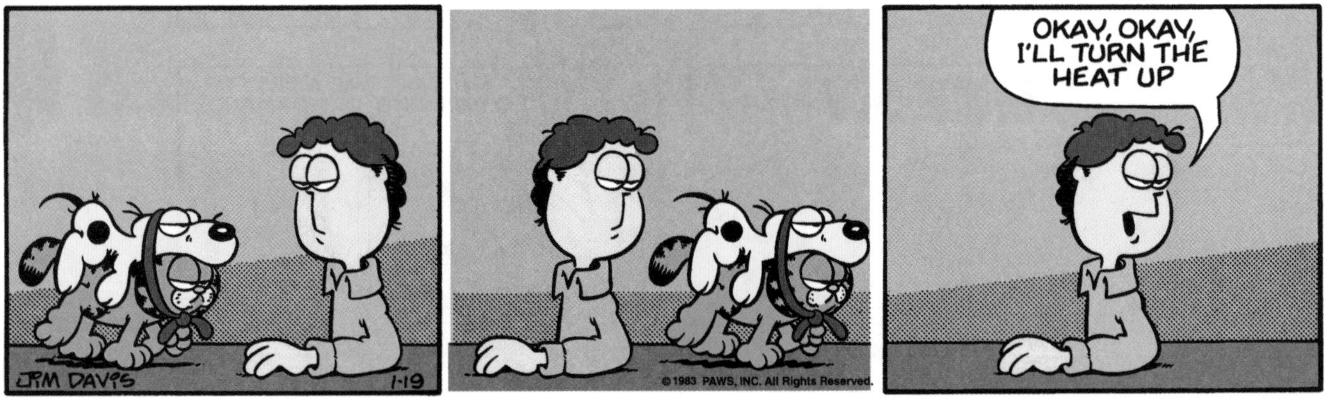
JIM DAVIS
1-19
©1983 PAWS, INC. All Rights Reserved.
OKAY, OKAY, I'LL TURN THE HEAT UP

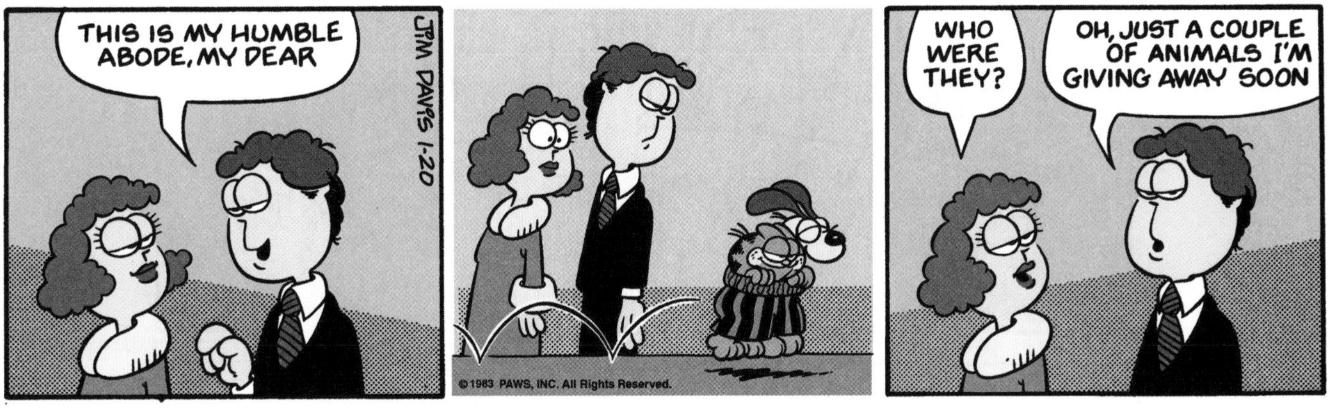
THIS IS MY HUMBLE ABODE, MY DEAR
JIM DAVIS 1-20
© 1983 PAWS, INC. All Rights Reserved.
WHO WERE THEY?
OH, JUST A COUPLE OF ANIMALS I'M GIVING AWAY SOON

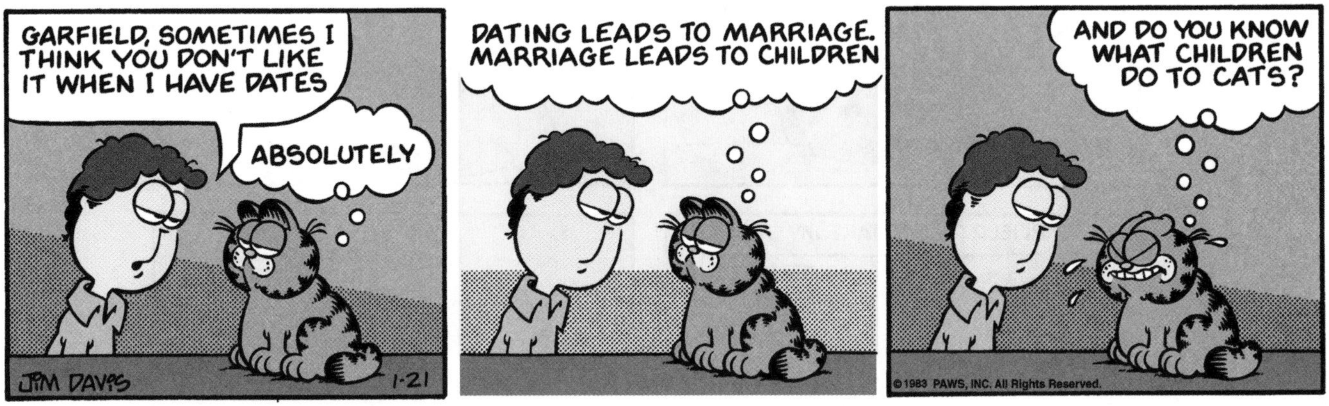
GARFIELD, SOMETIMES I THINK YOU DON'T LIKE IT WHEN I HAVE DATES
ABSOLUTELY
JIM DAVIS
1-21
DATING LEADS TO MARRIAGE. MARRIAGE LEADS TO CHILDREN
AND DO YOU KNOW WHAT CHILDREN DO TO CATS?
© 1983 PAWS, INC. All Rights Reserved.

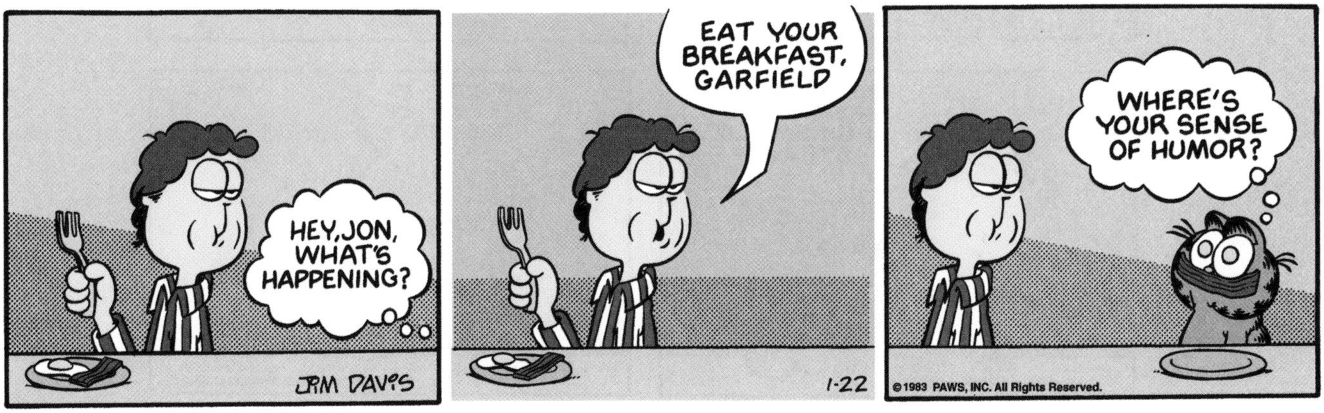
HEY, JON, WHAT'S HAPPENING?
JIM DAVIS
EAT YOUR BREAKFAST, GARFIELD
1-22
WHERE'S YOUR SENSE OF HUMOR?
© 1983 PAWS, INC. All Rights Reserved.

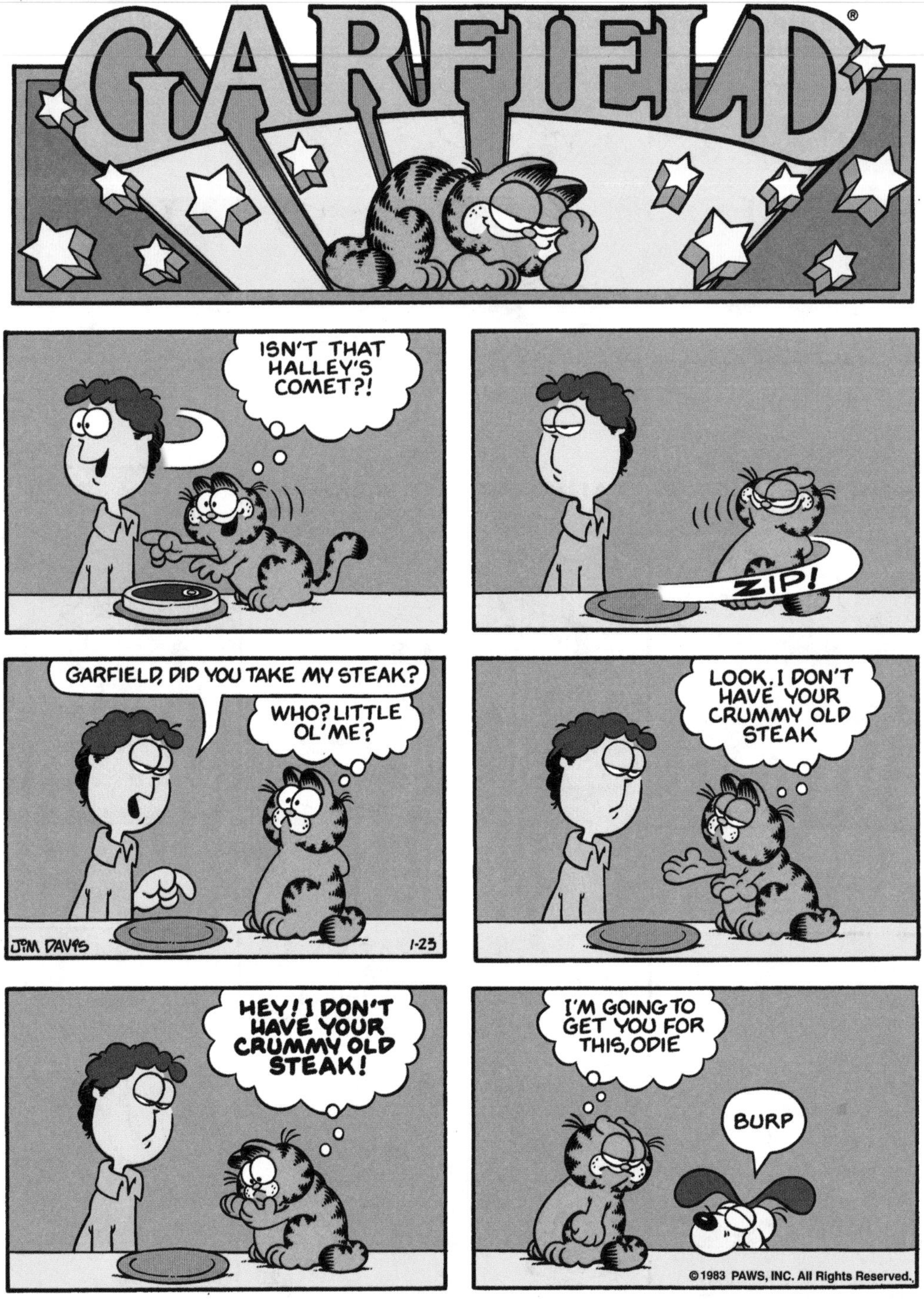
GARFIELD®
ISN'T THAT HALLEY'S COMET?!
ZIP!
GARFIELD, DID YOU TAKE MY STEAK?
WHO? LITTLE OL' ME?
JIM DAVIS
1-23
LOOK, I DON'T HAVE YOUR CRUMMY OLD STEAK
HEY! I DON'T HAVE YOUR CRUMMY OLD STEAK!
I'M GOING TO GET YOU FOR THIS, ODIE
BURP
© 1983 PAWS, INC. All Rights Reserved.

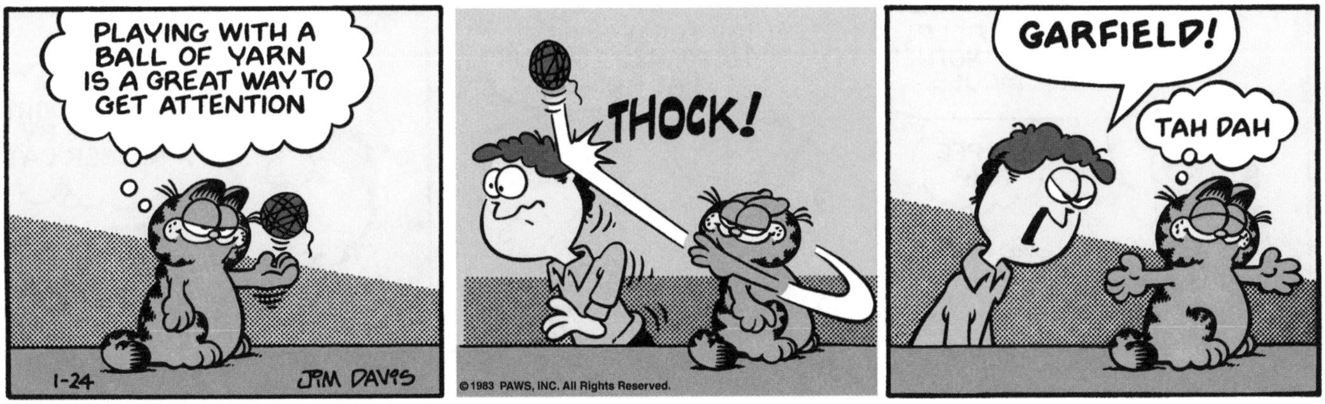
PLAYING WITH A BALL OF YARN IS A GREAT WAY TO GET ATTENTION
1-24
JIM DAVIS
THOCK!
© 1983 PAWS, INC. All Rights Reserved.
GARFIELD!
TAH DAH

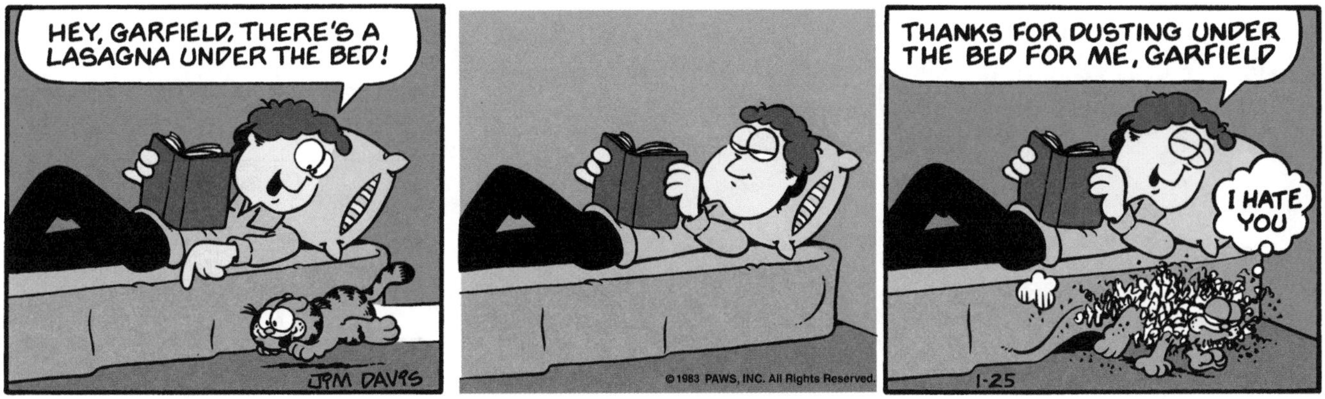
HEY, GARFIELD, THERE'S A LASAGNA UNDER THE BED!
JIM DAVIS
© 1983 PAWS, INC. All Rights Reserved.
THANKS FOR DUSTING UNDER THE BED FOR ME, GARFIELD
I HATE YOU
1-25

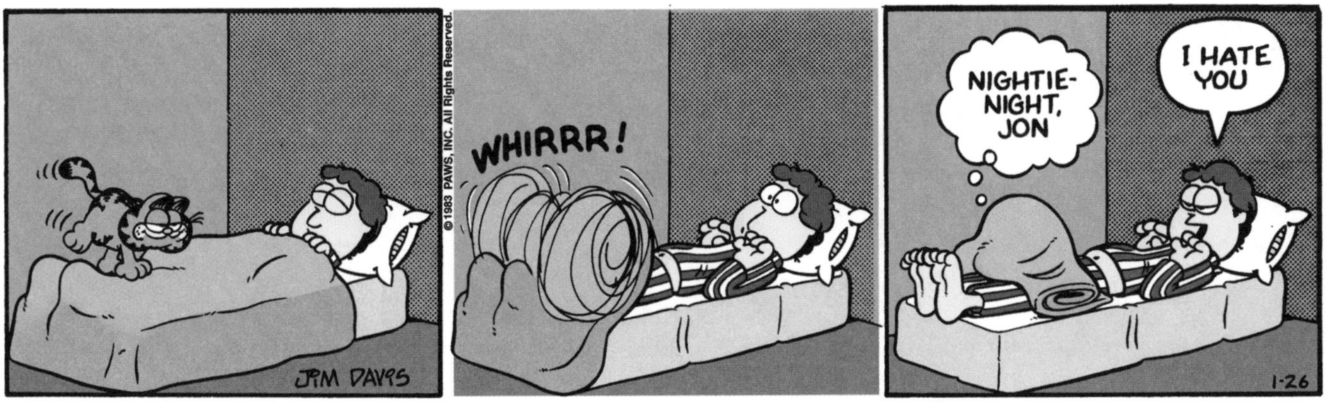
JIM DAVIS
© 1983 PAWS, INC. All Rights Reserved.
WHIRRR!
NIGHTIE-NIGHT, JON
I HATE YOU
1-26

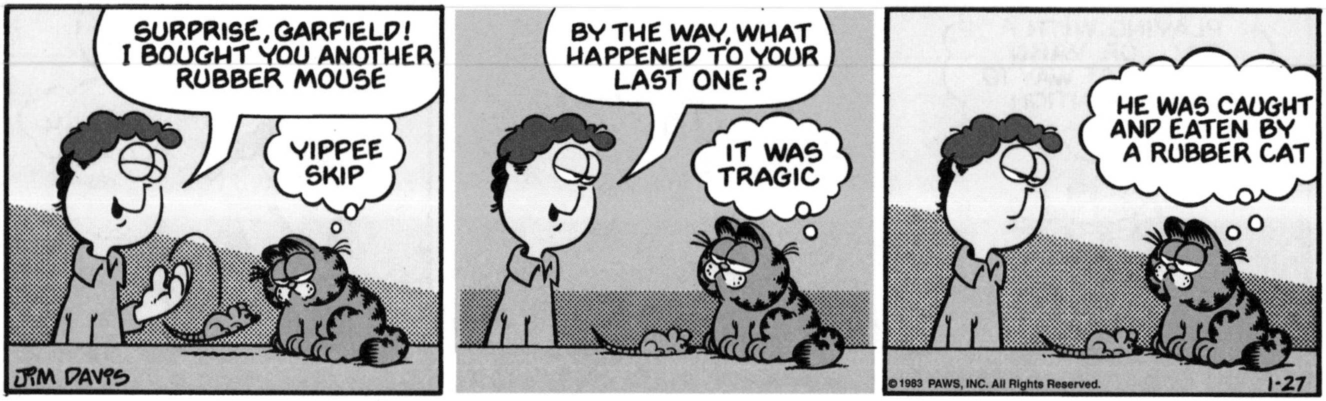
SURPRISE, GARFIELD! I BOUGHT YOU ANOTHER RUBBER MOUSE
YIPPEE SKIP
JIM DAVIS
BY THE WAY, WHAT HAPPENED TO YOUR LAST ONE?
IT WAS TRAGIC
HE WAS CAUGHT AND EATEN BY A RUBBER CAT
© 1983 PAWS, INC. All Rights Reserved.
1-27

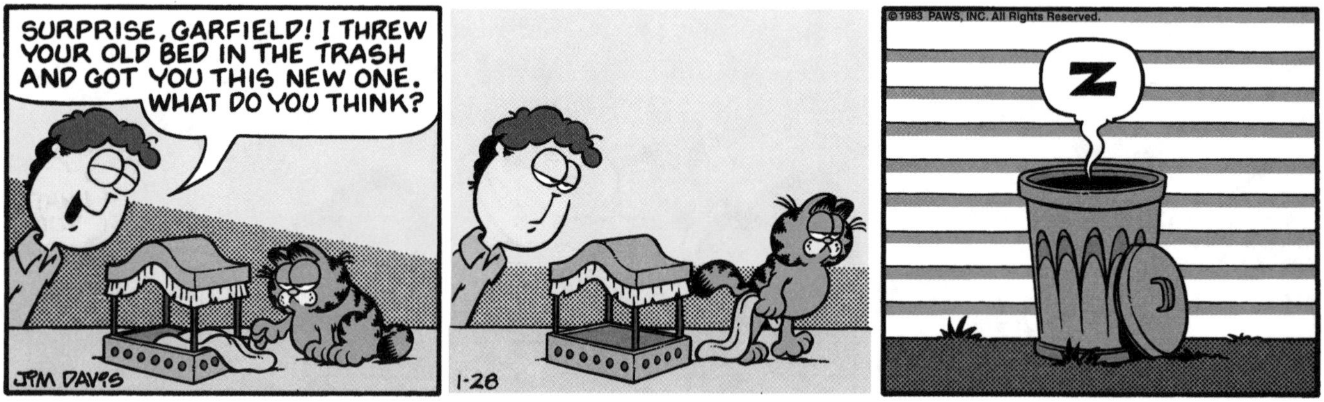
SURPRISE, GARFIELD! I THREW YOUR OLD BED IN THE TRASH AND GOT YOU THIS NEW ONE. WHAT DO YOU THINK?
JIM DAVIS
1-28
© 1983 PAWS, INC. All Rights Reserved.
Z

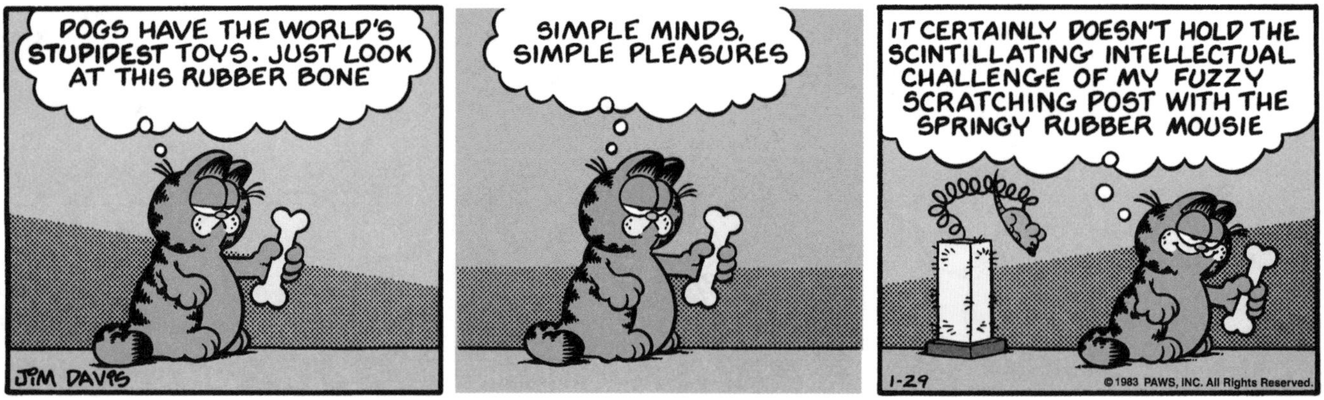
DOGS HAVE THE WORLD'S STUPIDEST TOYS. JUST LOOK AT THIS RUBBER BONE
JIM DAVIS
SIMPLE MINDS, SIMPLE PLEASURES
IT CERTAINLY DOESN'T HOLD THE SCINTILLATING INTELLECTUAL CHALLENGE OF MY FUZZY SCRATCHING POST WITH THE SPRINGY RUBBER MOUSIE
1-29
© 1983 PAWS, INC. All Rights Reserved.

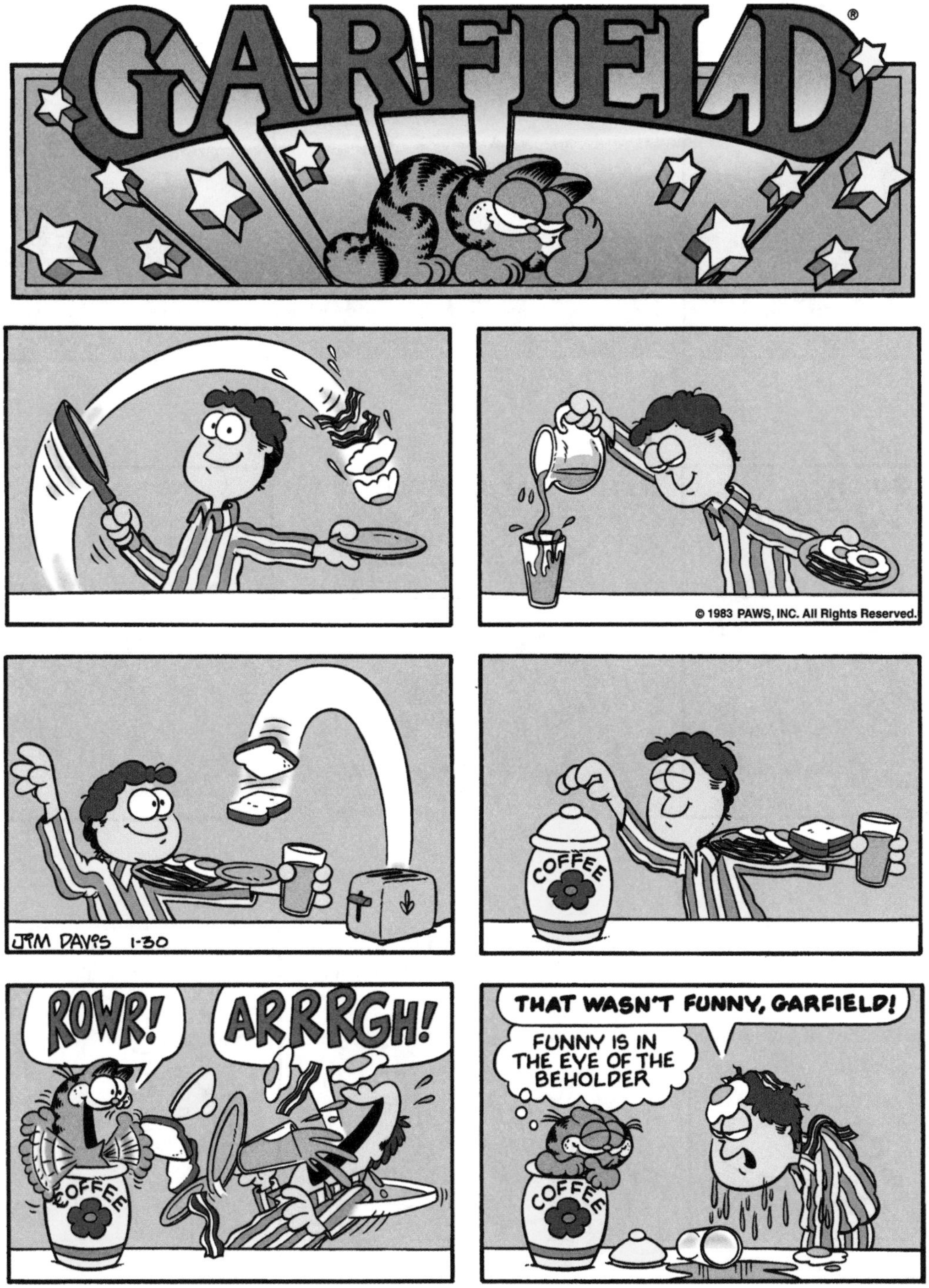
GARFIELD
© 1983 PAWS, INC. All Rights Reserved.
JIM DAVIS 1-30
COFFEE
ROWR!
ARRRGH!
COFFEE
THAT WASN'T FUNNY, GARFIELD!
FUNNY IS IN THE EYE OF THE BEHOLDER
COFFEE

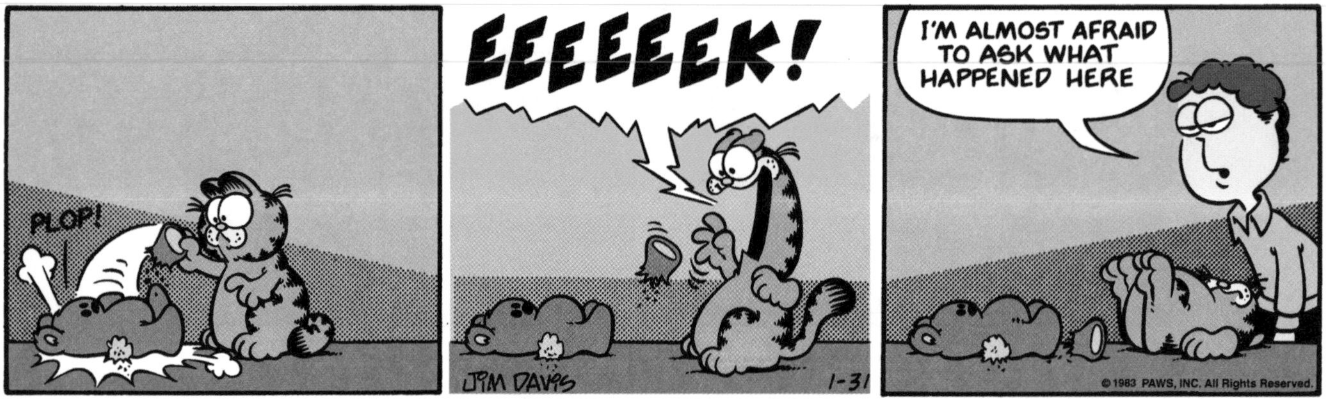
PLOP!
EEEEEEK!
I'M ALMOST AFRAID TO ASK WHAT HAPPENED HERE
JIM DAVIS
1-31
© 1983 PAWS, INC. All Rights Reserved.

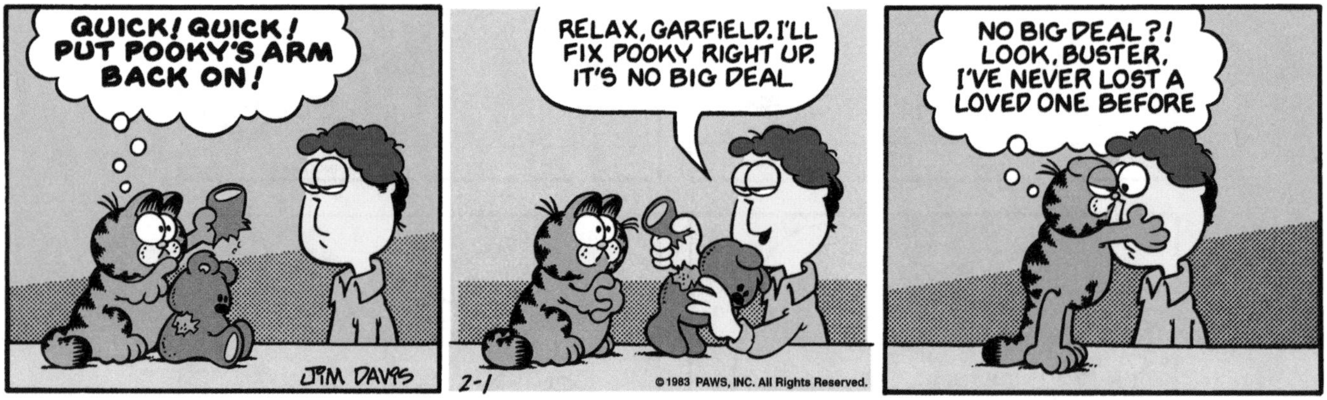
QUICK! QUICK! PUT POOKY'S ARM BACK ON!
JIM DAVIS
RELAX, GARFIELD. I'LL FIX POOKY RIGHT UP. IT'S NO BIG DEAL
2-1
© 1983 PAWS, INC. All Rights Reserved.
NO BIG DEAL?! LOOK, BUSTER, I'VE NEVER LOST A LOVED ONE BEFORE

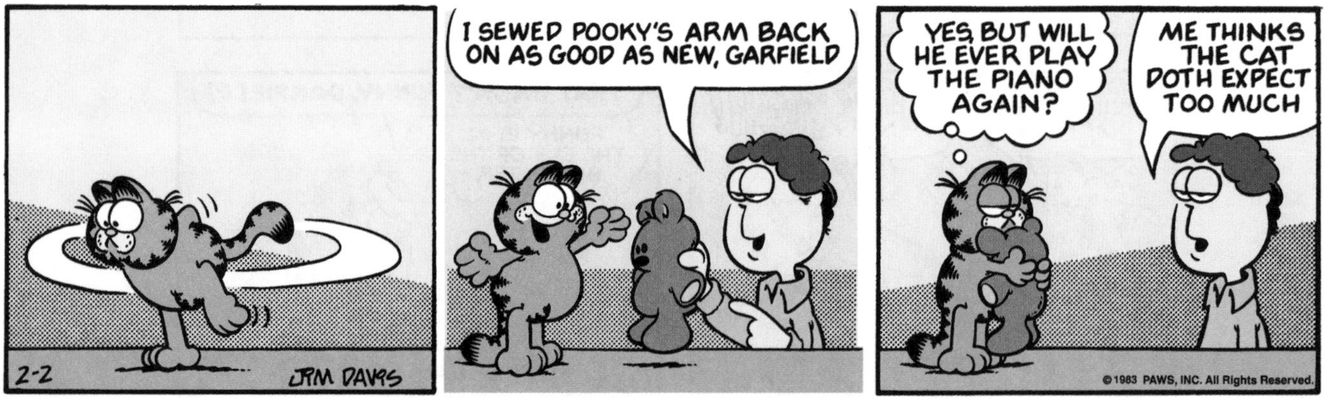
2-2
JIM DAVIS
I SEWED POOKY'S ARM BACK ON AS GOOD AS NEW, GARFIELD
YES, BUT WILL HE EVER PLAY THE PIANO AGAIN?
ME THINKS THE CAT DOTH EXPECT TOO MUCH
© 1983 PAWS, INC. All Rights Reserved.

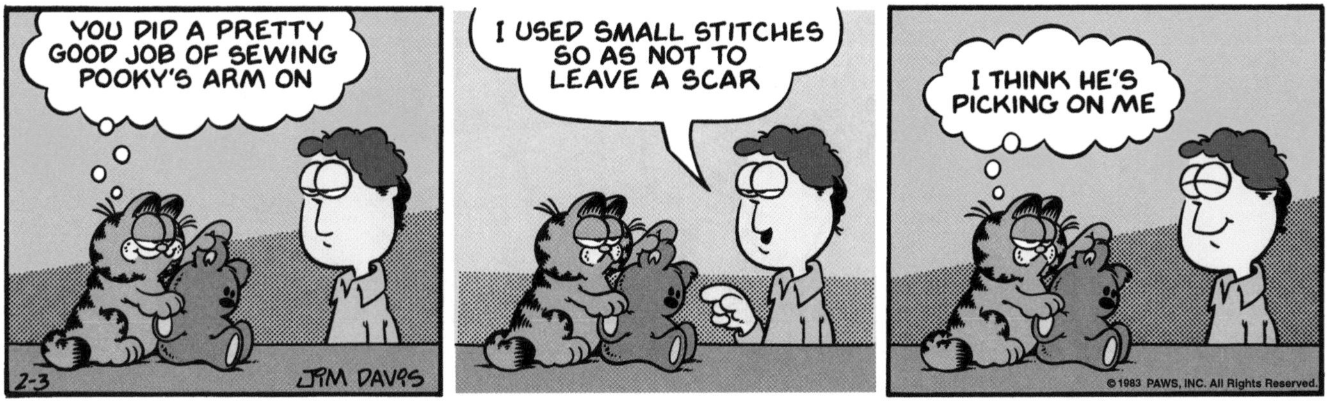
YOU DID A PRETTY GOOD JOB OF SEWING POOKY'S ARM ON
2-3
JIM DAVIS
I USED SMALL STITCHES SO AS NOT TO LEAVE A SCAR
I THINK HE'S PICKING ON ME
© 1983 PAWS, INC. All Rights Reserved.

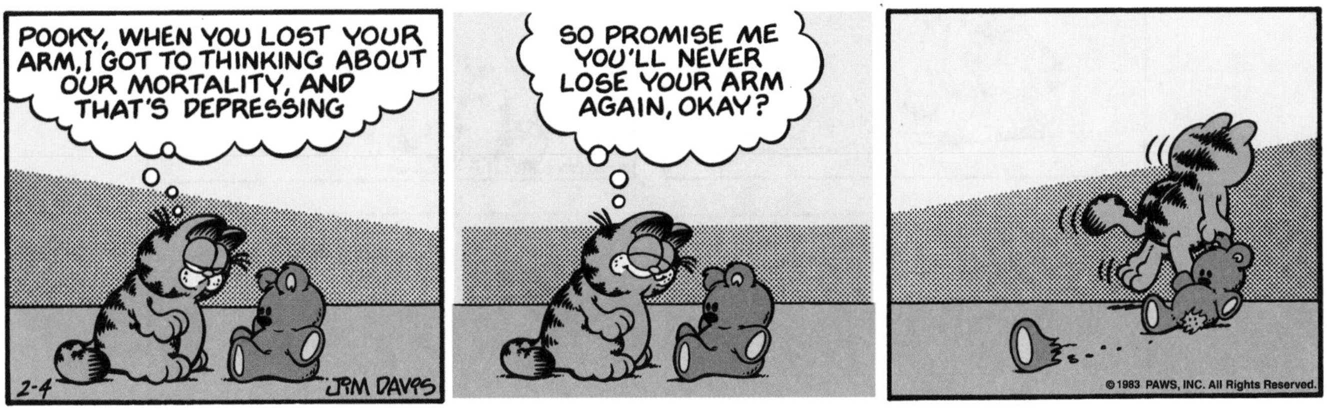
POOKY, WHEN YOU LOST YOUR ARM, I GOT TO THINKING ABOUT OUR MORTALITY, AND THAT'S DEPRESSING
2-4
JIM DAVIS
SO PROMISE ME YOU'LL NEVER LOSE YOUR ARM AGAIN, OKAY?
© 1983 PAWS, INC. All Rights Reserved.

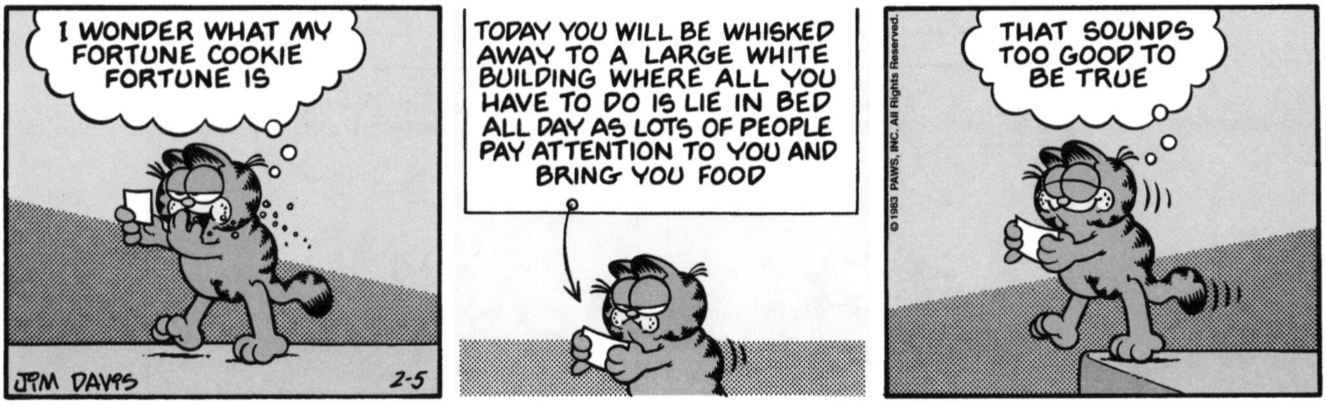
I WONDER WHAT MY FORTUNE COOKIE FORTUNE IS
JIM DAVIS
2-5
TODAY YOU WILL BE WHISKED AWAY TO A LARGE WHITE BUILDING WHERE ALL YOU HAVE TO DO IS LIE IN BED ALL DAY AS LOTS OF PEOPLE PAY ATTENTION TO YOU AND BRING YOU FOOD
© 1983 PAWS, INC. All Rights Reserved.
THAT SOUNDS TOO GOOD TO BE TRUE

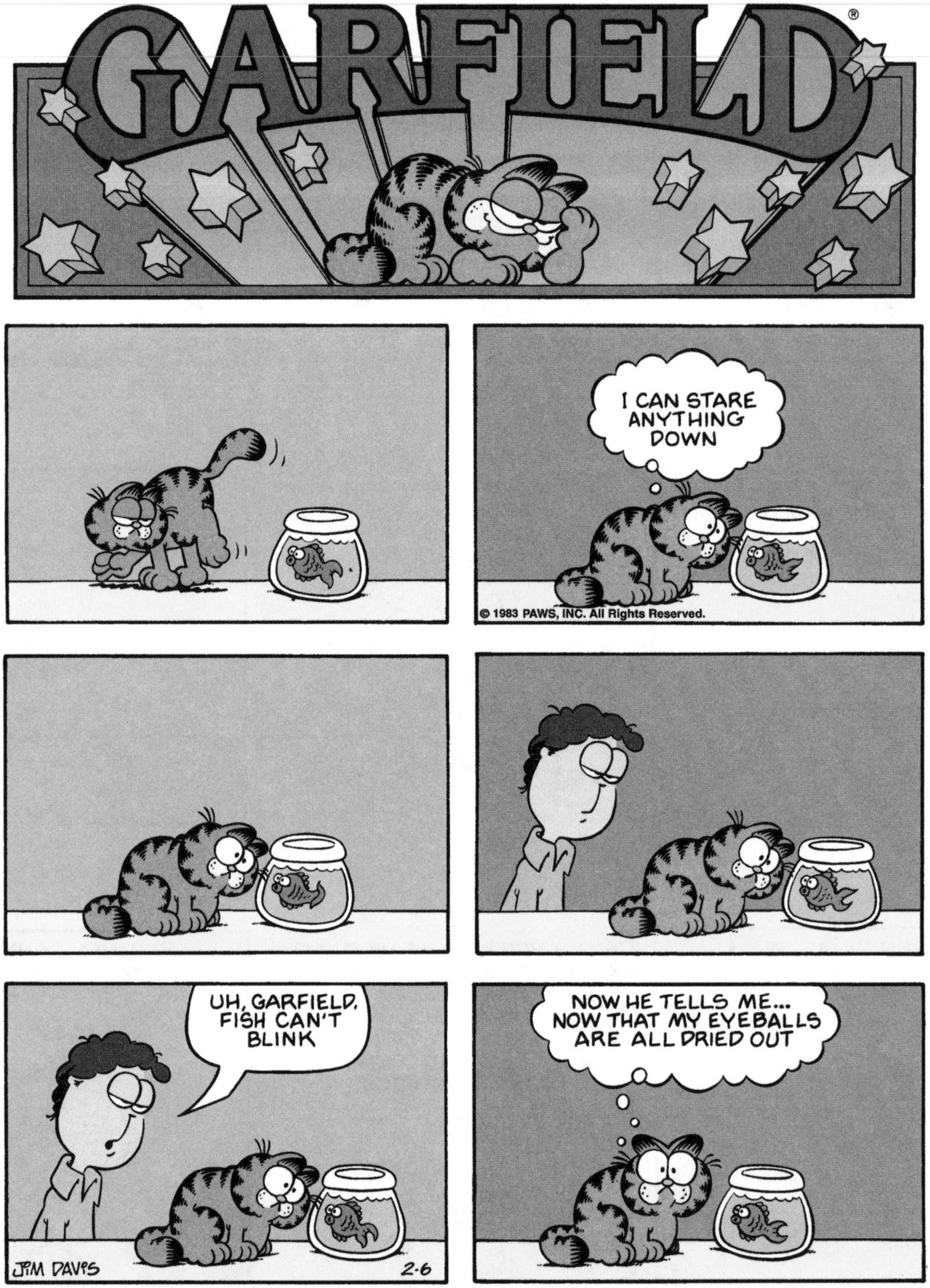
GARFIELD®
I CAN STARE ANYTHING DOWN
© 1983 PAWS, INC. All Rights Reserved.
UH, GARFIELD, FISH CAN'T BLINK
JIM DAVIS
2-6
NOW HE TELLS ME... NOW THAT MY EYEBALLS ARE ALL DRIED OUT

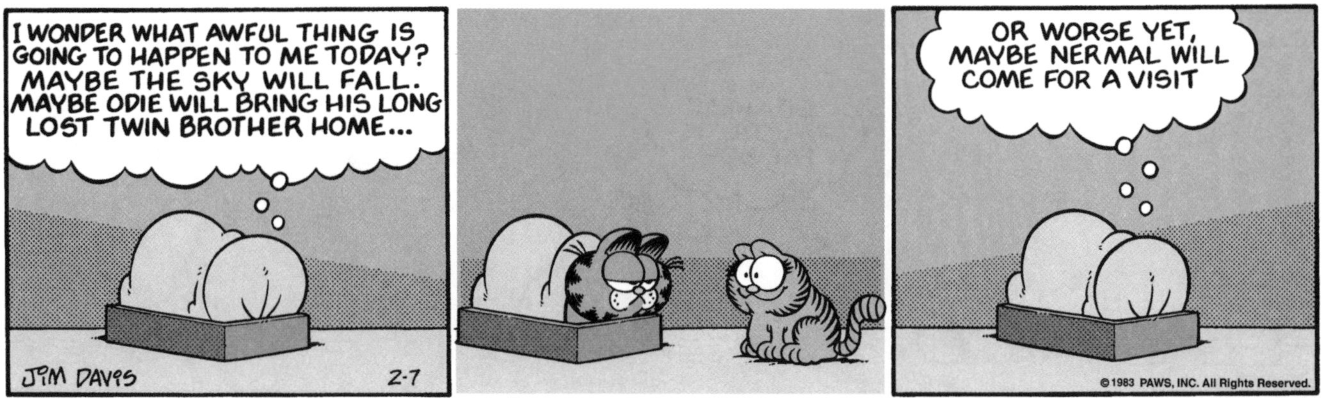
I WONDER WHAT AWFUL THING IS GOING TO HAPPEN TO ME TODAY? MAYBE THE SKY WILL FALL. MAYBE ODIE WILL BRING HIS LONG LOST TWIN BROTHER HOME...
JIM DAVIS
2-7
OR WORSE YET, MAYBE NERMAL WILL COME FOR A VISIT
© 1983 PAWS, INC. All Rights Reserved.

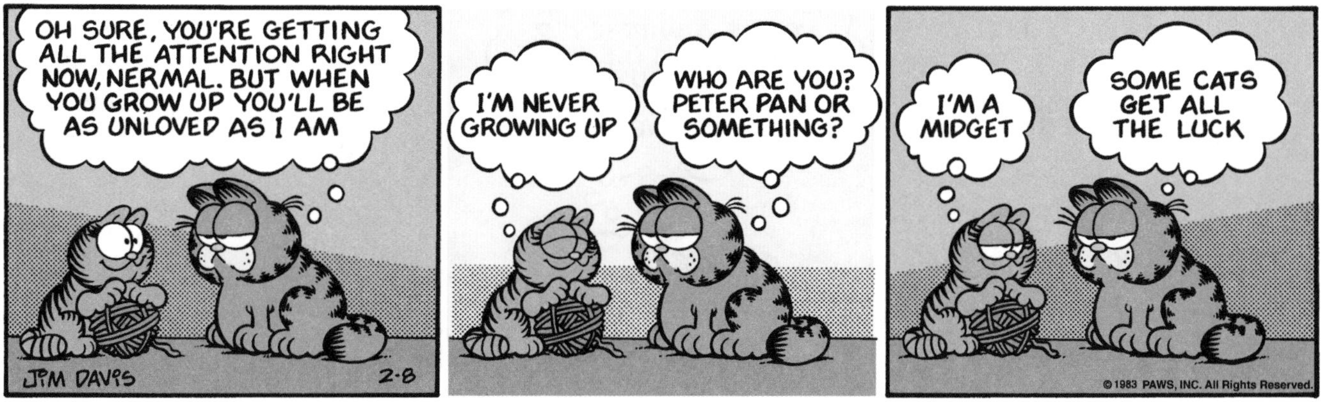
OH SURE, YOU'RE GETTING ALL THE ATTENTION RIGHT NOW, NERMAL. BUT WHEN YOU GROW UP YOU'LL BE AS UNLOVED AS I AM
JIM DAVIS
2-8
I'M NEVER GROWING UP
WHO ARE YOU? PETER PAN OR SOMETHING?
I'M A MIDGET
SOME CATS GET ALL THE LUCK
© 1983 PAWS, INC. All Rights Reserved.

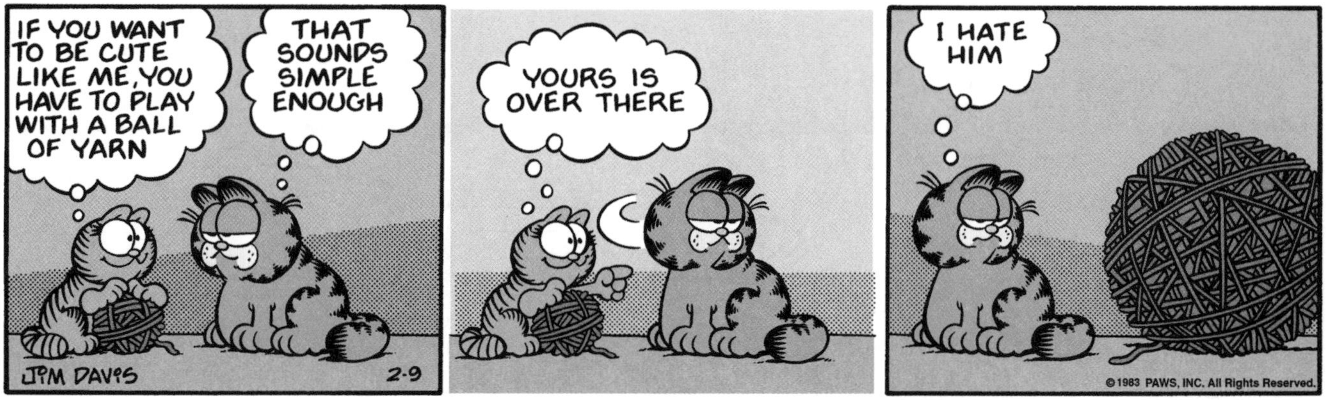
IF YOU WANT TO BE CUTE LIKE ME, YOU HAVE TO PLAY WITH A BALL OF YARN
THAT SOUNDS SIMPLE ENOUGH
JIM DAVIS
2-9
YOURS IS OVER THERE
I HATE HIM
© 1983 PAWS, INC. All Rights Reserved.

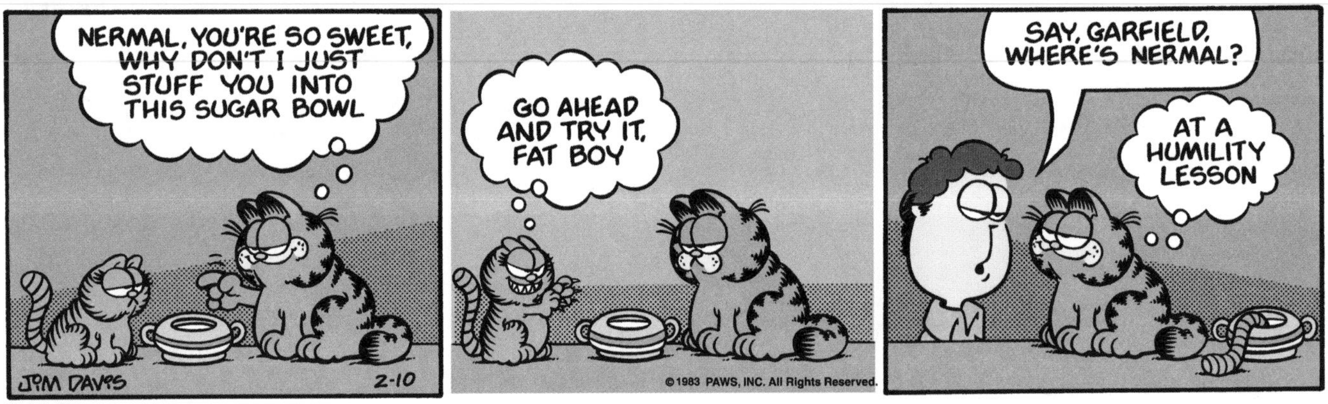
NERMAL, YOU'RE SO SWEET, WHY DON'T I JUST STUFF YOU INTO THIS SUGAR BOWL
JIM DAVIS
2-10
GO AHEAD AND TRY IT, FAT BOY
© 1983 PAWS, INC. All Rights Reserved.
SAY, GARFIELD, WHERE'S NERMAL?
AT A HUMILITY LESSON

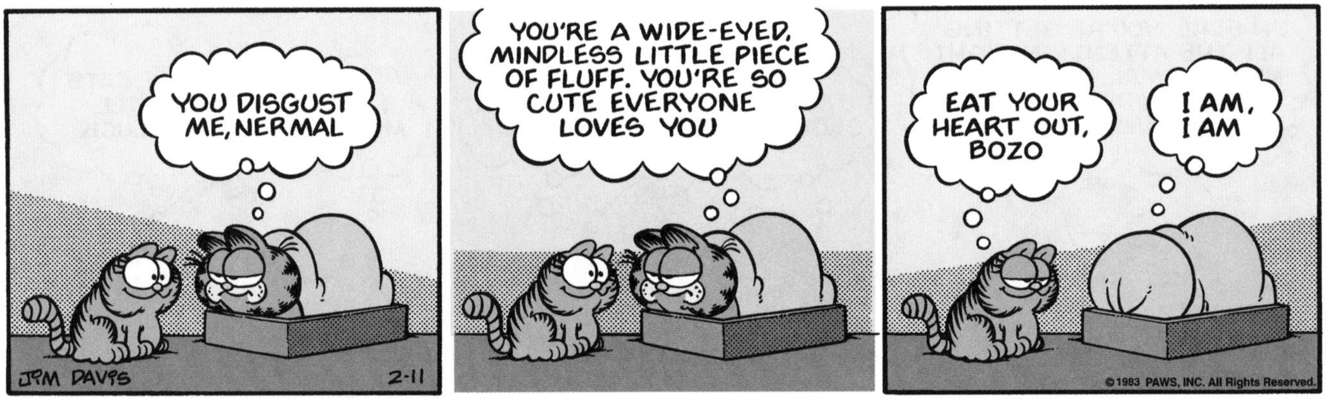
YOU DISGUST ME, NERMAL
JIM DAVIS
2-11
YOU'RE A WIDE-EYED, MINDLESS LITTLE PIECE OF FLUFF. YOU'RE SO CUTE EVERYONE LOVES YOU
EAT YOUR HEART OUT, BOZO
I AM, I AM
© 1983 PAWS, INC. All Rights Reserved.

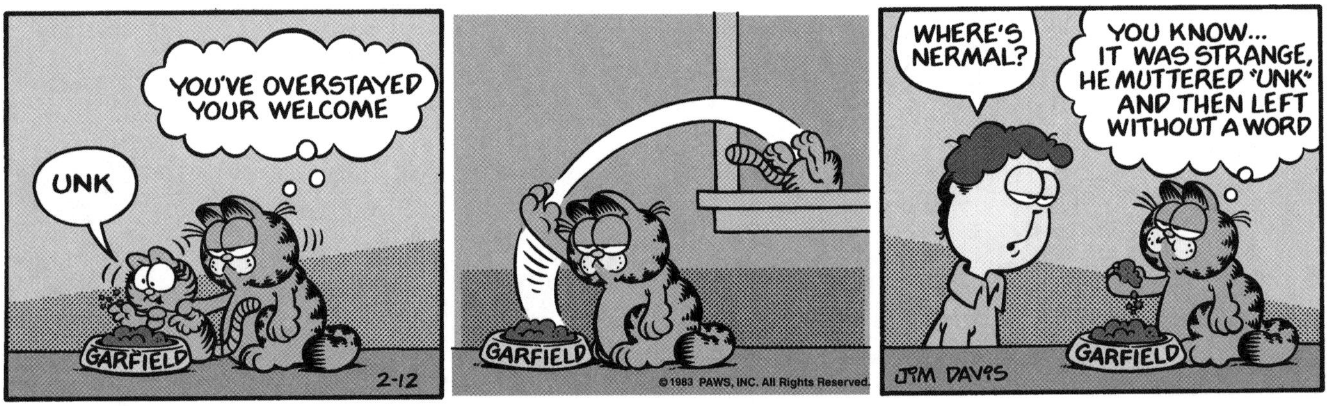
YOU'VE OVERSTAYED YOUR WELCOME
UNK
GARFIELD
2-12
GARFIELD
© 1983 PAWS, INC. All Rights Reserved.
WHERE'S NERMAL?
YOU KNOW... IT WAS STRANGE, HE MUTTERED "UNK" AND THEN LEFT WITHOUT A WORD
GARFIELD
JIM DAVIS

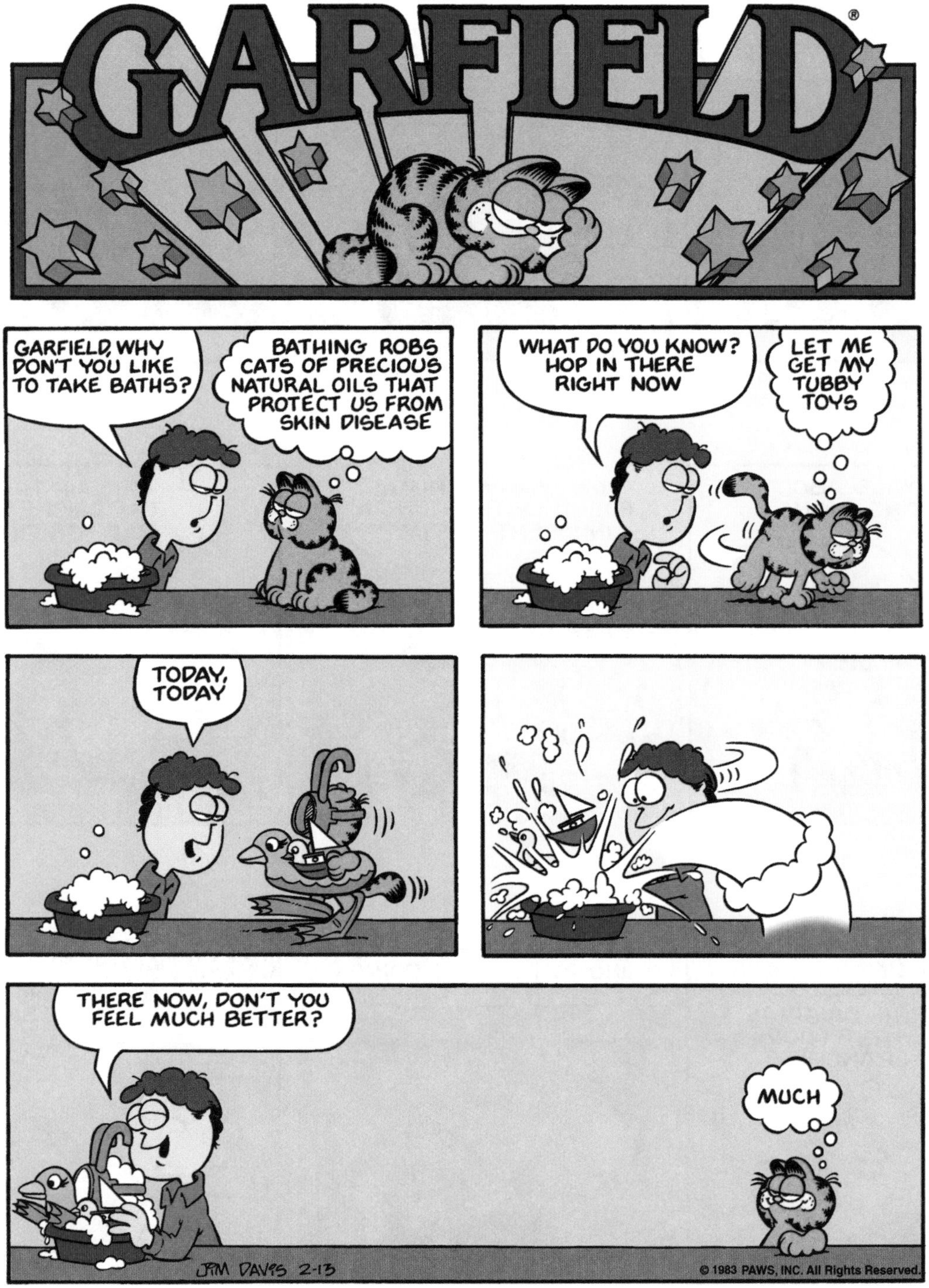
GARFIELD
GARFIELD, WHY DON'T YOU LIKE TO TAKE BATHS?
BATHING ROBS CATS OF PRECIOUS NATURAL OILS THAT PROTECT US FROM SKIN DISEASE
WHAT DO YOU KNOW? HOP IN THERE RIGHT NOW
LET ME GET MY TUBBY TOYS
TODAY, TODAY
THERE NOW, DON'T YOU FEEL MUCH BETTER?
MUCH
JIM DAVIS 2-13
© 1983 PAWS, INC. All Rights Reserved.

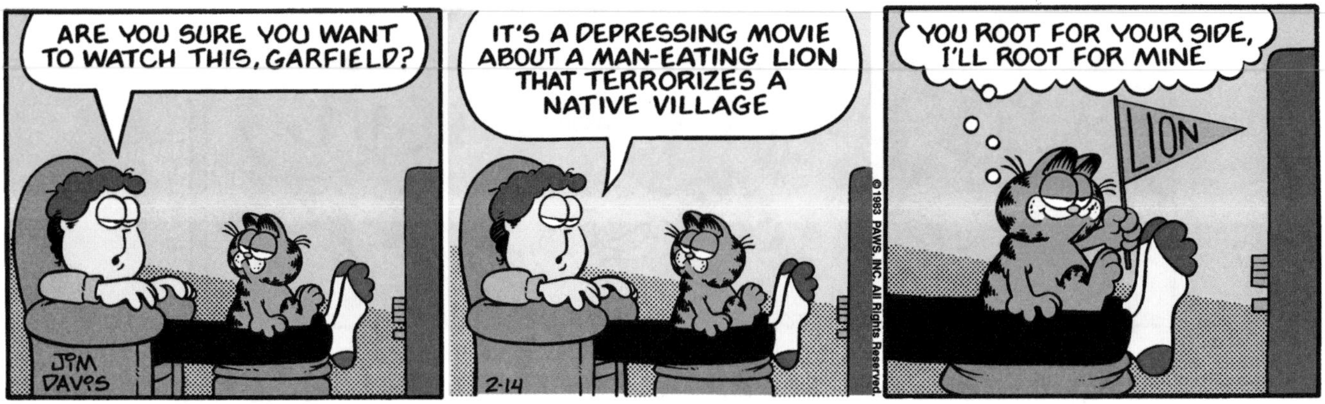
ARE YOU SURE YOU WANT TO WATCH THIS, GARFIELD?
JIM DAVIS
IT'S A DEPRESSING MOVIE ABOUT A MAN-EATING LION THAT TERRORIZES A NATIVE VILLAGE
2-14
© 1983 PAWS, INC. All Rights Reserved.
YOU ROOT FOR YOUR SIDE, I'LL ROOT FOR MINE
LION

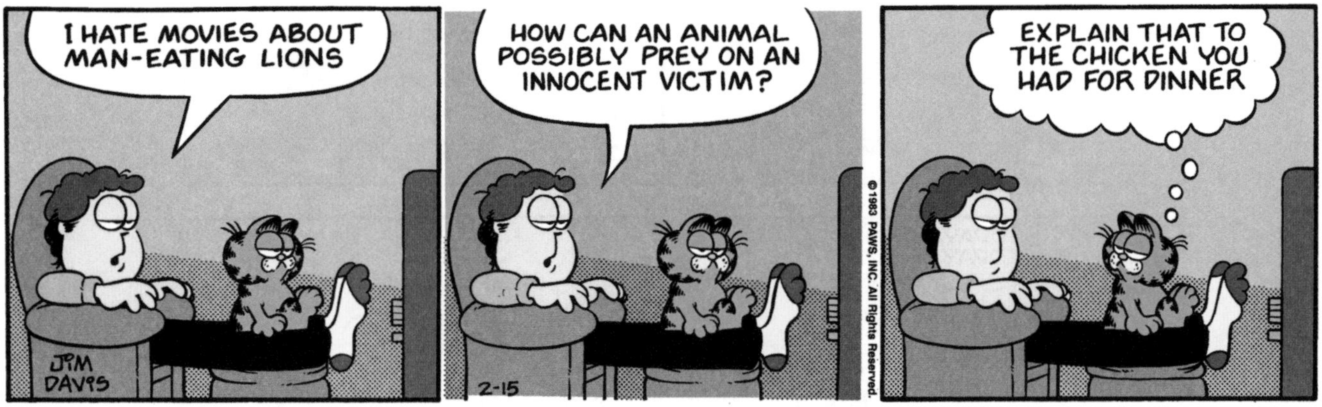
I HATE MOVIES ABOUT MAN-EATING LIONS
JIM DAVIS
HOW CAN AN ANIMAL POSSIBLY PREY ON AN INNOCENT VICTIM?
2-15
© 1983 PAWS, INC. All Rights Reserved.
EXPLAIN THAT TO THE CHICKEN YOU HAD FOR DINNER

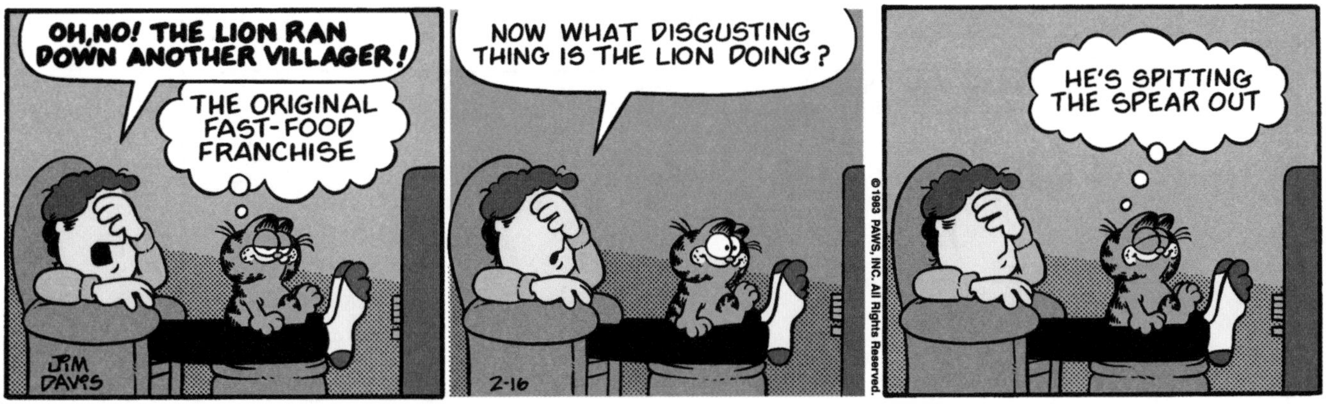
OH, NO! THE LION RAN DOWN ANOTHER VILLAGER!
THE ORIGINAL FAST-FOOD FRANCHISE
JIM DAVIS
NOW WHAT DISGUSTING THING IS THE LION DOING?
2-16
© 1983 PAWS, INC. All Rights Reserved.
HE'S SPITTING THE SPEAR OUT

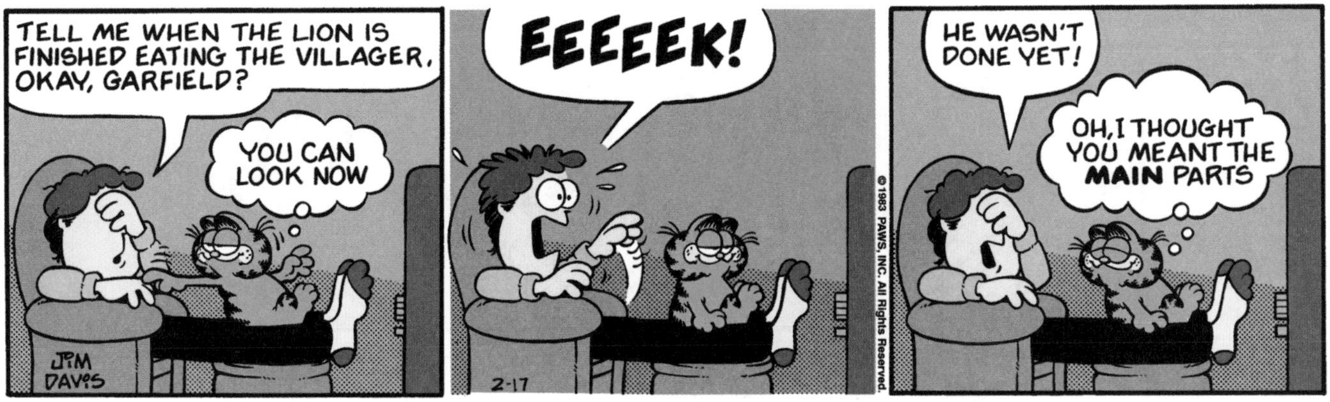
TELL ME WHEN THE LION IS FINISHED EATING THE VILLAGER, OKAY, GARFIELD?
YOU CAN LOOK NOW
JIM DAVIS
EEEEEK!
2-17
© 1983 PAWS, INC. All Rights Reserved.
HE WASN'T DONE YET!
OH, I THOUGHT YOU MEANT THE **MAIN** PARTS

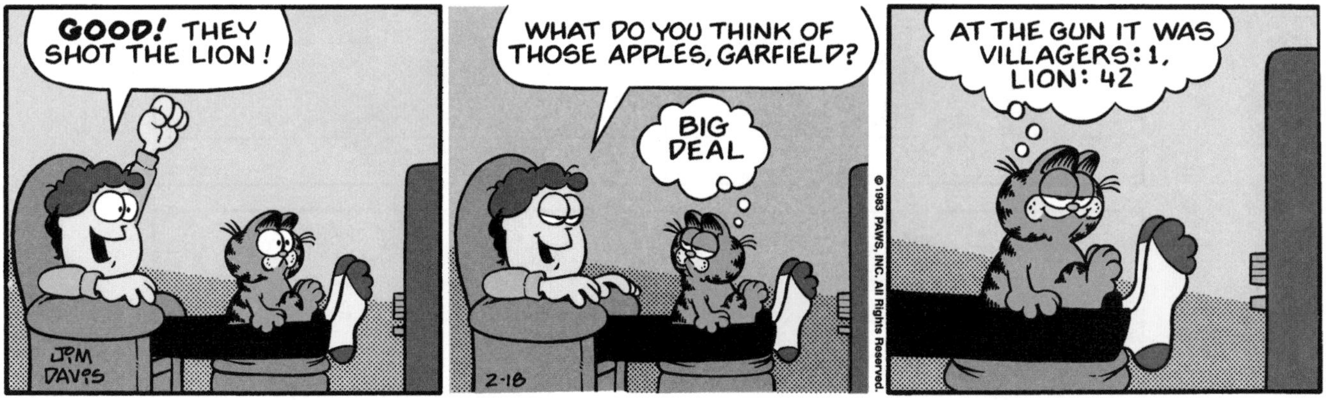
GOOD! THEY SHOT THE LION!
JIM DAVIS
WHAT DO YOU THINK OF THOSE APPLES, GARFIELD?
BIG DEAL
2-18
© 1983 PAWS, INC. All Rights Reserved.
AT THE GUN IT WAS VILLAGERS: 1, LION: 42

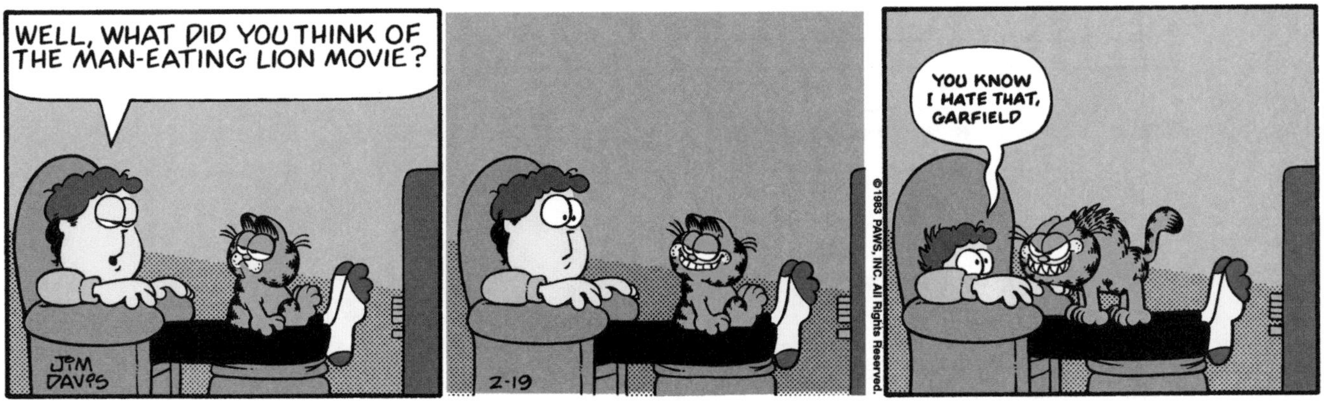
WELL, WHAT DID YOU THINK OF THE MAN-EATING LION MOVIE?
JIM DAVIS
2-19
© 1983 PAWS, INC. All Rights Reserved.
YOU KNOW I HATE THAT, GARFIELD

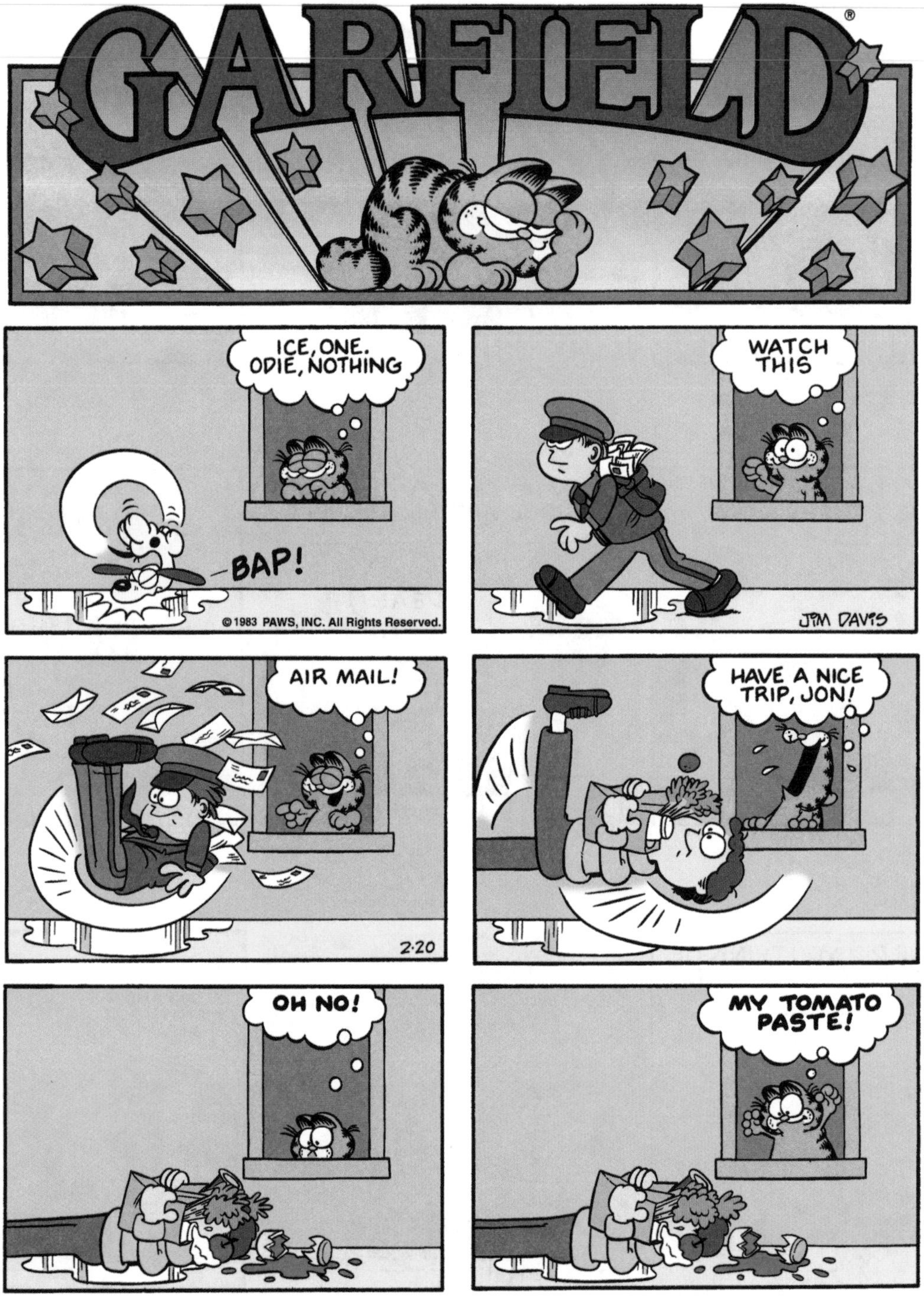
GARFIELD®
ICE, ONE. ODIE, NOTHING
BAP!
© 1983 PAWS, INC. All Rights Reserved.
WATCH THIS
JIM DAVIS
AIR MAIL!
2·20
HAVE A NICE TRIP, JON!
OH NO!
MY TOMATO PASTE!

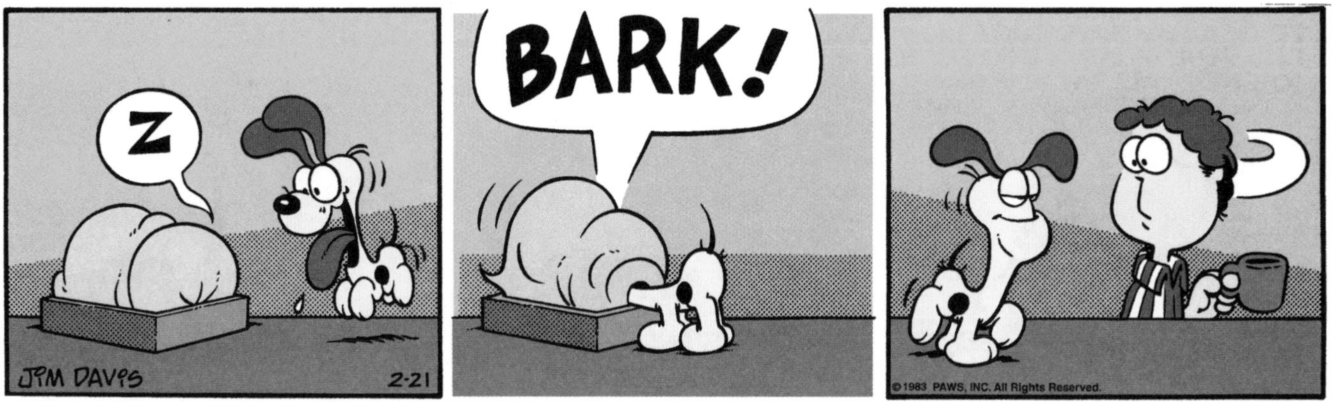
Z
JIM DAVIS
2·21
BARK!
©1983 PAWS, INC. All Rights Reserved.

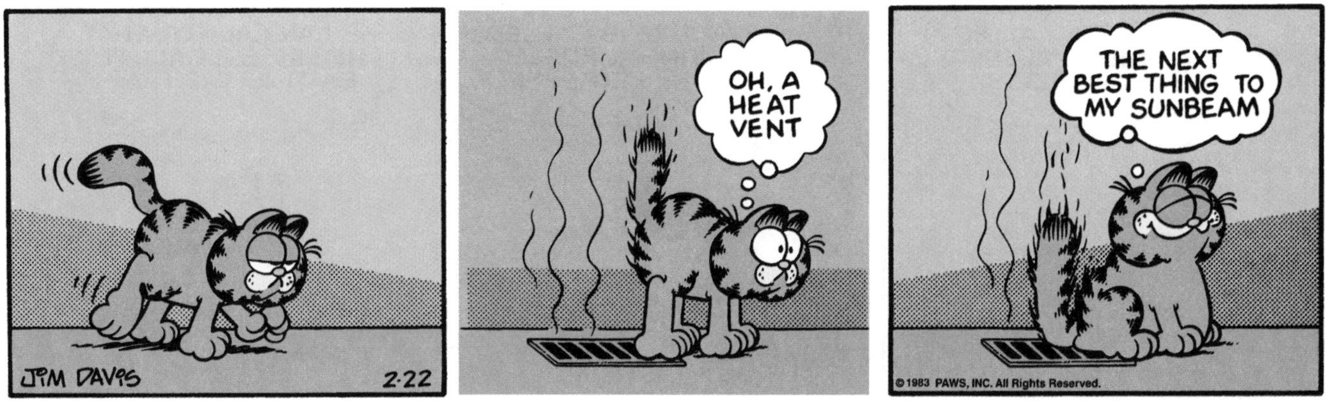
JIM DAVIS
2·22
OH, A HEAT VENT
THE NEXT BEST THING TO MY SUNBEAM
©1983 PAWS, INC. All Rights Reserved.

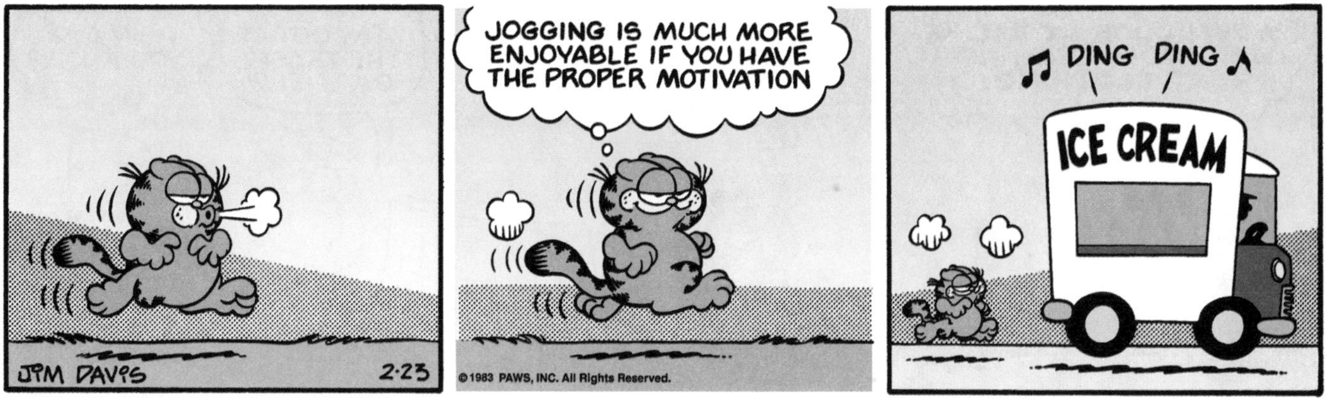
JIM DAVIS
2·23
JOGGING IS MUCH MORE ENJOYABLE IF YOU HAVE THE PROPER MOTIVATION
©1983 PAWS, INC. All Rights Reserved.
DING DING
ICE CREAM

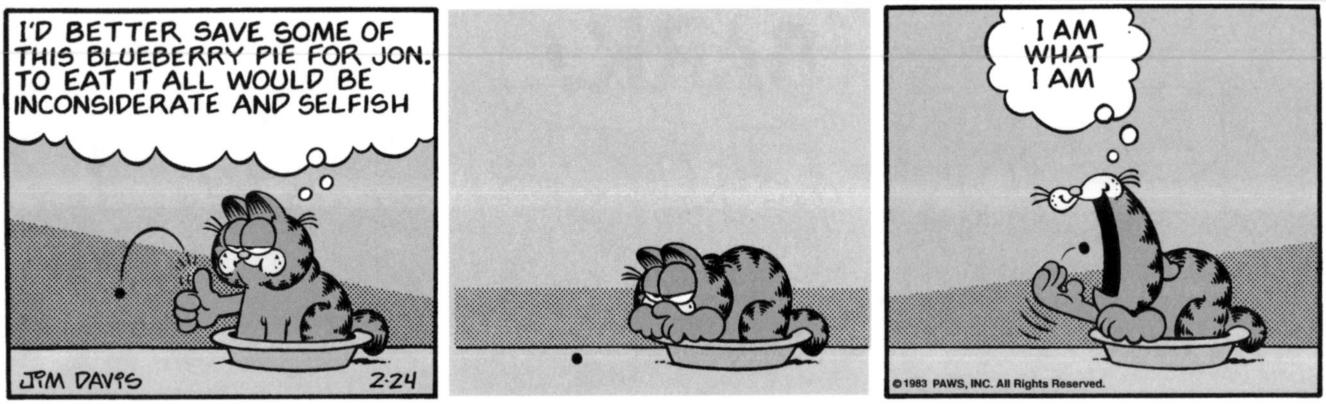
I'D BETTER SAVE SOME OF THIS BLUEBERRY PIE FOR JON. TO EAT IT ALL WOULD BE INCONSIDERATE AND SELFISH
JIM DAVIS
2-24
I AM WHAT I AM
©1983 PAWS, INC. All Rights Reserved.

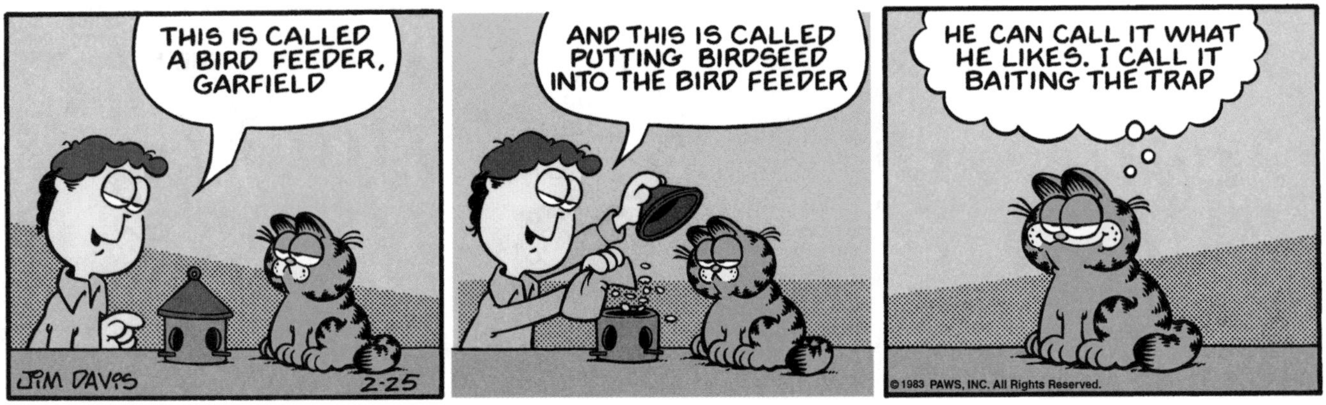
THIS IS CALLED A BIRD FEEDER, GARFIELD
JIM DAVIS
2-25
AND THIS IS CALLED PUTTING BIRDSEED INTO THE BIRD FEEDER
HE CAN CALL IT WHAT HE LIKES. I CALL IT BAITING THE TRAP
©1983 PAWS, INC. All Rights Reserved.

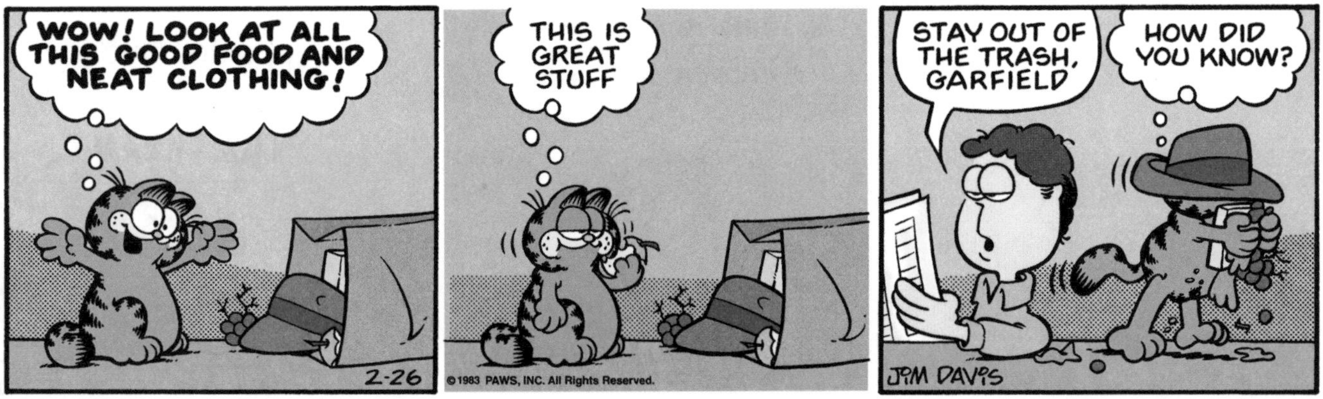
WOW! LOOK AT ALL THIS GOOD FOOD AND NEAT CLOTHING!
2-26
THIS IS GREAT STUFF
©1983 PAWS, INC. All Rights Reserved.
STAY OUT OF THE TRASH, GARFIELD
HOW DID YOU KNOW?
JIM DAVIS

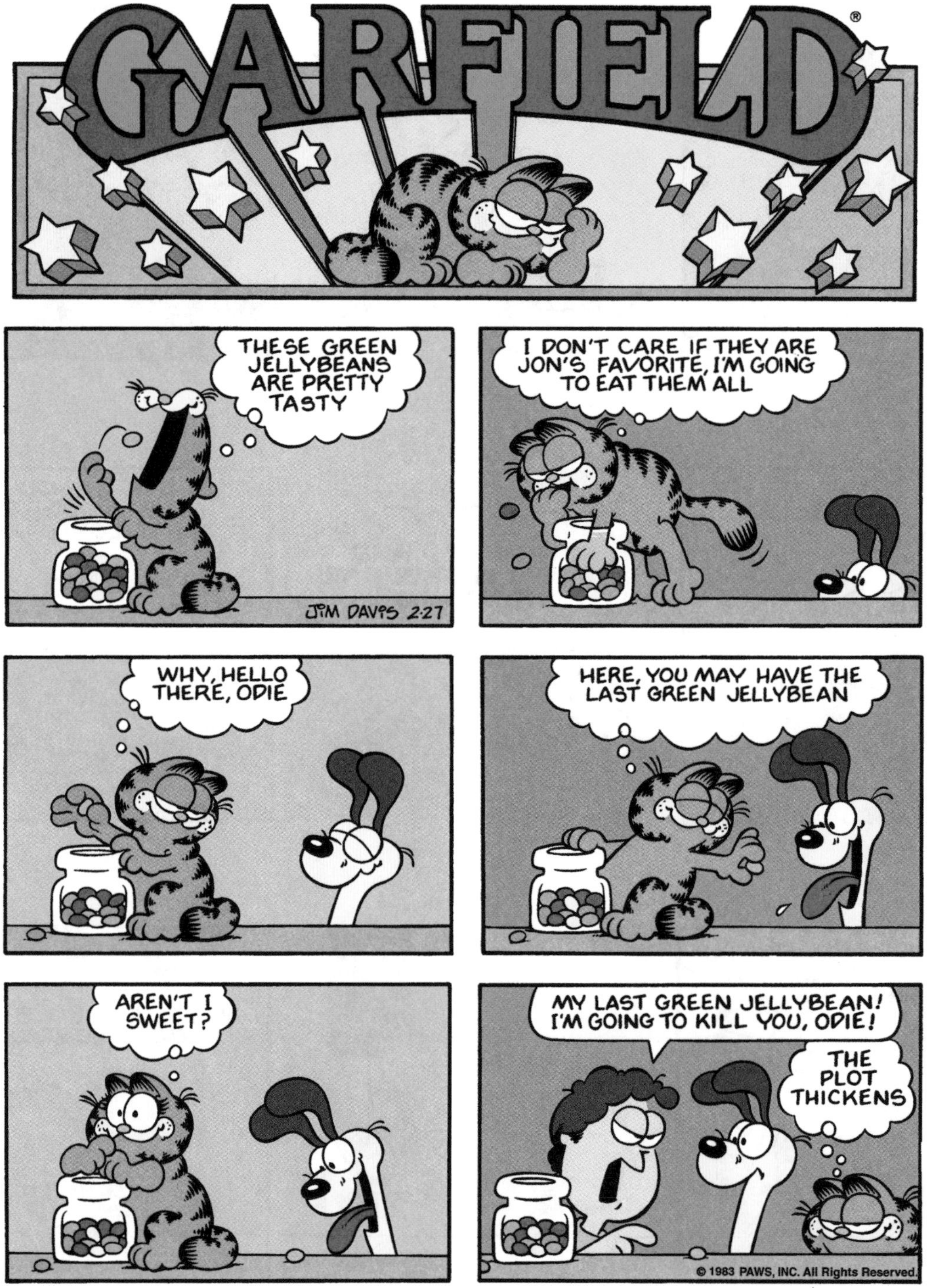
GARFIELD®
THESE GREEN JELLYBEANS ARE PRETTY TASTY
JIM DAVIS 2-27
I DON'T CARE IF THEY ARE JON'S FAVORITE, I'M GOING TO EAT THEM ALL
WHY, HELLO THERE, ODIE
HERE, YOU MAY HAVE THE LAST GREEN JELLYBEAN
AREN'T I SWEET?
MY LAST GREEN JELLYBEAN! I'M GOING TO KILL YOU, ODIE!
THE PLOT THICKENS
© 1983 PAWS, INC. All Rights Reserved.

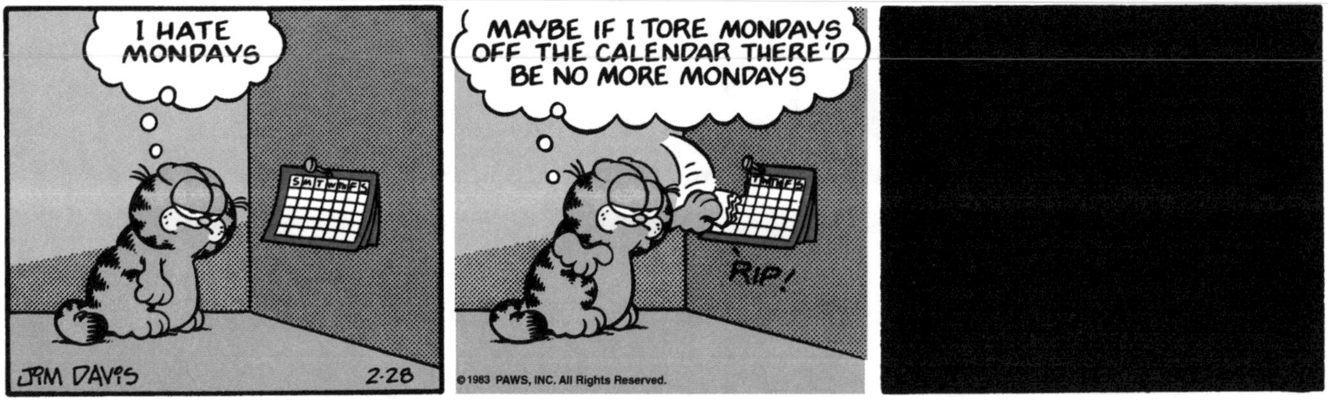
I HATE MONDAYS
JIM DAVIS
2-28
MAYBE IF I TORE MONDAYS OFF THE CALENDAR THERE'D BE NO MORE MONDAYS
RIP!
©1983 PAWS, INC. All Rights Reserved.

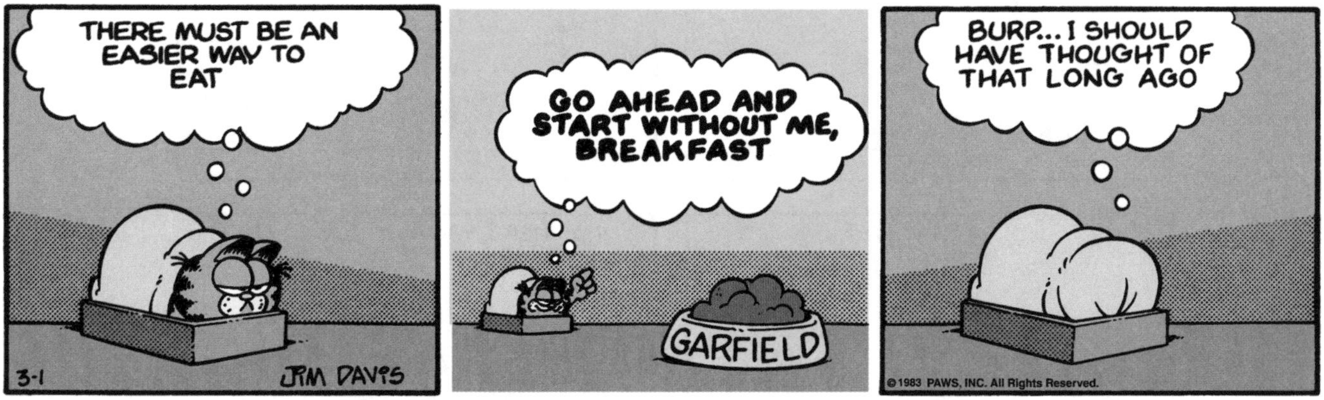
THERE MUST BE AN EASIER WAY TO EAT
3-1
JIM DAVIS
GO AHEAD AND START WITHOUT ME, BREAKFAST
GARFIELD
BURP... I SHOULD HAVE THOUGHT OF THAT LONG AGO
©1983 PAWS, INC. All Rights Reserved.

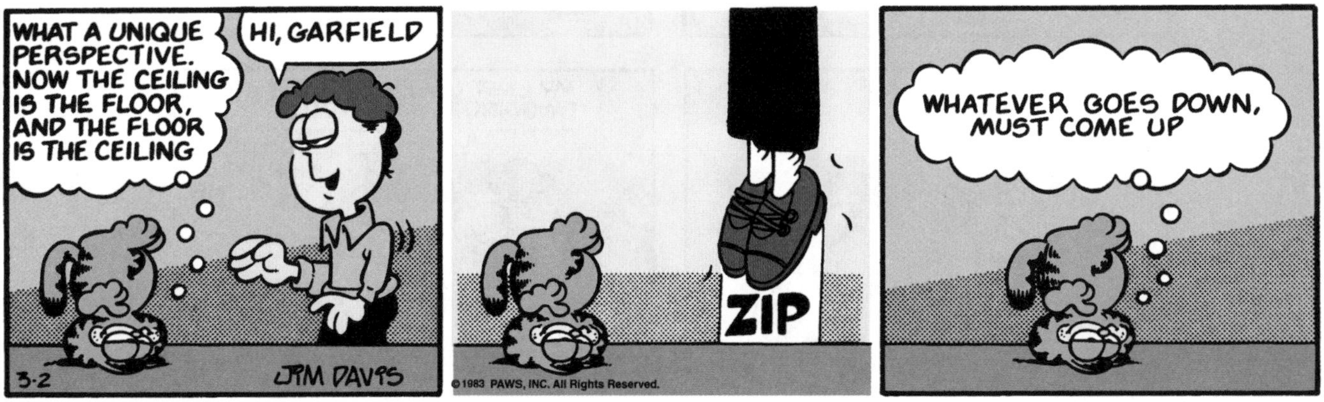
WHAT A UNIQUE PERSPECTIVE. NOW THE CEILING IS THE FLOOR, AND THE FLOOR IS THE CEILING
HI, GARFIELD
3-2
JIM DAVIS
ZIP
©1983 PAWS, INC. All Rights Reserved.
WHATEVER GOES DOWN, MUST COME UP

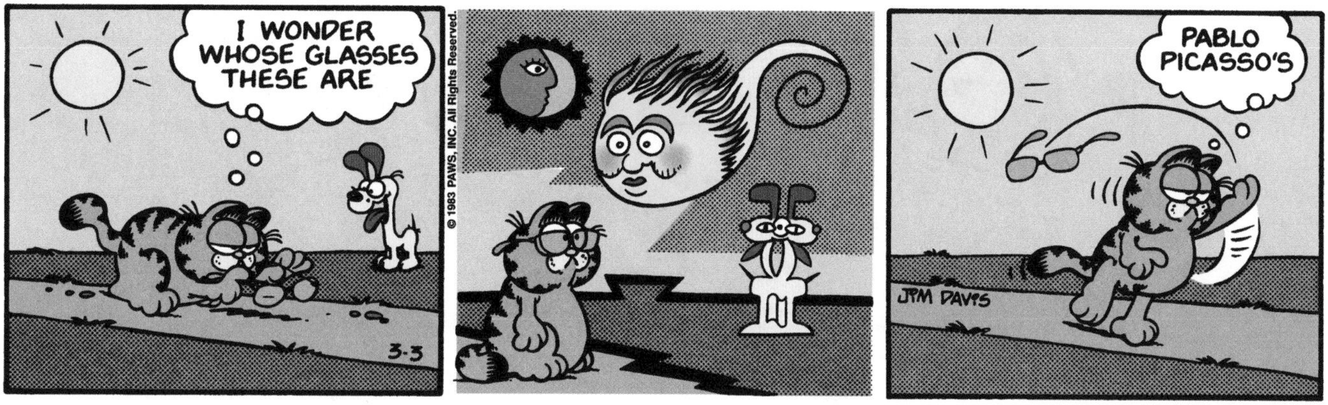
I WONDER WHOSE GLASSES THESE ARE
3-3
© 1983 PAWS, INC. All Rights Reserved.
PABLO PICASSO'S
JIM DAVIS

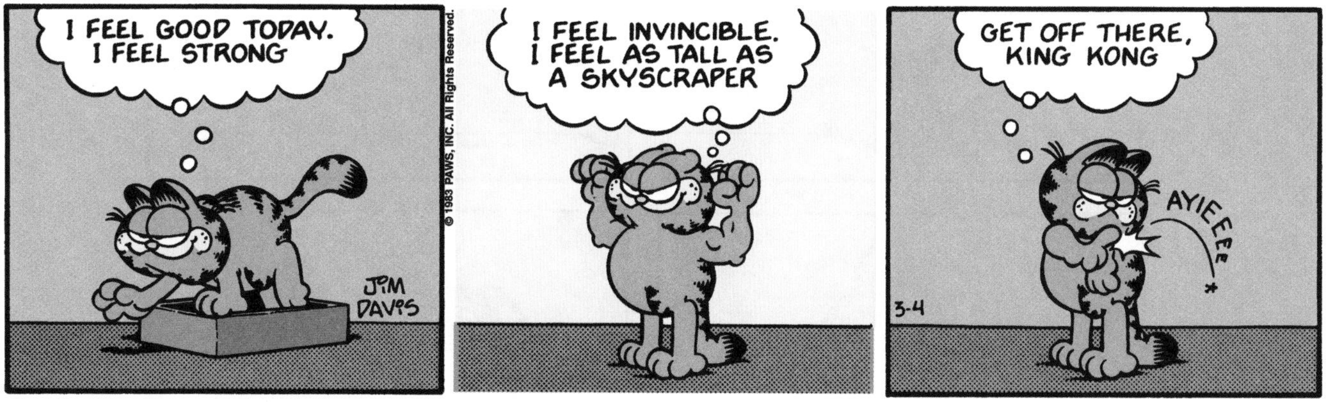
I FEEL GOOD TODAY. I FEEL STRONG
JIM DAVIS
© 1983 PAWS, INC. All Rights Reserved.
I FEEL INVINCIBLE. I FEEL AS TALL AS A SKYSCRAPER
GET OFF THERE, KING KONG
AYIEEEEE
3-4

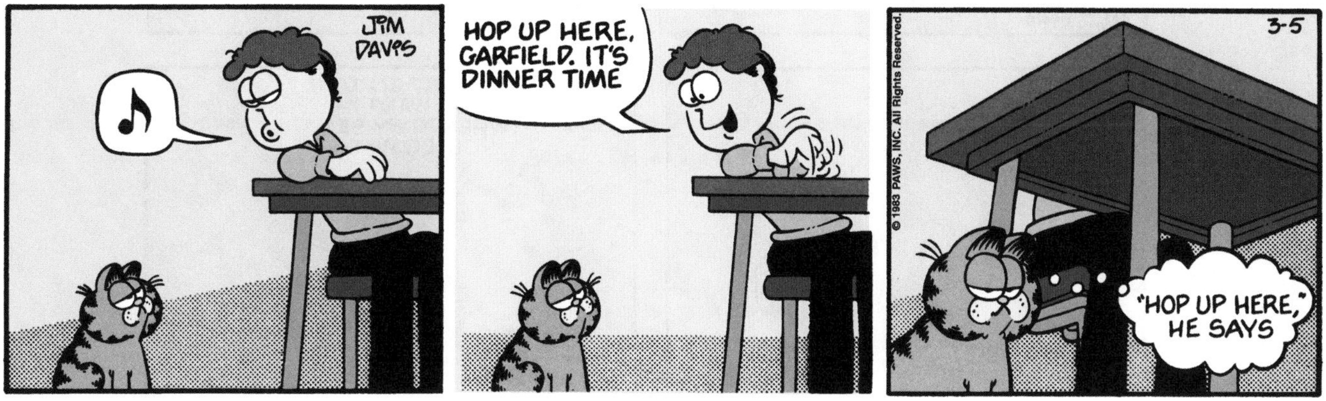
JIM DAVIS
♪
HOP UP HERE, GARFIELD. IT'S DINNER TIME
© 1983 PAWS, INC. All Rights Reserved.
3-5
"HOP UP HERE," HE SAYS

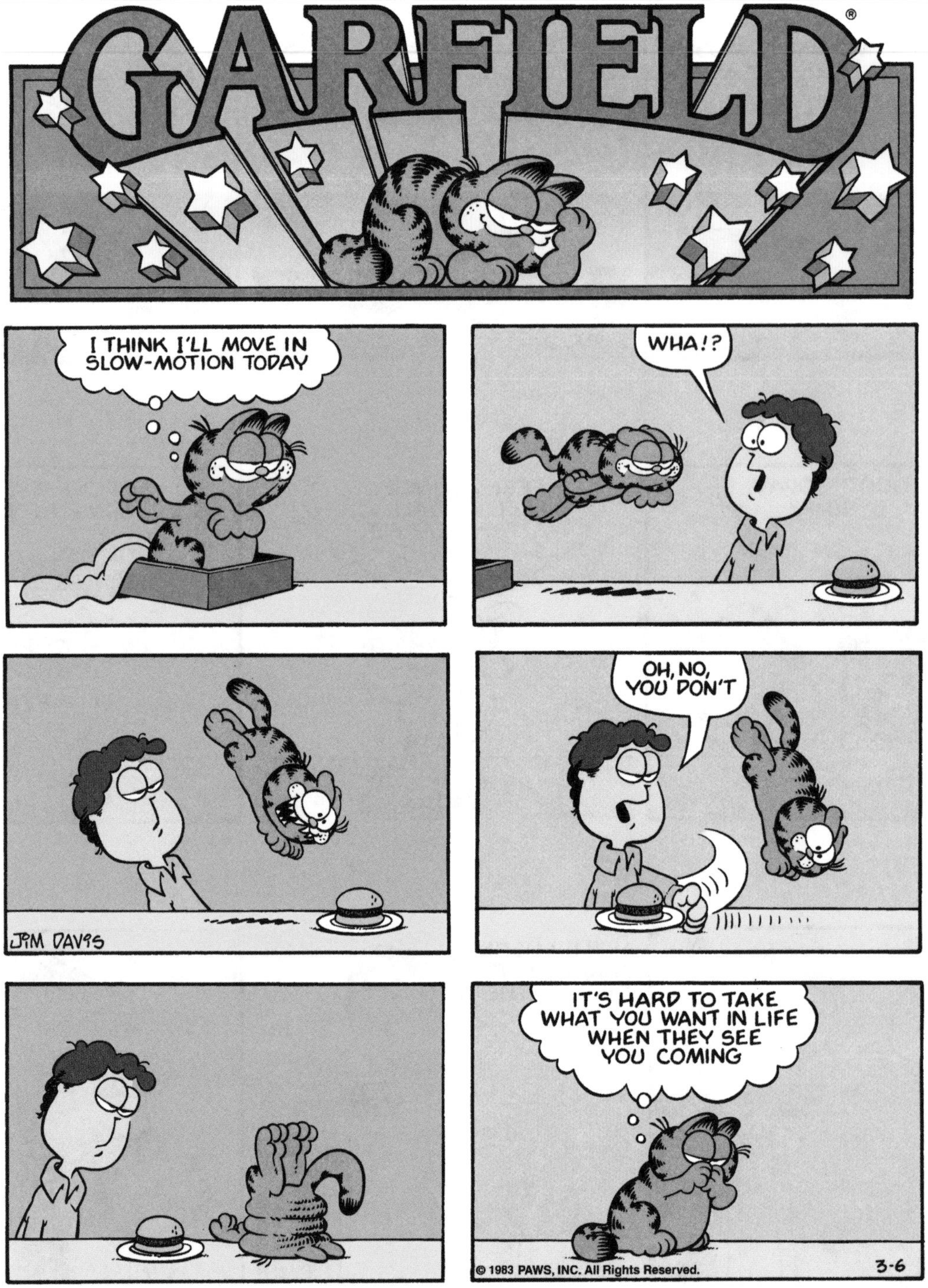
GARFIELD®
I THINK I'LL MOVE IN SLOW-MOTION TODAY
WHA!?
JIM DAVIS
OH, NO, YOU DON'T
IT'S HARD TO TAKE WHAT YOU WANT IN LIFE WHEN THEY SEE YOU COMING
© 1983 PAWS, INC. All Rights Reserved.
3-6

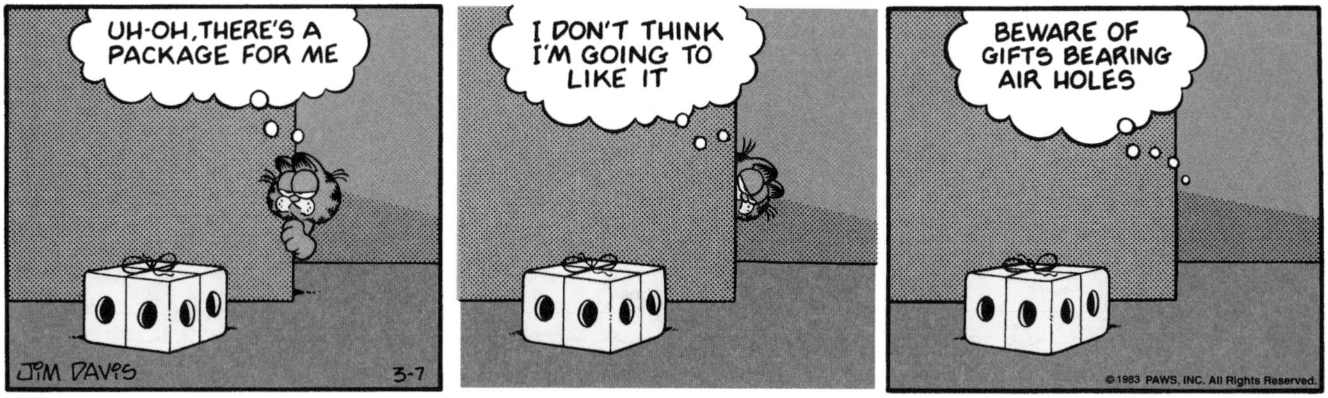
UH-OH, THERE'S A PACKAGE FOR ME
JIM DAVIS
3-7
I DON'T THINK I'M GOING TO LIKE IT
BEWARE OF GIFTS BEARING AIR HOLES
© 1983 PAWS, INC. All Rights Reserved.

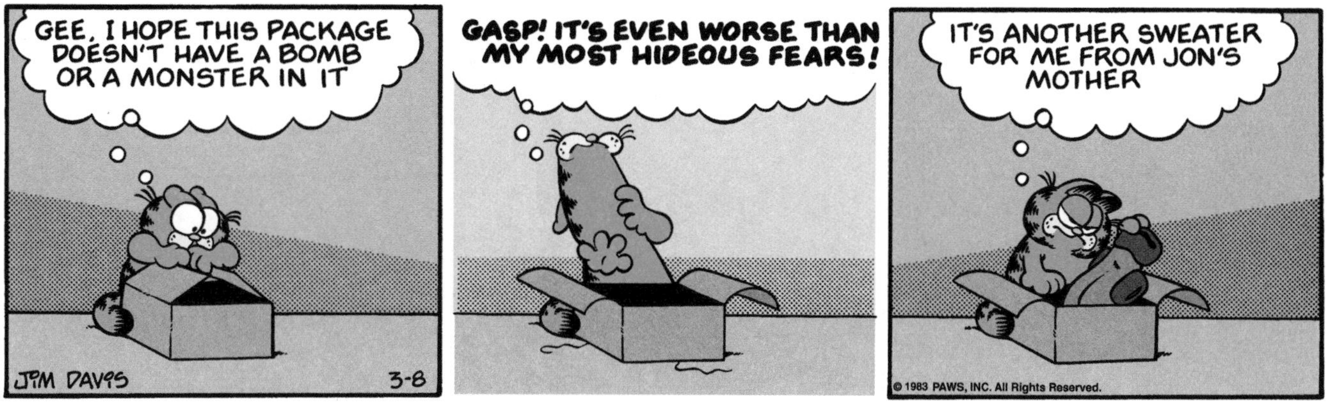
GEE, I HOPE THIS PACKAGE DOESN'T HAVE A BOMB OR A MONSTER IN IT
JIM DAVIS
3-8
GASP! IT'S EVEN WORSE THAN MY MOST HIDEOUS FEARS!
IT'S ANOTHER SWEATER FOR ME FROM JON'S MOTHER
© 1983 PAWS, INC. All Rights Reserved.

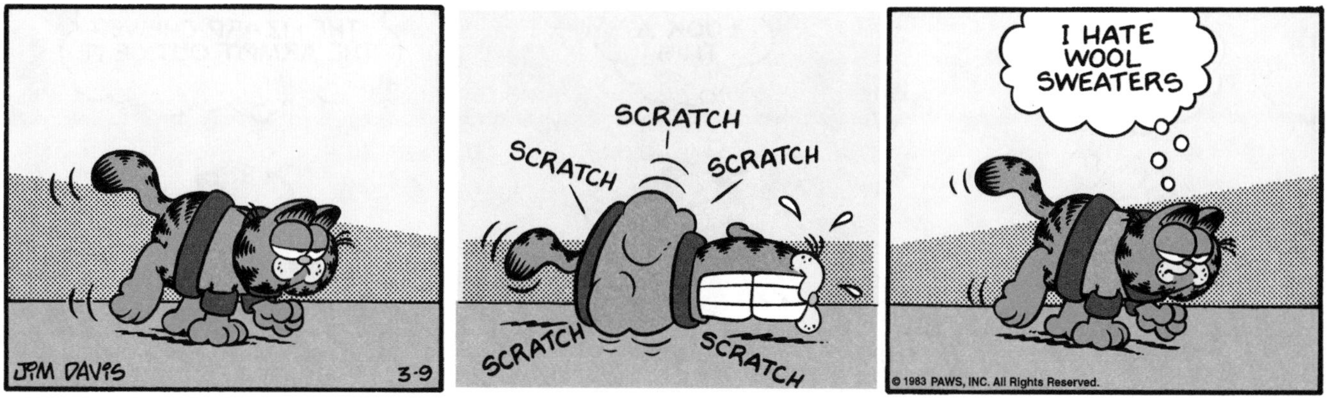
JIM DAVIS
3-9
SCRATCH
SCRATCH
SCRATCH
SCRATCH
SCRATCH
I HATE WOOL SWEATERS
© 1983 PAWS, INC. All Rights Reserved.

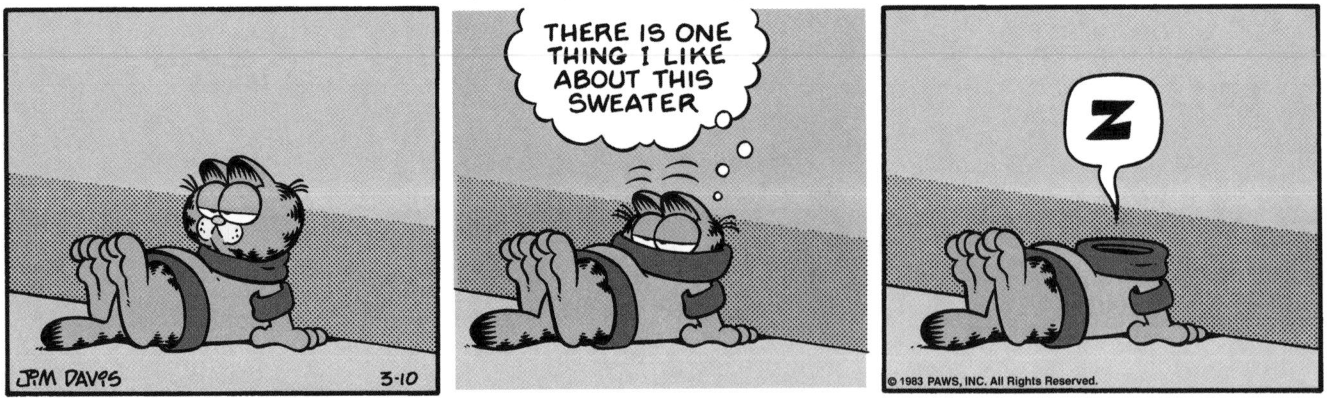
JIM DAVIS 3-10
THERE IS ONE THING I LIKE ABOUT THIS SWEATER
Z
© 1983 PAWS, INC. All Rights Reserved.

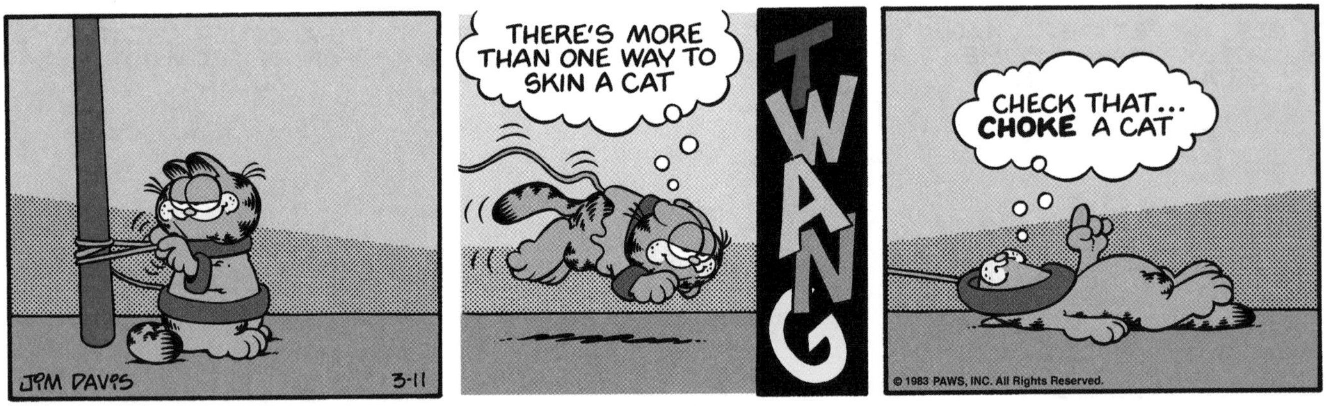
JIM DAVIS 3-11
THERE'S MORE THAN ONE WAY TO SKIN A CAT
TWANG
CHECK THAT... **CHOKE** A CAT
© 1983 PAWS, INC. All Rights Reserved.

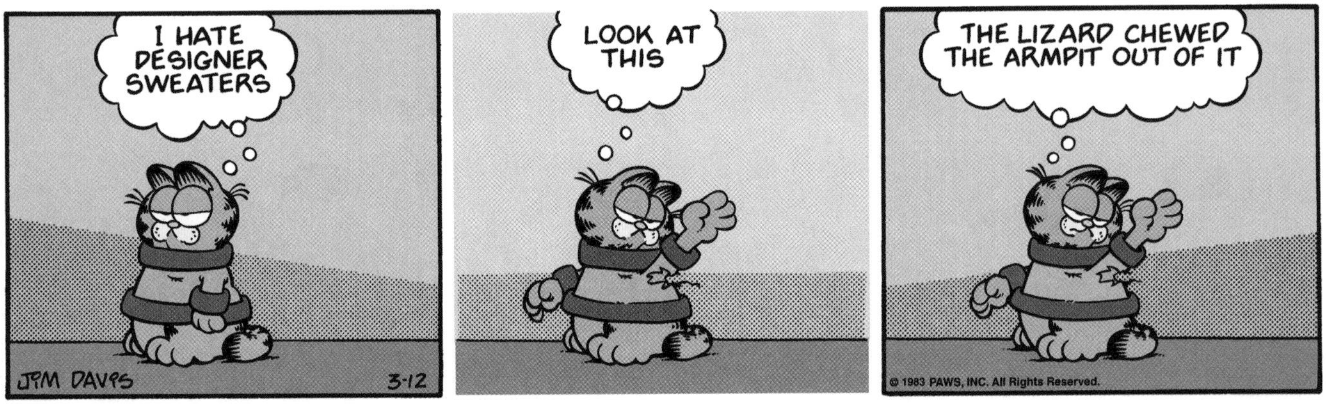
JIM DAVIS 3-12
I HATE DESIGNER SWEATERS
LOOK AT THIS
THE LIZARD CHEWED THE ARMPIT OUT OF IT
© 1983 PAWS, INC. All Rights Reserved.

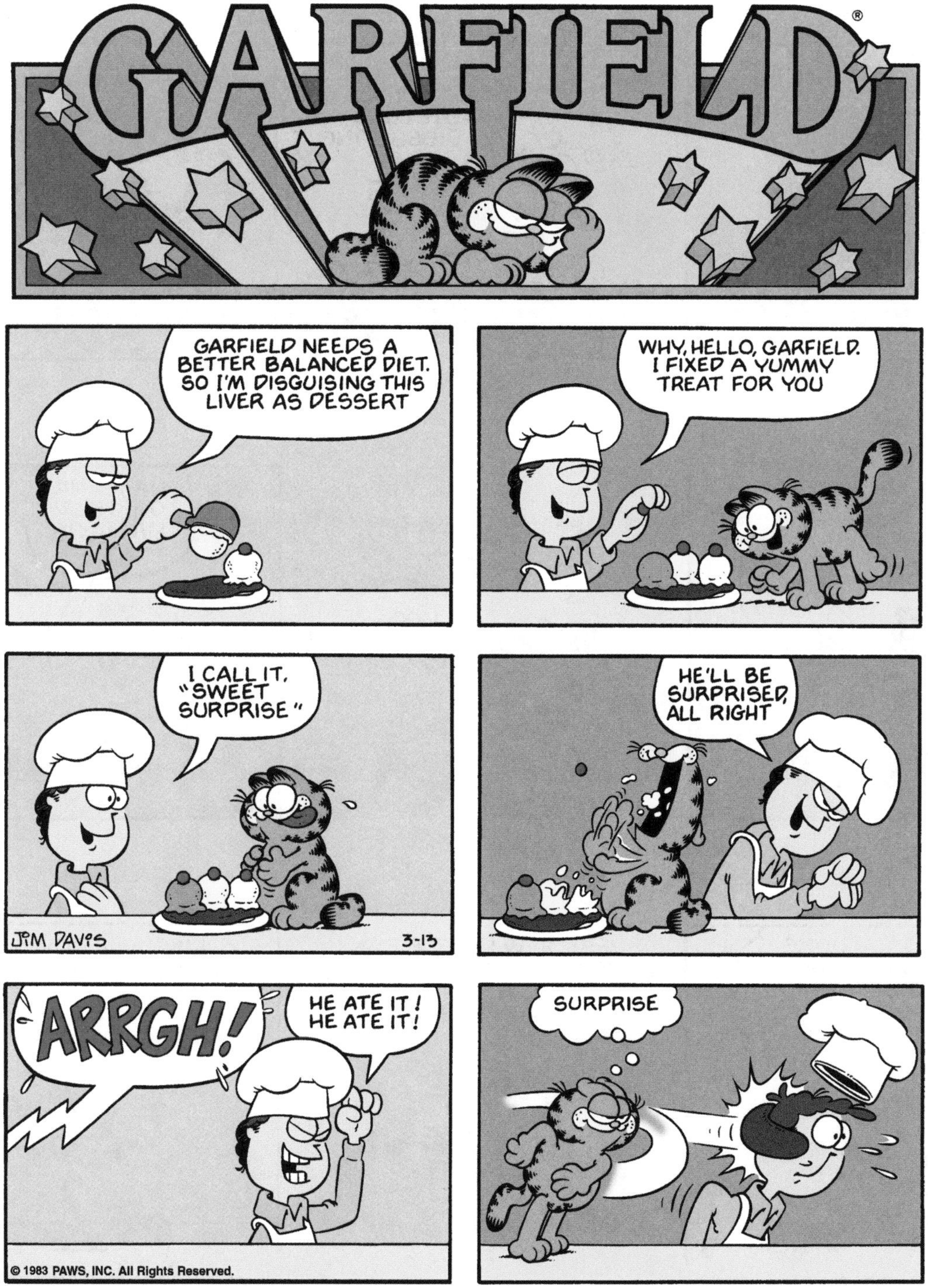
GARFIELD
GARFIELD NEEDS A BETTER BALANCED DIET. SO I'M DISGUISING THIS LIVER AS DESSERT
WHY, HELLO, GARFIELD. I FIXED A YUMMY TREAT FOR YOU
I CALL IT, "SWEET SURPRISE"
JIM DAVIS
3-13
HE'LL BE SURPRISED, ALL RIGHT
ARRGH!
HE ATE IT! HE ATE IT!
SURPRISE

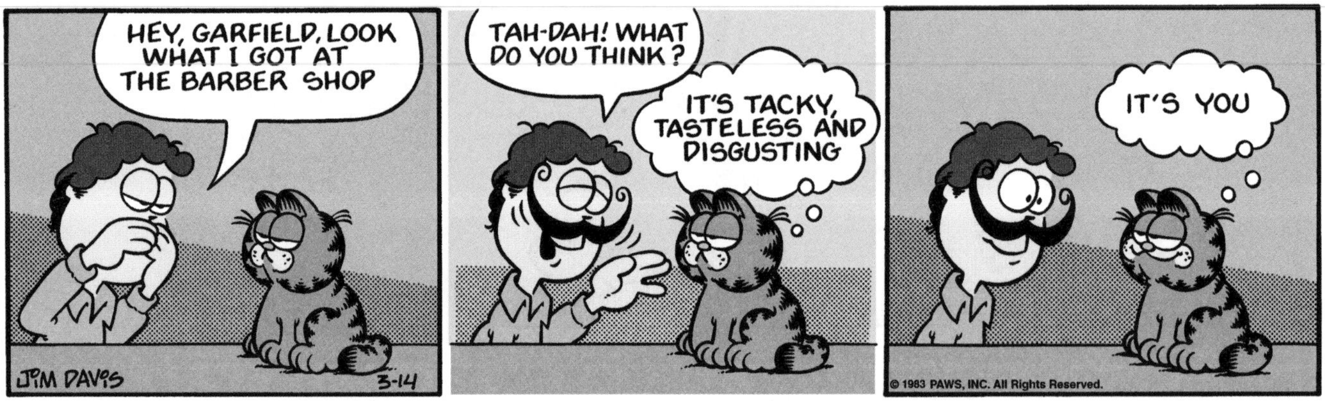
HEY, GARFIELD, LOOK WHAT I GOT AT THE BARBER SHOP
JIM DAVIS
3-14
TAH-DAH! WHAT DO YOU THINK?
IT'S TACKY, TASTELESS AND DISGUSTING
IT'S YOU
© 1983 PAWS, INC. All Rights Reserved.

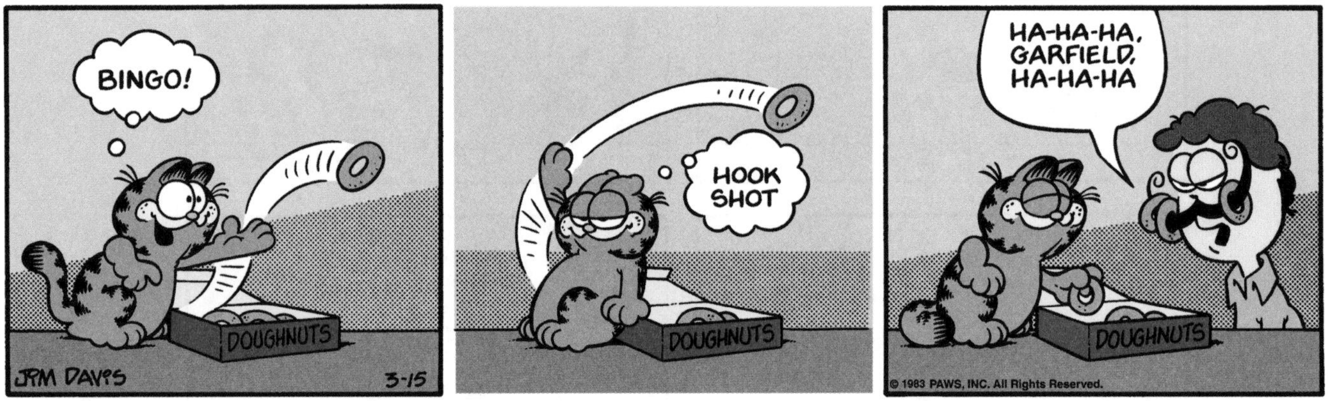
BINGO!
DOUGHNUTS
JIM DAVIS
3-15
HOOK SHOT
DOUGHNUTS
HA-HA-HA, GARFIELD, HA-HA-HA
DOUGHNUTS
© 1983 PAWS, INC. All Rights Reserved.

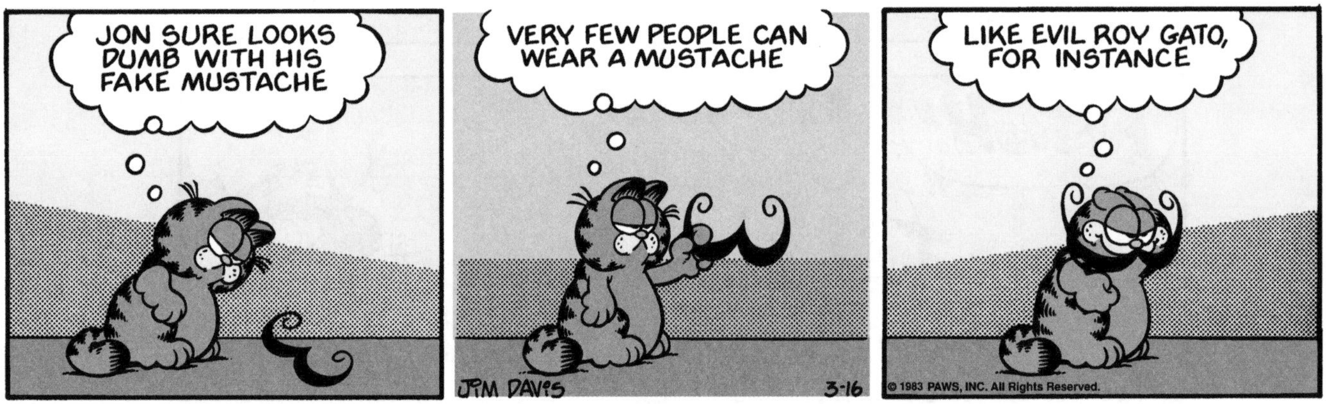
JON SURE LOOKS DUMB WITH HIS FAKE MUSTACHE
VERY FEW PEOPLE CAN WEAR A MUSTACHE
JIM DAVIS
3-16
LIKE EVIL ROY GATO, FOR INSTANCE
© 1983 PAWS, INC. All Rights Reserved.

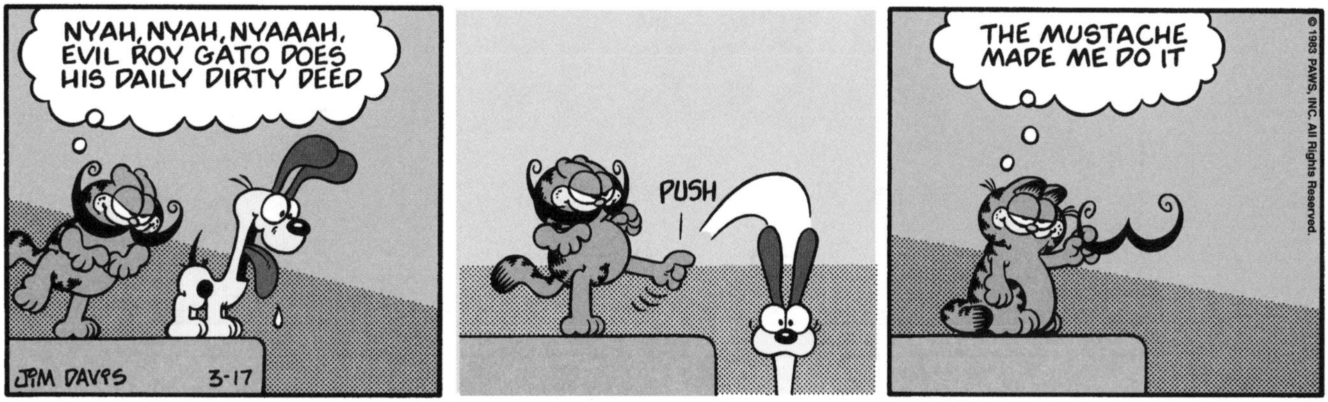
NYAH, NYAH, NYAAAH, EVIL ROY GATO DOES HIS DAILY DIRTY DEED
JIM DAVIS 3-17
PUSH
THE MUSTACHE MADE ME DO IT
© 1983 PAWS, INC. All Rights Reserved.

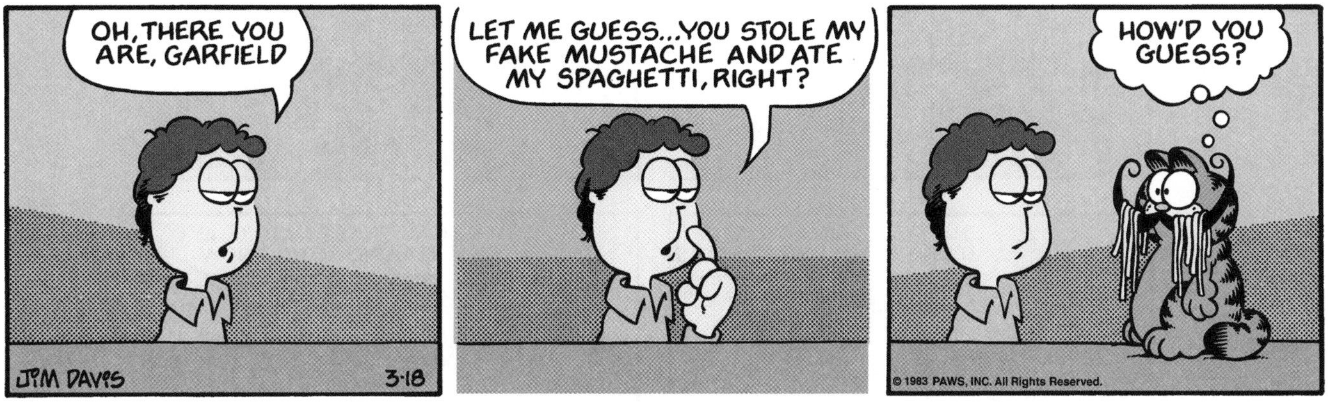
OH, THERE YOU ARE, GARFIELD
JIM DAVIS 3-18
LET ME GUESS... YOU STOLE MY FAKE MUSTACHE AND ATE MY SPAGHETTI, RIGHT?
HOW'D YOU GUESS?
© 1983 PAWS, INC. All Rights Reserved.

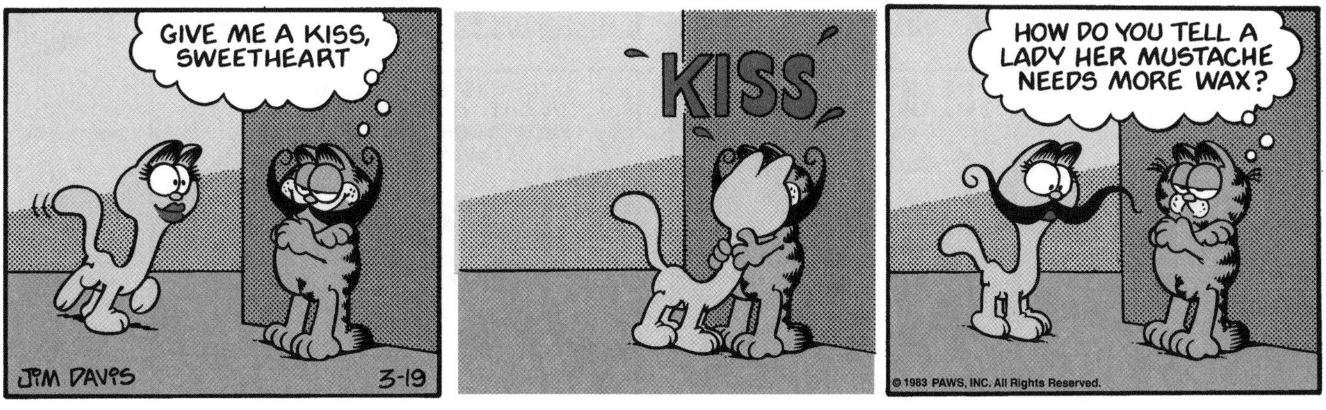
GIVE ME A KISS, SWEETHEART
JIM DAVIS 3-19
KISS
HOW DO YOU TELL A LADY HER MUSTACHE NEEDS MORE WAX?
© 1983 PAWS, INC. All Rights Reserved.

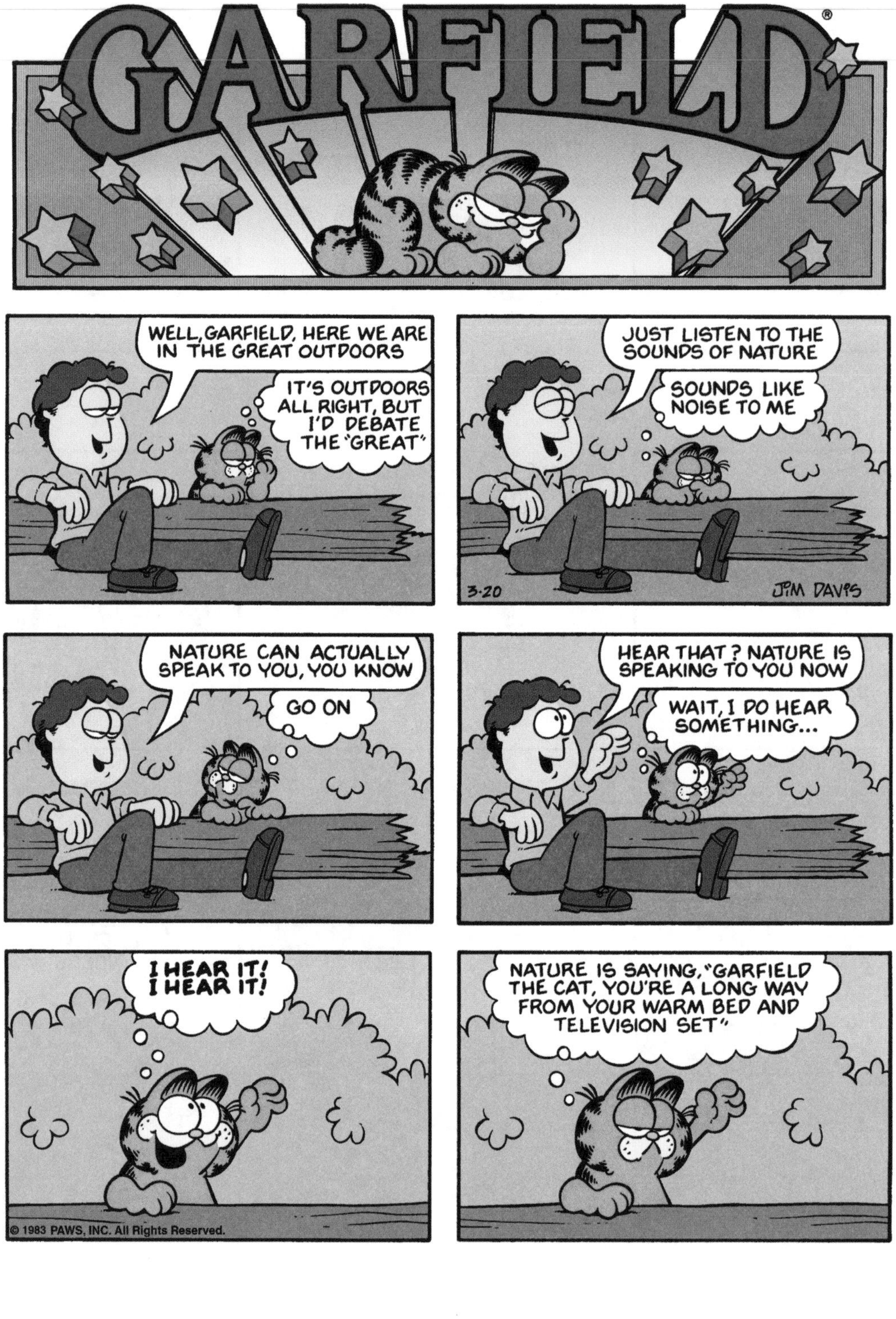
GARFIELD®
WELL, GARFIELD, HERE WE ARE IN THE GREAT OUTDOORS
IT'S OUTDOORS ALL RIGHT, BUT I'D DEBATE THE "GREAT"
JUST LISTEN TO THE SOUNDS OF NATURE
SOUNDS LIKE NOISE TO ME
3-20
JIM DAVIS
NATURE CAN ACTUALLY SPEAK TO YOU, YOU KNOW
GO ON
HEAR THAT? NATURE IS SPEAKING TO YOU NOW
WAIT, I DO HEAR SOMETHING...
I HEAR IT! I HEAR IT!
NATURE IS SAYING, "GARFIELD THE CAT, YOU'RE A LONG WAY FROM YOUR WARM BED AND TELEVISION SET"
© 1983 PAWS, INC. All Rights Reserved.